*To my parents, Martha and James, who showed
so much love and understanding in equal measure
to preceding and succeeding generations*

AGEING AND CARING

A Guide for Later Life

Professor Des O'Neill

ORPEN PRESS

Published by
Orpen Press
Lonsdale House
Avoca Avenue
Blackrock
Co. Dublin
Ireland

e-mail: info@orpenpress.com
www.orpenpress.com

Paperback ISBN 978-1-871305-31-9
ePub ISBN 978-1-909895-16-4
Kindle ISBN 978-1-909895-17-1
PDF ISBN 978-1-909895-18-8

Printed in Ireland by SPRINT-print Ltd.

DISCLAIMER

This book is designed to increase knowledge, awareness and understanding of ageing issues. It is not intended to replace the advice that your own doctor can give you. If you are concerned by any of the issues raised in this book make sure you consult your GP, who is there to help you.

Whilst every effort has been made to ensure the accuracy of the information and material contained in this book, nevertheless it is possible that errors or omissions may occur in the content. The author and publishers assume no responsibility for and give no guarantees or warranties concerning the accuracy, completeness or up-to-date nature of the information provided in this book.

Ageing and Caring

'A timely and reflective publication. As an organisation which promotes the value of older people's contribution in Irish society, we particularly welcome Professor O'Neill's comments on combating ageism and the value of social activity.'
Mary Nally, founder of Third Age

FOREWORD

It comes as no surprise that Professor Des O'Neill has written this self-help guide to ageing.

As a geriatrician who has been a fearless advocate for older people in Ireland, Professor O'Neill has played a key role in helping to shape and improve policies for older people in Ireland. From his work in helping develop policy on elder abuse prevention, to his report on the Leas Cross nursing home scandal, he has played a very public role in the fight for the rights of older people. When you add to this his talent for writing and communication, he was always a likely candidate to produce an important book like this.

Writing a guide to ageing is a daunting task. No two of us will age the same way. So many factors impact on how each of us will age. But Professor O'Neill has captured the major issues in this broad-reaching publication.

It is so encouraging to read a book about ageing which views the ageing process in a positive light. The fact that we are all living longer is something to celebrate. The fact that ageing presents challenges for some older people is something to plan for, rather than something to scaremonger about. This book not only deals with ageing for those already facing age-related issues, but also addresses the need for younger people to plan for when they will be older.

My colleagues in Age Action work each day with older people and their families who are living life to the full, adapting their lives to meet the challenges of ageing, and sometimes struggling with age-related issues. We try to empower older people and their families. Information is a key factor in empowering people. It enables them to decide how they will address their issues and live their lives. Hopefully this book will help empower many people and their families.

Ageing and Caring is a publication that could act as a conversation starter about pending issues. It could help each of us focus on, and plan for, issues ahead of us. In a society where the numbers of over-65s are predicted to increase steadily in the coming decades, this guide to ageing is certainly welcome and timely.

Eamon Timmins
Head of Advocacy and Communications,
Age Action

Acknowledgements

My clinical work over many years has been enriched by the lives of the many older people and their families I have encountered. The origins of this book lie primarily in their remarkable narratives of care, warmth, individuality and endurance in the face of often daunting adversity.

The practice of geriatric medicine, one of the most intellectually stimulating and professionally rewarding of medical disciplines, attracts a truly diverse and interesting following. I am forever indebted to the influence and solidarity of many inspiring colleagues whom I have encountered in geriatric medicine, gerontological nursing, old age psychiatry and associated therapies in Ireland, the UK, Europe and North America over two decades of practice as a geriatrician.

In addition, my energy is constantly renewed by the pleasure of watching the enthusiasm and discovery of generations of medical students and trainees as they 'get' the concept of how age-attuned care for this group of patients can make a big difference to patients and clinicians alike.

However, writing a book in the midst of a busy clinical and academic life entails the security and support of trusted colleagues. I owe a deep debt of gratitude to the support of my senior colleagues in Tallaght and Naas Hospitals – Drs Rónán Collins, Tara Coughlan, Anne O'Driscoll, Paul O'Brien and Seán Kennelly – who together make up a formidable font of expertise, drive and advocacy in a professional environment marked by warmth and humour. This support is mirrored among the wonderful nurses, therapists, social workers and many others who have supported the development of geriatric medicine, initially in the Meath Hospital and subsequently Tallaght Hospital.

A special mention must be made of helpful insights from Dr Shaun O'Keeffe, of the patience, tolerance and professionalism of Eileen O'Brien as editor for Orpen Press, and of Marian Hughes for providing brio, organisation and support in her key role in our department.

Finally, life is a zero-sum game, and I am deeply aware that the time and energy spent on this project is a gift, involuntary as it may have been, from my tolerant and loving family, and the deepest gratitude of all is owed to my wife, Mary, and my children, Liam, Aisling, Ciara, Siobhán, Conor, Ruairí and Éilis.

Desmond O'Neill, MA MD FRCPI AGSF FRCP(Glasg) FRCP
Dublin, August 2013

CONTENTS

Contents

Contents

Contents

Contents

Contents

Poem from a Three-Year Old
Brendan Kennelly

And will the flowers die?

And will the people die?

And every day do you grow old, do I
grow old, no I'm not old, do
flowers grow old?

Old things – do you throw them out?

Do you throw old people out?

And how you know a flower that's old?

The petals fall, the petals fall from flowers,
and do the petals fall from people too,
every day more petals fall until the
floor where I would like to play I
want to play is covered with old
flowers and people all the same
together lying there with petals fallen
on the dirty floor I want to play
the floor you come and sweep
with the huge broom.

The dirt you sweep, what happens that,
what happens all the dirt you sweep
from flowers and people, what
happens all the dirt? Is all the

dirt what's left of flowers and
people, all the dirt there in a
heap under the huge broom that
sweeps everything away?

Why you work so hard, why brush
and sweep to make a heap of dirt?
And who will bring new flowers?
And who will bring new people? Who will
bring new flowers to put in water
where no petals fall on to the
floor where I would like to
play? Who will bring new flowers
that will not hang their heads
like tired old people wanting sleep?
Who will bring new flowers that
do not split and shrivel every
day? And if we have new flowers,
will we have new people too to
keep the flowers alive and give
them water?

And will the new young flowers die?

And will the new young people die?

And why?

Legendary Figures, in Old Age
Thomas Kinsella

I saw there a number of elders
in intimate companionship,
their old shapes without shame,

playing with one another
– with all that remained
of the barbed shafts of Love.

And I heard one of them saying
to those around her:
'We cannot renew the Gift

but we can drain it to the last drop.'

Reproduced with permission. 'Legendary Figures, in Old Age'
by Thomas Kinsella, *PN Review* 165, Volume 32, Number 1,
published by Carcanet Press, September–October 2005.

Preface

Introduction

To paraphrase Peter Pan, growing old ... is a very big adventure. The fact that most of us will grow to old age evokes awe and trepidation for the most part. Yet this ageing of populations is a tremendous feat for our society and has provided an extraordinary reservoir of achievement and life skills for us. Ageing means growth and loss at every age; we accept this as children but are predisposed to dwell on the negative aspects of later life. It is as if the citizens of Dublin were oblivious to the grandeur of their wonderful mediaeval cathedrals and could only think of them in terms of the difficulties and costs of repairing the roofs. We need to make this shift of perspective if we are to come to terms with the reality of old age. Life in our later years does represent higher maintenance needs, but the gains in other aspects of life more than justify the investment.

Nevertheless, as you may have bought this book because you need some guidance on problems relating to later life, then this will be the focus of this book. However, this support is provided in a society that is still coming to terms with the concept of ageing. Since the possibility that so many of us will live to old age is a relatively new phenomenon for Irish society, it is not always easy to get information on how to make the best of our added years.

There is also a need to guide older people and those who care for them on how to react and adapt when illness or frailty strikes. Increasingly, those in middle age will begin to wonder about a preparation strategy for their later years. The aim of this book is to act as just such a guide for older people (at all stages of their development) and those close to them. The over-riding principle is *start early, but it's never too late*. This emphasises that while the best life plan is to develop positive life strategies as early as possible, there is nearly always some possibility of improving any situation, no matter how bad it may seem.

No book can provide all the answers, particularly as one of the hallmarks of ageing is an extraordinary increase in the diversity of experiences. However, I hope that some of the insights will provide a starting point for what is at times (often simultaneously) the most fascinating, frustrating, enriching and difficult stage of life.

Reader's Guide

Who Is this Book For?

This book was prompted by the increasing number of requests from friends, peers, patients and their relatives for some form of a guide to the complexities of ageing. In particular, many people feel disempowered when faced with the challenges of illness or loss of function (such as difficulties with walking or continence) that may occur in later life. They find themselves in new situations: older people with new disabilities that reduce their independence, spouses taking on a caring role, adult children and loved ones negotiating new roles with regard to their parents. The traditional care patterns that both have been accustomed to up to that point – one predominated by parents looking after children, progressing to a relationship between older adults and older children – become less distinct. Both sides need to adapt, and as old age brings experience and wisdom, often it is the adult children who have more difficulty in adapting to the change in circumstances. They are also often coping with raising families themselves, negotiating their way in the workplace and now coming to terms with the change in their relationship with their parents, and their parents' evolving situation.

In addition, access to supports and care is challenging, there is a lack of clarity regarding access and entitlements to such supports, and various parts of the health and social care system communicate poorly with each other.

Although this book is predominantly aimed at older adults and their spouses or partners, my hope is that adult children will also find it of use. Older adults have the most direct stake in their own well-being and care, and any guide to health and care in later life must emphasise the need to put the wishes of older people at the centre of all decisions about their care. They also need access to information about ageing and ways to pre-empt, remedy or alleviate the effects of disease in later life. In the main, older adults are themselves responsible (and indeed want to be responsible) for their own health and care. This is the huge difference between this manual of care for later life and those for the beginning of life, such as the manuals by Penelope Leach or Sheila Kitzinger. All sections aimed predominantly at adult children involved with care will be placed in shaded boxes (see below); older adults might also find it interesting to read these to gain another perspective on the increasingly complex relationships that arise out of disability in later life.

This Is Not a Childcare Manual for Older People

Not only do babies not read childcare manuals (although they are the reason that they are written), but also they are not fully fledged adults with powers of reasoning and all the advantages (and discomforts) of free will. This is a key message to adult children that will permeate the book

– all care and support in later life must have as its primary principle the wishes of the older person. At times this may be difficult to accept, and the book will try to explore the complexities of negotiating care with the wishes of older people as the central tenet of any package.

However, adult children need to appreciate this concept for many reasons. At the very least, they need to come to the realisation that older people are not some ethnically distinct group of 'other' people but are, in fact, 'us as we age'. We all have a vested interest in ensuring that philosophies and mechanisms of care for older people will develop with our own wishes as a central tenet for when we ourselves are in the same situation. More importantly, an understanding of ageing and its effects at a personal level are important to empathise with your older parent; they are not passive recipients of care but rather wish to have support in making their own responses to their own individual situation. This is even true for older people with dementia; the vast majority will retain some decision-making abilities, even quite late into their illness.

Agenda Slide

An understanding of the primary need to support the wishes of older people will help to allay one of the many challenges in helping older people, that of 'agenda slide'. This is a mismatch between what the older person sees as an appropriate solution to whatever difficulties they are experiencing and the solution that the adult child sees as appropriate. As we will discuss later, this classically occurs over issues of safety. A phrase such as: 'It isn't safe for my mother to be at home on her own' is often representative of how adult children and older people view independence and risk in very different ways. In general, older people value their independence very highly and are willing to accept more risk than their adult children are comfortable with to achieve this aim. In only exceptional circumstances should this wish be overridden. Remember, we all have the right to make what others would see as foolish or risky decisions, whether this is smoking, failure to install a smoke alarm or risky sexual behaviour.

A part of the challenge of care for older people is exploring the agenda slide, looking for the reasons underlying the gap; for adult children this means acknowledging the components that reflect our need for security and stability rather than the independence of the older person and hopefully initiating some discussion between family members.

How Should I Use this Book?

Although several chapters of this book will link specifically to issues which may be of direct concern to you when you buy this book – memory problems, incontinence, stroke, etc. – I would recommend that you start by trying to understand some of the more general issues about ageing in Section I, especially the first three chapters. This is important because the welcome possibility that so many of us will live into later life is relatively new for us as a society and for each of us individually. This means that we have not fully adapted to both the positive and negative implications of this radical change and may not understand that our initial responses, and those of our society and health and social care systems, may actually be poorly adapted to the new reality.

One of the most important concepts you will encounter is that of ageism. This is a failure to recognise the intrinsic worth and value of older people and to accord equal rights and privileges to them. This has largely arisen as a failure of ourselves and our society to evolve as rapidly as the increase in older people has occurred and is largely an unconscious sin of omission. However, the harmful effects of ageism are not in any way lessened for older people because they are not deliberate, and it is important for those looking for help to understand the impact of ageism and to learn how to start combating it.

This failure of society to evolve to take account of the complexity of ageing also accounts for the relatively fragmented and often inadequate support system you will encounter on your journey. If you are reading this from the perspective of an adult child, I hope that some of you will be moved to some form of activism to improve the shape, form, transparency and effectiveness of the system, if not for your older parent then at the very least for yourself when you will encounter the system yourself in later life.

Chapters 4, 5 and 6 deal with preparing for ageing, particularly in terms of health and finance, two important determinants of successful ageing. On the basis of the book's motto, *start early, but it's never too late*, these chapters will be of interest and use to both older people and their adult children.

The final chapters of Section I deal with planning and coordinating your interaction with the health and social care services in Ireland, and ageing and the family, exploring the new roles that mass population ageing have afforded us.

Section II focuses on health concerns and ageing. It is perhaps important to stress that this is not an attempt to medicalise old age; rather it is a recognition that illness rather than old age is the cause of many of the difficulties associated with later life. Modern healthcare should use a bio-psycho-social model to respond to these illnesses; that is to say that we recognise that social and psychological factors are hugely important in determining the impact of disease in later life and we try to ensure that care packages will be directed towards each of these components. This means physical treatment of the illness, as well as psychological and social assessment and support. Over-emphasis on a single component at the expense of the others will be harmful in the long term. A classical example is the provision of a Zimmer frame to an older person with walking difficulties without a detailed assessment. While probably well-meaning, a failure to diagnose the cause of walking difficulties may mean that a treatable cause may be ignored and get worse, and methods to restore function, such as therapy, may be missed out on.

Section III deals with the more complex and difficult aspects of ageing: when home is no longer possible, elder abuse and death. Information is power in all of these issues, and nearly all those I know personally who have dealt with these have felt that they did not have access to a useful guidebook or information source at the time.

Adult Children and Other Carers

Chapter 8 is specifically geared towards carers (but should be read by both groups). Throughout the other chapters, when there is a specific focus for the adult child or carer, it will be outlined in grey, like this section.

Keeping Up to Date

This book is a guide to how best to find paths through the complexity of later life. Given the nature of modern life, changes will occur even as the book is being published. For example, the structure of the health system is under constant review. Given both the fallibility of the author and the likelihood of change, it is important to realise that a book such as this is only one component of your approach. Use it as a basis for discussion with your family, doctor, public health nurse and any other resources you find. Feedback on any section that you think could be improved would be gratefully appreciated, by contacting me through the publishers.

Section I

Ageing: What You Need to Know

1

What Is Ageing?

Trying to describe ageing is similar to St Augustine's famous observation on the nature of time –'*What, then, is time? If no one asks me, I know what it is. If I wish to explain it to him who asks me, I do not know.*' We all have a sense of what it is; yet will have significant difficulties in explaining to other people what it is. When we do try, our explanations will vary remarkably from one to another; it is also likely that many will emphasise the negative aspects of ageing at the expense of the positive aspects. As you may have bought this book because of an unwelcome aspect of ageing or an age-related disease, you might be in sympathy with this negativity. A balanced view is important: illness and bad things happen to people at all stages of life, and most of us wish to rise above an illness and affirm our innate humanity and personality. Also, many of the intrinsic qualities of ageing – wisdom, stoicism, good strategic thinking – are generally helpful aids in dealing with the difficulties associated with age-related disease and disability.

Growth and Loss

Ageing is at once complex and simple. It occurs not only from the moment we are conceived, but ageing in previous generations can also affect us directly. The egg that formed each of us was present in our mother's ovary from the time that her ovaries were formed, giving rise to the paradox that we are born very young from eggs that are very old. In a most general sense, ageing at all stages is associated with growth and loss. For example, at the age of seven there are things that we can no longer do that we could do with ease at the age of two – learn a language, learn to walk and put our toes in our mouth! In general, we have grown accustomed to unconsciously doing the calculation that the growth side of the equation more than adequately makes up for the losses, to the point that we do not even consciously recognise the losses. This occurs to such an extent that most people unconsciously associate the word 'ageing' with old age, and this usually in negative terms.

Why is it important to discuss ageing in the context of it occurring at all ages? Precisely because much of the negative attitude to old age is due to a failure to recognise the positive and negative sides of ageing at all ages. An emphasis on the negative side only colours the climate within which you or your loved one will (or will not) receive care services as well as the standard of those services. If society diminishes the value of ageing, then the political emphasis dwells less on health and social services for older people, the adult group for whom these services are most clearly needed.

Positive Aspects of Ageing

One of the ways of reminding ourselves of the positive is to look at the incredible achievements of older people and of the ways in which their age contributes to the output of later life. If you walk into the National Gallery of Ireland, you may be struck by the wonderful Louis le Brocquy tapestry which spans the height of the new entrance hall. Vibrant and glowing, it is the product of his eighty-second year. Further into the gallery is the celebrated portrait of Bono, painted in le Brocquy's eighty-third year and showing the artist in his prime yet still catching the zeitgeist. Move along to the Yeats room and you will find another great Irish artist, Jack B. Yeats. In his case, all of his greatest paintings date from the age of seventy onwards. The National Gallery has a range of similar great paintings from artists such as Titian, Cézanne, Tiepolo and Corot, all painted after the age of sixty.

Late life skills are not confined to painting – great sculptors (Louise Bourgeois), architects (Frank Lloyd Wright), writers (Seamus Heaney, Brendan Kennelly, P.D. James, Samuel Beckett, W.B. Yeats, Jennifer Johnston), musicians (Handel, Haydn, Wagner, Liszt, Janacek) and political leaders (Golda Meir, Winston Churchill during World War II, Ronald Reagan) also figure. But closer to everyday experience is an increasing body of knowledge that points out how older workers are among the most cost-effective and useful of workers. They tend to cause fewer problems with absenteeism and are mature and pragmatic in how they deal with work issues, such as faults in the system.

These skills might seem far removed from you or your frail parent, but it is worth reflecting that many of these positive achievements are mirrored in a more everyday way in how older people achieve their goals in later life. They use their wisdom and life experiences in a very positive way to steer their way around what others might see as obstacles. A classic example is a study by a psychologist called Salthouse on younger and older typists. Older typists might be thought to be disadvantaged by slower reaction speeds, changes in eyesight and theoretically slower physical agility. Yet the older typists not only held their own but even beat the younger typists at their game. How can this be? It turns out that the older typists used other strategies, such as looking further along the line of text to be transcribed than did the younger ones.

These advantages have shown in other common-place examples. Older drivers, for instance, despite having slower reaction times, more arthritis and eyesight difficulties, are the safest group of drivers on the road. All this goes to show that older people have their own ways for dealing with their own problems.

These strategies are effective in their own way, and as an adult son or daughter you will serve them best by supporting them in dealing with issues in their life in their own way.

What Are the Characteristics of Ageing in Later Life?

The hallmarks of ageing that we can definitely identify are four-fold:

- Positive aspects
- Increased inter-individual differences
- Reduced reserve
- Complexity

The positive aspects we have discussed above. The increased inter-individual difference is a fascinating theme. Basically, it means that the difference between any of us and our peers will increase with time. It is a product of the interaction of the years, your genes and all the influences of your environment and family surroundings. A group of baby boys are very like one another in terms of things like grip strength, lung capacity and strength of yell. These group similarities tend to remain fairly constant until somewhere between the twenties and the thirties. From then on, differences in our genetic make-up, lifestyle choices (exercise, smoking, etc.), education, wealth and environment begin to have a chance to exert their influence. At the age of seventy, the factors (grip strength, lung capacity and yell strength) that were quite similar in twenty-year-olds now begin to diverge quite widely. We can see this in everyday phrases such as 'He is a very young ninety-year-old' or 'She is very old for fifty'.

Why is it important to know about this? Quite simply, it means that older people's problems will tend to be much more individual and different from each other than younger people's. This means that not only may this book not cover the ailments of later life in a way that corresponds to the problems in your life, but also that the health and social care services need to have a more individualised and sophisticated approach when dealing with older people than when dealing with younger people. 'When you have seen one older person, you have seen one older person' is a useful variation of the stock phrase which emphasises this heightened individuality. Failure to recognise this increased difference between individual older people is at the heart of many of the problems that older people face with the health service, as traditional services tend offer more simple 'one-size-fits-all' solutions, whether in day centres (do we have these for middle-aged people?), the hospital or nursing homes.

The third widely recognised quality of ageing in later life is reduced reserve. An example is that while an older person may easily walk for the bus, they may not be able to run for the bus. This is replicated in a lot of other ways. In the health setting, it is seen in the way older people tolerate the side effects of medications less well than younger people. Another manifestation is that illnesses such as pneumonia may stress other systems to the point that they do not function as well. For example, an older person with severe pneumonia may develop a degree of (hopefully transient) kidney, heart or brain failure. It is a point of some considerable discussion as to whether this reduced reserve occurs as a result of ageing, age-related disease or lifestyle. The answer is almost certainly a combination of all three. While we can't stop ageing, we can modify the amount and impact of age-related disease and change our lifestyle to maximise our chances of withstanding the stresses of everyday life and of illness in a more robust manner.

Finally, complexity – which arises from the three features listed above. Older people are more individual, more likely than younger people to have more than one illness and more likely to have more medications but be less tolerant of the side effects of these medicines, and have reduced reserve. Therefore, policies and strategies for older people need to become more sophisticated and subtle to react to the contributions and needs of older people. This is a major challenge: for example, much of the medical system is based on the concept that you have a single illness – heart attack, stroke, stomach ulcer, etc. – and many guidelines for care fail to recognise that a therapy that is good for one problem may actually create or exacerbate another problem. A classic example is the treatment for high blood pressure, usually a good thing in itself for younger people; for older people it is complicated by the fact that it will cause some people to fall more easily.

So, more individually tailored therapy is needed, and this concept is at the heart of both geriatric medicine and old age psychiatry, and one of the reasons that we need to train all healthcare providers – in particular public health nurses and family doctors – in the basics of gerontology, the study of ageing.

What Causes the Negative Aspects of Ageing?

One of the biggest difficulties in this area is the separating out of the changes in later life that are due to ageing and those that relate to age-related disease and lifestyle. To a great extent this difficulty arises from our society's fatalism about loss of function in later life. If through a negative view of later life we think that it is normal to be incontinent, forgetful or have difficulties with walking in later life, then we will not make an effort to change these states and instead will try to compensate for them; the negative aspects are considered to be intrinsic to ageing. Nowadays we have a greater understanding that problems with continence, memory or mobility are likely to be due to overt and subtle forms of disease, in particular stroke disease and neurodegenerative diseases. Damage from the environment may also be an issue. It was formerly thought that a loss of hearing for high tones was part of normal ageing. It is now established that in some populations (in particular those with low levels of ambient noise) this does not occur.

There is some contribution, both positive and negative, from genes. The most dramatic form of this influence, an extreme form of accelerated ageing known as Werner's syndrome, is linked to a specific gene. In this (thankfully rare) illness, negative aspects of ageing, such as baldness, heart disease and varicose veins, can occur by the time a child is ten. While this condition is of little direct relevance to most older people, a closer examination of how the genetic defect in Werner's syndrome causes these symptoms may help scientists to understand how to combat the negative changes of ageing. On the credit side, having parents who lived to a ripe old age improves your own chances of longevity.

Apart from genetic influences, up to 300 possible theories have been advanced for the deterioration of systems that are seen with ageing – clear evidence that none of them are sufficient in their own right to explain ageing. Many focus on increasing amounts of small damage that accumulate over time. Others relate to an increasing tendency to faulty repair mechanisms, while yet another line of reasoning promotes the idea of damage to the system from free radicals. Free radicals are a form of oxygen with an extra atom and there is good evidence in experiments with fruit flies that increasing the body's ability to neutralise free radicals leads to longer life spans for fruit flies. However, we are not fruit flies, and it is not at all certain that taking foods that are rich in antioxidants will prolong life.

So can anything else prolong life? The answer is yes, and it is happening as we watch. Between 1996 and 2002, the life expectancy of older Irish people increased by 2.1 years for men and 1.8 years for women, and it increased further in 2006 and 2012. However, most of this improvement is not directly due to medical advances but relates to general trends in improved wealth, hygiene, nutrition and education. As we will see in later chapters, each individual has the capability of improving their health and well-being in later life through social engagement, exercise and diet.

Those who wish to learn more about the theories underlying ageing might usefully read Tom Kirkwood's book on ageing, *Time of Our Lives*,[1] a clear and interesting overview by one of the great experts on biological ageing.

---

[1] Tom Kirkwood, *Time of Our Lives: The Science of Human Aging*, Oxford University Press, 2002.

Social Aspects of Ageing

As previously mentioned, the phenomenon of mass ageing is relatively new, and our society is still coming to terms with it. There is much talk of 'demographic time bombs', 'greying tides' and other such apocalyptic terms. It is absolutely vital that all of us challenge these stereotypes, as they affect us all. Susan Sontag, discussing cancer and tuberculosis at a time when both suffered from a social stigma, has written eloquently about how the care and treatment of those affected was negatively influenced by the social attitudes of the time: 'It is impossible to take up one's residence in the kingdom of the ill without being prejudiced by the lurid metaphors with which it has been landscaped.' In today's terms, she could easily have been writing about ageing.

Those trying to understand the phenomenon might reflect on the changes from another time, when child mortality reduced greatly in late Victorian times. Did anyone complain about a 'wailing tide' or a 'squalling time bomb'? No, society welcomed these extra people as a bonus to society and adapted accordingly. We have been slow to understand that 'us as we age' is a bonus for our society in just the same way. A better term for ageing is the 'demographic bounty', but with an understanding that more complex and sophisticated societal responses to the contributions and needs of older people are required. As a society, we have embraced complexity in other areas. For example, we know that our transport systems have become more complicated, and are not surprised at the scale of investments needed, whether in airports, metro lines or motorways. In a similar manner, the increased complexity of an ageing population requires a more age-friendly system.

Portraying the costs of care for age-related disease and disability as a crippling burden is a factor which may exacerbate ageism, and this is a worrying trend for politicians in some countries. There is also a lot of loose talk about the 'cost of care' and how burdensome it has become for governments. This is outright nonsense, and represents a political choice rather than an inability to provide an adequate income and health and social services for older people. The wealth of the developed world (including Ireland) has been rising enormously over the last few decades and could easily provide the care needed. The political climate, however, has focused on a low-tax regime, and if we have one of the lowest direct taxation burdens of European Union member states we must understand that the services network will reflect this with a correspondingly lower level of public services.

Embracing Dualism

So how do we reconcile the positive and negative aspects of ageing? Perhaps the easiest way is to keep a constant sense of dualism in all matters with ageing. This is a position that emphasises that, at the same time, good and bad things occur when ageing. A corollary is the ability to accept later life as a time of particular skills and wisdom, and simultaneously as a time when older people require particular support to help them overcome the effects of age-related disease and disability. These are not

independent of each other: maximising the possibility of good health will allow older people to participate
in society – enabling that very important buzz word,
inclusion. This is important and will help to keep
a focus on the bigger picture. Sometimes fit older
people themselves may focus only on their preserved
abilities. Examples are pictures of 85-year-olds
pole-vaulting or running marathons – while clearly
admirable in their own right, these pictures are not
really representative of the everyday life and achievements of most older people. At the other extreme is
an over-emphasis on the most difficult cases, creating an image of dependency and passivity. The truth
lies in a constant sense of both patterns contributing
to one's later life.

Standing Up to Ageism

Despite what you now know about ageing, many
others will still see only the negative side and this
is expressed as ageism. This term will come up time
and again in your dealings with all aspects of society.
Although there are many trying to counter its effects
(older people's advocacy organisations and professional groups such as geriatricians), its influence is
pervasive. You may find it in many guises, whether
through the stopping of breast cancer screening at
the age of 65, the failure of an Accident & Emergency
department to take your loss of mobility seriously or
having difficulty hiring a car after the age of 70.

   You will not be able to undo decades of ageism on
your own, and in the broader context it is important that older people support their advocacy

organisations. In your immediate circumstances, the best weapons against ageism are knowledge, tact and firmness. Through self-help manuals such as this one you can get some sense of what is possible. Specific books on specific conditions, advocacy groups for certain illnesses (stroke, Parkinson's disease and dementia, for example) and the internet can all help. A discussion with the person who is dealing with you calmly outlining your concerns is the first step. Remember, they may not be aware of the ageist implications of what they are proposing. In health and social care settings, ageism may in fact be exacerbated by general shortages of resources, such as not enough hospital beds, not enough specialists or not enough nursing home beds.

Two good general principles might be of help in deciding whether or not your options in healthcare are being negatively affected by your age:

- *Age is not in itself a contraindication to any treatment; your condition at the time is the key factor.* Whether it is access to surgery, a bed in the Intensive Care Unit or getting chemotherapy for cancer, decisions should be based on your physical abilities and condition rather than your age. This is of vital importance – there is overwhelming evidence that a) this is appropriate and b) sadly, that it may be unrecognised or ignored by healthcare workers on the ground. A calm discussion outlining the reasons why you are not getting something which you think might be beneficial is the best way to start. If you feel that you are being negatively discriminated against, ask for the reasons why you are not getting the service, and discuss it with your family or GP.

- *Any sudden loss of function (sudden confusion, sudden loss of mobility, etc.) is a serious illness until proved otherwise.* It may be a subtle stroke, pneumonia or side effects of a medication. In any event, you or your carer should realise that you require medical attention. Again, a calm discussion outlining your wish to know the diagnosis for and management of this loss of function is the best way forward.

If you are not getting satisfaction with either of these approaches, you should ask to see a more senior person, for example the consultant, and, if necessary, ask for a second opinion.

Carers

While you have a role in keeping an eye out for ageism, remember that it is for the older person to decide how to deal with what you think might be ageism. In the first instance, you should discuss your concerns with the older person and support them in whatever they decide. Don't forget, decisions don't always have to be immediate, and you may actually add to the older person's concerns by taking hasty action, cathartic as it may be for you. Only if the older person is absolutely incapable of understanding and dealing with the situation should you step in. Again, remember the triad of knowledge, tact and firmness. You and your relative should be wary of having problems put down to 'ageing', and a particular cause for concern at hospital admission is the label of a 'social admission' or 'failure to cope', whereby your relative has lost function (e.g. the ability to walk or think straight, or continence), but the doctor seeing them has not enough training to recognise this as a sign of illness and ascribes their symptoms to some sort of breakdown in the social supports surrounding your loved one.

In other areas of life, you might consider approaching the Equality Authority or the Ombudsman if you find that you are being barred from accessing services or positions as a result of your age. Get involved and get active! Join an advocacy group, keep informing your elected representatives if you have unsatisfactory experiences with services and support systems, and join the public debate to combat ageism and welcome the inclusion of you and your peers in society as you age.

2

As You Age

Our own perception of ageing is complex and much coloured by our surroundings. Even the sense of belonging to our own age group is not secure – witness the reluctance of older people to identify in any significant numbers with their advocacy organisations, until the 2008 protest march against the withdrawal of the Medical Card. This is not confined to older people; distant hills are green at any age. As an older person you have already made many of the adaptations psychologically in an unconscious way and, for you, you may not have any particular sense of being an older person – just as you didn't consciously think of yourself of being a 'teenager' when you were 14, or 'middle-aged' when you were 43. Very often it is only when we encounter some barrier in the outside world (e.g. trying to get into an 18-cert film when you are 14) or test ourselves in some activity (e.g. running a marathon at 43) that we become aware of some sense of categorisation by age.

Although in some ways it is meaningless to you *personally* to belong to one of these rather broad categories, they do make some *societal* sense. Very often there are particular needs that a group has which, if not filled, will not allow it to participate in society to the maximum. So to ensure that children are not hampered by illness or poor education we provide vaccinations, developmental check-ups and heel-prick tests at birth, and invest in education. Similarly, retirement is relatively predictable for many types of jobs, and certain health services become more clearly needed after a certain age.

Arbitrary Cut-Offs

Arbitrary cut-offs may always cause some discomfort, particularly in view of our own absorbing of ageist and negative views of old age. There are several cut-off points for being an older person. The UN recognises 60+ as the age range in which someone is regarded as an 'older person'. The usual retirement age of 65 is somewhat fluid, and indeed under review internationally. The age of 70 is yet another gateway for being an older person: getting a Medical Card (until 2009) and the unnecessary medical screening of drivers at this age.

However, it does make sense to have some sort of cut-off point where we recognise that a significant number of issues arise. In health terms, at somewhere between 60 and 70 we begin to notice the onset of age-related diseases, gradually at first but the change is definitely perceptible. In employment terms, although there is some significant debate over its compulsory nature, there is a generally agreed viewpoint that the majority of people retire somewhere between 60 and 70. Both of these issues have very significant implications for society (and all of us) and it is reasonable to develop policies so that the negative impacts are minimised.

An example is dementia if the susceptibility to dementia did not increase in later life there would be a relatively small number of people who would suffer from the illness. However, it does increase with age and the very numbers mean that a more specific policy is needed. Although you may not be aware of it, or may consider the services you or your family are getting not to be sufficient, the government does have an *Action Plan for Dementia* (even if largely unimplemented), and the activities of old age psychiatrists (those who specialise in the psychiatric care of older people) and the Alzheimer Society of Ireland have built up a programme of care over the last twenty years, albeit not to levels that might be desired.

There are also many positive things that can be organised on the basis of a changed lifestyle from 60ish onwards – ongoing education, activities, leisure pursuits, part-time working, consultancy, volunteer working – that really require significant rethinking of policies and infrastructure to fulfil.

Lastly, if we are going to develop policies which are older-person friendly we need to get the voices of older people into the system. If sufficient older people do not find it in themselves to say, 'Yes, it's good to be the age that I am now with so many other people, but I also want to make sure that my society recognises this change in a positive way', then the progress to an older-person friendly society is going to be a slow one.

A Balanced View on Ageing

As you may have bought this book because you are faced with a difficulty with health or disability, you may get impatient with attempts to draw out the positive side of ageing. However, it is important to emphasise that the changes of ageing will have made you better able to deal with these changes than if they occurred twenty years previously. Also, no matter what your health or disability, you still wish to and should enjoy what you can still enjoy, participate in society in whatever way you can still participate and be recognised for who you are with dignity.

Boxing Clever

The most important change in ageing is probably improved strategic and adaptive skills when faced with difficulties in later life. This improvement in life strategies is usually carried out without consciously thinking it through. As you are usually unaware of it, it may be helpful to consider this skill in more depth. One of the ways of thinking of this is a theory called Selection–Optimisation–Compensation. This is one way of summarising the wisdom and strategic skills of older people. In the face of inevitable restrictions caused by age-related disease, *Selection* involves focusing on high-priority areas of life. These are areas that give you a feeling of satisfaction and personal control. *Optimisation* is deciding to take on behaviour that will enrich and enhance the abilities you still have. This helps you to make the most of what you want out of life. *Compensation* involves using resources – either your own or others' – to gain your objectives. This can involve casting aside vanity to get hearing aids or bifocal glasses. It may mean purposefully becoming dependent on others for routine needs, so you can save energy for things you want to do. Even in nursing homes, clients can allow themselves to be dressed by a nurse so they can engage in favoured activities – like playing cards – later.

The most classic example is the great concert pianist Arthur Rubinstein, who was active into his 90s. When Rubinstein was asked how he continued to be such an excellent concert pianist he named three reasons. He played fewer pieces, but practiced them more often, and he used contrasts in tempo to simulate faster playing than he could actually manage. To phrase this in selection, optimisation and compensation terms, Rubinstein reduced his repertoire (selection). This allowed him the opportunity to practice each piece more (optimisation). And, finally, he used contrasts in speed to hide his loss in mechanical finger speed, a case of compensation: by playing the slow passage before a fast passage more slowly than usual it was less obvious that he was playing the fast passage more slowly than previously.

Driving is another classic example, where, despite some degradation of vision and reaction times, older people are the safest group of drivers on the road. They select to drive less at night and during rush hour; they optimise by choosing routes that they know; and they compensate by limiting trips, using free travel passes for long journeys, and so on.

You can try to bear this strategy in mind as we consider certain areas of activity, such as work, recreation, social behaviour, spirituality and sexuality.

Work

As we age certain things become easier and other things become more difficult. Better life and social skills, good attention to detail, better strategic thinking and life experience can give people an edge in skilled labour and areas where social skills are important, such as sales. For example, one telesales company found that older people spent longer on the initial telephone call but not only made as many sales as their younger colleagues, but more importantly more second sales, which suggests a positive impact on the brand name. On the other hand, stamina and reaction time may be an issue, particularly for jobs with significant physical exertion, such as mining, and those with a need for fast reaction times, such as jet fighter pilots. But we are increasingly in a service economy, and ever smaller numbers of people are in these physical jobs. However, it is also recognised that older people can compensate well for some of the changes by good strategic skills. Another way of compensating is to reduce work hours, and some employers have been adapting their employment practices to be able to use the skills of older people.

In general, older people are sensible about the limitations they may find in their work as they get older. Perhaps the most important message is to make sure that any difficulties you are experiencing are not due to some disease that is remediable. Poor vision, depression and poor hearing can all make your job experience more difficult and you should discuss this with your family doctor or employer.

A graduated exit from the workforce would be the choice of many people, but few workplaces facilitate this, and such an arrangement may not work to the advantage of those with defined benefit pension arrangements.

Recreation

Many recreational activities are unaffected by age, especially those that do not make many demands on perceptual or motor coordination, attention capacity, memory or speed of processing (such as gardening and cooking). On the other hand, again we find that for others, such as bridge or golf, older people are expert at compensating with experience and using tricks like slowing down the overall pace.

For most of us, the best and easiest thing to be doing is that which we were doing already – golf, tennis, Scrabble, hill-walking, Bingo – whatever it was, keep doing it. You will almost certainly develop mechanisms to cope with whatever changes old age brings with it.

To those reading this at younger ages, please re-think your life–work–recreation balance now and start developing the habit of a recreational activity that you enjoy; in general, if you weren't doing it before you retired you are much less likely to take it up after you retire. Even with the 'Big Squeeze' (children, work, helping older parents), as you will read in the carer section, you need to carve out this time for yourself. The sooner you do develop this habit, the easier will be your own ability to enjoy your retirement and later life.

Compensations in later life are the availability of facilities, courses and activities during what was formerly the working week. As ever, on the principle of *start early but it's never too late*, you can begin a new activity, start a course, or go to a lunchtime concert or lecture. In my own practice I am constantly astounded at how some older people can make new starts in various activities and initiatives very late in life.

Travel is another area of potential discovery. Not only are you more flexible with your time, but there may be advantageous prices arising out of this flexibility, not only in Ireland but all around the world. You may be aware that a major UK company, Saga Holidays, has been very successful in matching the time flexibility of older people with slack periods in the travel industry. One fly in the ointment is the difficulty in getting travel insurance and hiring cars after the age of 65. This is outright ageism, particularly bearing in mind the good performance of older people as drivers.

Even with a significant disability, it is possible, with the help of friends and carers, to find activities that correspond to your present abilities. One of the greatest barriers may be within you, a reluctance to accept help for the transport side of these activities. Whether it is a visit to the cinema or going out to the pub for a drink, do not feel that you are imposing if someone else is providing the transport. If you are fortunate enough to have support for these activities don't forget that you would probably have done the same for them. However, it will require more coordination and time, and advance preparation will have to take priority over spontaneity.

Social Behaviour

The effects of ageing on social behaviour are complex. Some authors identify a trend towards disengagement, whereby the number of interactions with others decreases. However, it must be remembered in assessing such a feature of ageing that once you have retired from work the opportunities for social activity decrease. In addition, there are culturally imposed stereotypes that can lead to a reduction in social interaction, along with the gradual death of friends and acquaintances. Also, older people may decide to cut down on such contact as part of their selection–optimisation–compensation strategy.

In any event, it is clear that social contact is a valuable component of healthy ageing. As an older person it is likely that your patterns of socialisation will be similar to those when you were younger. However, many opportunities exist and again patterns laid down before old age will help. Clubs, associations and sporting activities are one possibility. Some groups have sections for retired members, which can extend your participation and interest. For example, if you have been a Rotary club member, their senior arm is Probus, which is strongly recommended. The University of the Third Age is a valuable avenue also for a fresh start for older people (see Useful Resources section for details).

There are also differences in social behaviour and roles between men and women which assume increasing importance in later life. Women tend to have a more clearly identified role in the home, even when they have worked outside the home. Men sometimes struggle with this after retirement and failure to develop their own role in terms of the house and maintenance can lead to marital stresses. Think hard about this! No two couples will approach this the same way, but men should start thinking about the rainy day. It may not be the best time to learn how to use the washing machine in the middle of a crisis.

Spirituality

It may be a little late to read this now, but a belief in God is associated with both longevity and health in later life. In many ways this is understandable: a religious philosophy is a highly developed model of strategic thinking, with a sense of goals and a philosophy of life which articulates approaches to life that are highly developed and reflective of life in its broadest sense. Religious observance also fosters an enhanced sense of belonging to a community. In a wider sense, spirituality and a sense of reflection are intrinsic to later life, and contribute to the wisdom of later life. These attributes continue to develop and hopefully you will feel free to use the opportunities of later life to deepen your own spirituality, whether by reading, retreats (in the widest sense of the word) or joining discussion or prayer groups. Some parishes in Ireland have recognised this with radio networks broadcasting Mass and other services, as well as ministers of the Eucharist who can visit you at home. These are important developments in maintaining a sense of purpose, community and belonging.

For adult children there is a relatively strong statistical likelihood that you may not share your parents' attachment to religious practice. However, for most of you, you will recognise it is important. In the event of a disability that restricts access, assistance with transport to participate in religious services can make a big difference to your older relative's life. If the disability prevents the older person from going out, visits from a minister of the Eucharist, pastoral worker, priest or minister can also add to the quality of life.

Sexuality

The biggest social challenge with sexuality and later life is to escape from the many social stigmas and myths that surround the topic of sexuality and its expression in older people. Sexuality includes a range of emotions, gestures and actions, not just sexual intercourse, and one challenge is to ensure that we do not overly focus on sexual intercourse at the expense of all other manifestations of sexuality. The need for physical and emotional intimacy does not end as we become older, but contemporary society seems to hold the mistaken belief that appropriate sexual expression can only be found in 'the young and the beautiful'. In a 1981 study of sexuality by Masters and Johnson we find the following quote:

For some inexplicable reason, society has been uncomfortable with any overt expression of an active interest in sexual function by an older man or woman, or unable to accept without reservation any ageing person's demands for freedom to express his or her basic sexuality.

This is reflected in the somewhat ribald media reporting of the sexual activity of older Irish people in more recent surveys.

These negative attitudes are yet another reflection of ageism and need to be overcome. When asked the question 'When should old people stop having sex?' the prominent sexologist Alex Comfort responded in his own inimitable way: 'Old folk stop having sex for the same reason they stop riding a bicycle – general infirmity, thinking it looks ridiculous, or no bicycle.'

There is good evidence that older people not only continue to enjoy sexual relationships but also describe them as improving. Older people tend to adapt well to the changes of ageing. Studies show that the numbers of orgasms tend to decrease. However, it is important to realise that sexual relationships do not have to stop at 60, 70 or 80. In both men and postmenopausal women the rate of arousal tends to slow down. In the male, the penis becomes less sensitive and the angle of the penile erection tends to be lower with the amount of ejaculate being reduced. In the female, the vulva, vagina and occasionally the breasts become less sensitive. The vaginal mucosa is a bit stiffer and less lubricant is produced. Some women complain of soreness during intercourse due to this dryness and some artificial lubricant (such as K-Y Jelly) may be of great help. There is much talk about the use of drugs such as Viagra in the press; while some caution is needed if you have other medical conditions (ask your doctor before you use it), these medications can be helpful, although it is a hugely personal choice between you and your partner and it is worth thinking of the wider context. Is it part of a performance anxiety or does it really add to the tenderness, emotional comfort and stimulation of your relationship? Is it something you both want? In the end, remember that emotional and physical tenderness and security are probably the most important expressions of sexuality at all stages of life.

Also, illness, disability and the effects of some medications can reduce sexual libido in both sexes and may cause impotence in some men. Among such drugs are sedatives, tranquillisers, alcohol, and some medications that are used to control high blood pressure, or oestrogens used to treat prostate cancer. Patients who undergo a mastectomy or an amputation may feel unattractive. Here, positive affirmation from their partner as well as from their carer is of paramount importance. It is important that patients be given clear guidance as to when they can resume their sex lives, particularly after sickness or surgery. After such an illness, your partner may need to understand that it can take a little time to regain stamina and interest. Family doctors are increasingly aware of and sensitive to the issue of sexuality and health, so if you have any concerns discuss them with your GP.

Sleep

In general, the human body has a remarkable capacity to manage its own affairs and adapt to each life stage. This is no different in later life and the vast majority of older people will get enough sleep to keep them healthy. However, the body needs less deep sleep and people tend to be more easily awoken after the age of 40. Most older people report sleeping less than previously, but sleep is only considered a problem when the person is not satisfied with their sleep, when the person feels drowsy the following day, or when the sleep problem suggests a serious underlying illness.

A discussion with your family doctor will help to determine if it is just a question of making a few simple lifestyle changes (sometimes called 'sleep hygiene') to improve your sleeping patterns. These include:

- Avoiding naps during the day
- Getting more exercise during the day
- Avoiding going to bed too early
- Avoiding alcohol and other drinks late at night
- Reviewing your medications with the doctor
- Not using the bedroom for reading and watching television, but becoming accustomed to using it for sleep only

However, life stresses or health problems such as depression or anxiety, dementia, prostate or bladder problems, or drinking alcohol may cause insomnia.

In these cases you will need to tackle the underlying disease to try to improve your sleeping.

The most common reason for a sudden change in sleep patterns is stress or nervousness. Depression can keep people up and wakes them at early hours. Dementia frequently alters sleep–wake patterns. A person with dementia may sleep during the daytime then stay awake and even wander at night. Medicines such as diuretics, antidepressants, anti-anxiety medicines, painkillers, and drugs for Parkinson's disease can also affect sleep patterns.

Sometimes people may have an actual sleep disorder called sleep apnoea. This may manifest itself by marked tiredness and sleepiness during the day, and it is caused by a disruption of sleeping whereby breathing actually stops for periods during the night. Your spouse or partner might notice these gaps or other odd behaviours while sleeping. Moving the arms or legs, kicking, loud snoring, or choking sounds are all signs of possible sleep disorders. These should be brought to the doctor's attention. It is important to recognise this condition as it can be treated and make you feel much better during the day.

At all costs, try to avoid sleeping tablets. These only give the illusion of sleeping longer, and start losing their effectiveness after several weeks. At this stage you are likely to have become dependent on them, and they may affect your balance and memory, or indeed your performance when driving a car. Worse, if they are stopped suddenly, you may go into withdrawal and become quite muddled. Unfortunately, Irish people seem to have developed a culture of accepting sleeping tablets. If you are currently on sleeping tablets, discuss a programme of phased withdrawal with your doctor and a review of the possible cause(s) of your sleep disturbances. An exception to this rule may be the sleep disorder of dementia, where there may have to be a compromise so that your partner or spouse can get sleep in order to look after you, and prescription of sleeping tablets for you might be reasonable.

Your Environment

The largest capital expense in life is the purchase of a house. It is quite shocking that the building regulations in Ireland have neglected 'inclusive design', whereby homes are suitable for both disabled and able-bodied people. Older people tend to live in older houses, and a major consideration for your later life is to consider whether or not to prepare your house for potential disability, or to consider a possible move or downsizing. In particular, the possibilities of living on one floor and of having level or ramp access to the outside and the garden, if you have one, are general features to think about. Within the house, the presence of a toilet and shower with generous space on the floor where you are likely to live are key requirements.

The time to be thinking about an age-friendly house is well before you become an older person. Grants are available through the county councils to adapt a house (Housing Adaptation Grant for People with a Disability Scheme), but can only be accessed when you have a disability rather than in anticipation of disability. These grants require an assessment by an occupational therapist, which is a good thing, as they will aim to match any proposed changes with your present and anticipated needs. Do not consider putting in any equipment, lifts or chairlifts without discussing this with an occupational therapist, as this particular solution may not, in fact, be best suited to you, and you and your family may only be engaging in significant extra expenditure with no benefit to you.

Thankfully We Are Not Old Dogs ... and Do Learn New Tricks!

From the above sections, you are now hopefully reassured that in general older people adapt well to the changes of later life and can lead happy and fulfilling lives. When this is not the case, it may in fact be disease and poverty which are the factors that are causing discomfort, rather than old age itself, and the responses to these will be dealt with in coming chapters. Older people are adaptable and flexible, and do respond to new technologies and changes in society whenever possible. Again, poverty may be an issue – the cost of a computer for internet access may be a significant strain, and older people may have to use public facilities rather than having such access at home.

There are many examples of older people making radical change – artists and writers, architects and film-makers have sometimes created their most radical works later in life – think of the wonderful giant spiders of the sculptor Louise Bourgeois, the Guggenheim Museum of Frank Lloyd Wright and the late nocturnes of Gabriel Fauré. Most of us will make smaller but, in their own way, equally radical changes in our lifestyle as we adapt. Perhaps the biggest challenge in later life is to feel empowered and enabled to make these changes, and hopefully you will feel encouraged to do so in a way that suits you. Simone de Beauvoir's insight is a helpful prompt: 'There is only one solution if old age is not to be an absurd parody of our former life, and that is to go on pursuing ends that give our existence a meaning.'

The somewhat tongue-in-cheek comments of Hokusai, the Japanese artist, are a good way to finish off this chapter. Hokusai painted his most radical works in his late 70s and early 80s and you can see this work at the Chester Beatty Library in Dublin. At the age of 73, he wrote:

Although I had produced numerous designs by my fiftieth year, none of my work done before my seventieth year is really worth counting. At the age of seventy-three I have come to understand the true forms of animals, insects and fish and the nature of plants and trees. Consequently, by the age of eighty-six I will have made more and more progress, and at ninety I will have got significantly closer to the essence of art. At the age of one hundred I will have reached a magnificent level and at one hundred and ten each dot and line will be alive. I would like to ask you who outlive me to observe that I have not spoken without reason.

3

Ageing in Ireland

This chapter tries to give some sense of the wider picture of ageing in Ireland and some of the responses from society and government to the new phenomenon. You have approached this book most likely because you (or a loved one) have a problem with an age-related disease, or frailty, and you may wish to go straight to the chapters dealing with those issues. However, some of the problems relating to the experience of ageing in Ireland stem from the relative unpreparedness of Irish society for the complexities, upsides and downsides of ageing. So the provision of everything from pensions to health services has a lag in its planning, and society often either views older people as a disproportionate burden, or provides systems of care that underestimate the complexity of the care needs of older people.

A Country of Young People?

Although by European standards Ireland is a relatively youthful nation (11.7 per cent of the population were aged over 65 in 2011), this is still more than one in ten people. Life expectancy is continually increasing: that of men at the age of 65 increased from 13.8 years in 1995–1997 to 15.4 years in 2001–2003 and to 16.6 in 2005–2007; the corresponding figures for women were 17.4, 18.7 and 19.8 years.

Ageing-Specific Policies in Ireland

Although certain branches of government have developed policies specific to older people (in particular in health), the overall level of awareness of ageing as a core issue for government policy is low. Ireland was one of the last countries in Europe to respond with a National Ageing Strategy, in 2013, to the UN Madrid International Plan of Action on Ageing, and the key UN concept of intergenerational solidarity (whereby strengthening the links between and recognising the interdependency of the various age groups is to the benefit of all) finds little echo in official policy.

Although there has been a Junior Minister for Older People for over a decade, and an Office of Older People was initiated in 2008 to develop a National Strategy on Positive Ageing, no new line of funding was organised for this work, and the Office has incorporated the work and staff of the National Council on Ageing and Older People, which was dissolved in 2009. Founded in 1981 as an advisory body to the Department of Health, the National Council was a vital catalyst in the development of policies on ageing, acting as a centre for social and health gerontology when such activity was at an embryonic stage in Irish universities. It published over 150 reports on various aspects of ageing in Ireland, including health, mental disease, disability, and the law and older people, which are excellent source books on ageing in Ireland and many of which remain accessible on its website (www.ncaop.ie) despite the fact that the National Council is now defunct.

Are Older People Seen as Valued Members of Irish Society?

In some areas, Ireland does seem to recognise older people as an important part of our society, and some gestures have been made such as free public transport and free television licences. However, these can be also seen as gestures that are relatively inexpensive but also which do not respond to the real needs of older people, and an improvement in income, as well as health and social care provision, would be more appropriate. In European surveys, older people in Ireland rate respect from other generations somewhat more highly than in most other European countries, with 44 per cent reporting more respect and 22 per cent reporting less respect.

Income and Finances

Income and support for older people in Ireland arise from a combination of pensions and benefits in kind. The public pension system is what is called the Beveridge type, aimed at providing a safety net rather than income replacement; older Irish people rank second highest for risk of relative poverty in the EU after social transfers and pensions are taken into account. Older women are at a higher risk of poverty than men. However, consistent poverty rates are significantly lower than for people of working age. There were some improvements in the period 2004–2010, and in particular in the risk of poverty (now affecting one in ten older people), but in general the income of older people is significantly lower than that of other adult age groups.

Between 1996 and 2005 there was a considerable shift from State (Non-Contributory) Pensions (a means-tested basic pension) to State (Contributory) Pensions (a taxable, but higher, flat-rate basic pension linked to social insurance payments). Overall, the take-up of private pensions is low in Ireland, with less than half of all workers covered by such schemes.

The most important benefit in kind had been the provision of free access to primary care, medications and hospitals to those over 70, not means tested, which had been shown to have had a dramatic effect on the uptake of preventive healthcare for older people in the first Irish longitudinal study on ageing (Health and Social Services for Older People II (HeSSOP II)); unfortunately, this was removed in 2008. More controversial are the benefits in kind of free public transport, free telephone rental and an allowance for electricity, with critics pointing to the inevitable erosion of access that occurs with piecemeal benefits, given that people need to apply for each one separately, and challenges to less able-bodied older people in using existing public transport. A helpful initiative in this regard has been support from the Department of Transport for social economy models of rural transportation.

Advocacy

Popular advocacy for older people is still developing. It is divided among five groups with, as yet, relatively modest political impact: the most active is Age Action Ireland, and the others are the Irish Association of Older People, the Irish Senior Citizens' Parliament, the National Federation of Pensioners and the Federation of Active Retirement Associations. A number of these organisations joined an umbrella organisation in 2006, Older and Bolder (www. olderandbolder.ie), which provided a more focused approach to advocacy until it ceased operation in June 2013. The government has instituted a national organisation to promote positive attitudes to ageing, Age and Opportunity, which has had some impact, particularly with its programme for exercise for older people, Go For Life (see Chapter 4) and a month-long festival of ageing and the arts, Bealtaine, which is held each May. The under-developed state of popular advocacy on ageing issues may explain the relatively low level of outcry at deficits in community care and long-term care, as well as the indifference to some of the overt ageism in the healthcare system. These include a breast cancer screening programme that has an upper cut-off age of 65 (despite protestations from geriatricians and some advocacy organisations) and clear evidence of less aggressive treatment for older people with many forms of cancer. It is a tribute to the foresight and determination of a handful of figures in Irish public life that a number of positive developments have taken place in this context.

Health Status of Older People in Ireland

The health status report card contains both good and bad news. Several studies find that older Irish people generally report good health. In the first Irish longitudinal study on ageing (HeSSOP II, 2004), more than half of respondents reported no major illnesses while 75 per cent considered their health to be good or very good. In the first wave of the study (HeSSOP I, 2001), 80 per cent rated their quality of life as very good or good. However, as in many other countries, the level of disability rises with advancing age. Almost half of older people reported having at least one major illness, 12 per cent had at least two conditions and almost 2 per cent said they had three or more. That these reports conflict is not surprising: it is common for older people to adapt to illness or disability and rate their health as good overall.

There is also evidence from Irish health surveys that mental ill health increases with later life. Studies of dementia in the community suggest that between 5 and 8 per cent of older people living in the community suffer from dementia.

Structure of the Health Service

It is only in the last two decades that explicit global strategies for ageing and the whole health service have been articulated by the Irish Department of Health. The most important of these was *The Years Ahead,* adopted as official policy in 1993. The main emphasis is on supporting older people to live in their own homes.

At the time of writing (2013), health and social services are run by the Health Service Executive (www.hse.ie). Although there is a National Director of Services for Older People based in HSE Head Office, it is not clear as to how the coordination of services for older people will happen nationally.

Health and social services tend to be relatively poorly coordinated. Surveys confirm the perceptions of older people with disabilities that access to and availability of both health and social services are limited. There is also a major manpower problem on the way, with shortages likely among doctors, nurses, therapists and care staff. According to a 2001 report prepared for the Department of Health and Children, an additional 1,300 chartered physiotherapists and 875 occupational therapists will be needed if adequate services are to be provided in the years ahead. This has led to the opening of new therapy schools in several Irish universities since then.

For many years the Irish healthcare system has been underfunded. The number of specialists is low by international standards. Although healthcare spending rose during the economic prosperity of the Celtic Tiger, many areas of the health service, including care for older people, remain underdeveloped. In 2010 Ireland spent 9.2 per cent of gross domestic product on health, compared to an average of 9.5 per cent in OECD countries, 11.4 per cent in Canada and 17.6 per cent in the United States.

Older people are relatively heavy users of certain health services; in one survey almost half had seen a doctor in the previous four weeks and only 11 per cent had not seen a doctor within the previous year.

Access to Healthcare

There is a mixed public and private healthcare system in Ireland. Approximately one-third of the population has access to universal primary medical and hospital care, including free medication, on the basis of low income. This is known as the General Medical Scheme. Although this scheme was extended to cover everybody over the age of 70 years in 2001, a move which removed one major cause of concern for older people, this was revoked in 2008 and a means-tested system put in place.

Those without Medical Cards are entitled to virtually free access to all public hospital services (a maximum annual payment of €750 (as of Budget 2013) must be paid), and will have all medication costs over €144 a month (as of Budget 2013) reimbursed by the state. However, if they have a GP Visit Card they have to pay for primary care from their own resources and may not have access to the (limited) community services. All healthcare expenses are deductible against income tax. One-third of the population subscribe to private healthcare insurance, at present with four companies; but unfortunately there has been a steady, if subtle, erosion of the community rating basis (i.e. no adverse loading for increased age) which has existed up to now. This insurance is predominantly directed towards elective hospital care. The main advantage of private health insurance is avoiding the relatively long waiting lists for elective surgical procedures in the public system. There is very little allowance for the specialist demands of geriatric medicine. Few, if any, private hospitals have departments of geriatric medicine.

The nursing home scheme, the so-called 'Fair Deal', is perhaps typical of the recurring ageism in the Irish health system. In reality, it replaced an eligibility for state-funded nursing home care, less 80 per cent of the State (Non-Contributory) Pension. Unfortunately, this eligibility was not clarified to many older people and their families, with the consequence that they may have paid the nursing home costs themselves, often causing great distress. To such people, the new scheme is an improvement; however, the lack of outcry at the failure to clarify the existing eligibility, and the use of older people as a test-bed for first removal of a health eligibility in Ireland, speaks volumes for the relatively low priority given to their needs.

Specific Healthcare Policies for Older People

Government policy for the health of older people started with a White Paper, *The Care of the Aged* in 1968; but it is really with *The Years Ahead*, published in 1988, that the first signs of a dedicated policy emerged. This was the report of a working group, with input from many disciplines and healthcare administrators, appointed by the Minister for Health to develop a blueprint for services for the elderly with the goals of a) maintaining older people at home where possible at an optimal level of health and independence, and b) enabling those who cannot live at home to receive treatment, rehabilitation and care as near as possible to home. The report made extensive recommendations regarding the social and medical needs of older people, including the need for adequate housing and income; health promotion; partnership between carers, volunteers and statutory agencies; and the development of comprehensive and coordinated services for all older people whether at home, in hospital or in institutional care. The special needs of older mentally ill patients were also recognised.

The report was adopted as official government policy in 1993 and although it has been influential in shaping health policies for older Irish people, a review of its impact after eight years found that many recommendations remained unfulfilled and noted that almost no extra spending had been directed to older people. This is in stark contrast to childcare services, which expanded greatly following specific legislation in 1991. It was the opinion of the National Council on Ageing and Older People (and of many geriatricians) that specific legislation will be required to underpin the development of appropriate levels of services for older people.

Geriatric Medicine

The Years Ahead emphasised the need to provide specialist expertise for older people and advocated the development of geriatric medicine in general hospitals. These arguments have been accepted by the government, and it is now official policy that each general hospital should have a department of geriatric medicine. The first consultant geriatrician in Ireland was Dr Michael Hyland, who was appointed to Cork University Hospital in 1969. There are now over 70 geriatricians in the country, the number having more than trebled over the last decade, and geriatric medicine is now the largest medical speciality in the country. However, provision of the facilities and staff necessary for true multidisciplinary geriatric medical care has lagged behind in many areas.

The scientific body associated with ageing in Ireland is the Irish Gerontological Society, which was founded in 1951 and is one of the oldest gerontological societies in Europe. It was founded by Dr John Fleetwood Snr, one of the great pioneers of ageing studies in Ireland and the author of one of the first books on ageing and health. The Irish Gerontological Society has an interdisciplinary membership and a strong healthcare orientation, and much of the research presented at its meetings has been instrumental in promoting better care for older people in Ireland.

Psychiatry of old age has developed relatively recently as a specialty and it is unstated government policy to appoint psychiatrists in old age in each region.

Community Care Services

Community care services, although developing rapidly, have been underdeveloped in Ireland. Roughly 18 per cent of all older people receive some form of ongoing formal care at home. In a 2004 survey, 15 per cent had been visited by a public health nurse and 5 per cent by other home-based services. In *The Years Ahead* it was proposed that each health board appoint a coordinator for services for the elderly. The precise role and responsibilities of such posts have not been clearly identified and there is little evidence of positive or negative impact on community services. The cornerstone of community care services is the public health nurse system and family doctors supported by home help services. A relatively small number of older Irish people avail of home help, but this increases significantly with age: 6.2 per cent of those aged between 70 and 79, rising to 19 per cent for those over 80. There are various models of organisation of this service and this can lead to considerable frustration among older people and their carers in terms of adequacy and access. A major step forward was the institution of Home Care Packages, for which older people with disabilities in many parts of the country can apply.

Community therapists are in general limited to physiotherapists and occupational therapists, with very limited, and sometimes no, access in the community to speech therapy, clinical nutrition and social work for older people and their carers. Waiting lists can be long for community physiotherapy and occupational therapy, and there is an element of chance as to the degree of availability of these services in any one area. An initiative of the HSE was to group therapists into primary care teams, but there does not appear to be a common core set of services applying to all primary care teams, or indeed a common method of accessing their services.

Day centres can be very helpful from a social and community perspective for those who wish to avail of them, but may not suit all older people. There are approximately 212 day centres in Ireland which provide social, nutritional and community support for older people, but not health-based interventions. About 1.8 per cent of the older Irish population receive domiciliary meal services – 'Meals on Wheels' – whereby meals provided by voluntary organisations, with financial assistance from the HSE, are delivered to people's houses. In certain areas, however, these services are not available.

Long-Stay Care

Long-stay care is divided between institutions administered directly by the HSE (9,573 beds – 49 per cent of the total) and private nursing homes (6,209 beds – 32 per cent of the total), with a small but significant sector provided by the voluntary sector (religious orders and charities) (3,786 beds – 19 per cent of the total). The HSE institutions are categorised as geriatric homes and hospitals (6,126 beds), welfare homes (1,056 beds) and district/community hospitals (2,391 beds). Unfortunately, there was little impetus to renovate often outdated buildings and facilities in public nursing homes during the Celtic Tiger boom, and there appeared to be a policy to significantly reduce the number of public nursing home places; the HSE National Service Plan 2012, for example, proposed closing between 500 and 900 public nursing home places.

Although the vast majority of staff providing care in these settings are dedicated and kind, there was little articulation of clear standards of care until after the Leas Cross Report in 2006. Following this report, the Health Information and Quality Authority

(HIQA), together with representatives of older people's organisations, nursing home providers and healthcare professionals, drew up standards of care in Irish nursing homes that represented a quantum leap forward. In addition, all nursing homes, whether public, private or voluntary, are inspected regularly by HIQA to ensure that these standards are maintained, and reports of these inspections are posted on the HIQA website (www.hiqa.ie).

Some work remains on some of the recommendations of the Leas Cross Report, including the level of training for doctors who provide medical care in nursing homes. The Irish Society of Physicians in Geriatric Medicine has produced a position paper on standards of assessment, treatment and care in extended care, including the proposal that doctors working in nursing homes should have a Diploma in Medicine of the Elderly or a similar qualification.

In Summary

Overall, it is clear that at the very least, the Irish people and government have a road map, *The Years Ahead*, for good care and health for older people. That they should have lost their way somewhat and have failed to invest does not mean that we should throw away the map. Some good things have happened, in particular the offering of Medical Cards to the over-70s (but sadly snatched away again), the development of geriatric medicine and old-age psychiatry, the National Care Programme for Older People, the provision of Home Care Packages, and the overall increase in fitness of our older population. Urgent development of both community and nursing home services are required, as you will be likely to discover, and many of the succeeding chapters try to advise on strategies to navigate the shoals and reefs of the system. The proposed division of the HSE into seven service divisions raises some concerns over coordination and integration of services but it is too early to say what will happen.

4

Active Ageing

Several interconnected activities are the mainspring for maintaining maximal well-being in later life. As will become obvious, the more that all of these become the habits of a lifetime, the greater will be the gain. However, it really is never too late, and even the frailest older person will gain from developing their activity profile. Of course, this is not an absolute protection against disease and disability, but all can benefit. The very simplicity of these components may pose a difficulty for some – surely it can't be that simple? No technology, no tablets, no vitamins ...? In fact, the evidence from international studies is overwhelming – active ageing strategies are the key pathway to giving yourself a healthy and happier old age.

The components of active ageing are:

- Exercise
- Mental activity
- Social activity

Ideally, it would be more pleasurable and more productive to combine two or three of these components together, for example by way of dancing, exercise classes or walking to your bridge class. Active retirement groups or informal groups of friends may be a good way of attending and maintaining this level of activity: Active Retirement Ireland can direct you to an active retirement group in your area (www.activeirl.ie). Another way to access exercise is to make use of a countrywide exercise programme for older people called Go for Life (www.ageandopportunity.ie/go-life). Run by Age and Opportunity in conjunction with the HSE, it provides a network of Go for Life coordinators who can inform you of a physical activity leader in your area. These are often older people themselves, and the activities can span from tai chi through bowling to exercise programmes suitable for those who can only perform activity when sitting down. Go for Life also produces some excellent leaflets on exercise and walking, with a helpful motivational chart.

Exercise

Exercise has never been more important, and the most effective of all the possible ways of maximising your chances of healthy old age. Living in a society with an increasingly sedentary lifestyle, we are not prompted to exert ourselves to the same extent that occurred a generation previously. We also live in a society in which ever more of us will reach old age. Exercise has been described as the nearest thing we have to an anti-ageing remedy. While this must not be taken too far, there is no doubt that exercise improves health and appearance. It can restore functions which have already declined and delay the onset of many illnesses. Among the benefits of exercise are:

- Developing greater stamina
- Improving balance and lessening the tendency to fall (in particular balance exercises such as tai chi)
- Strengthening bones (weight-bearing exercise)
- Beneficial effects on the heart and circulation, including lower blood pressure and possibly lower cholesterol levels
- Improving diabetes
- Improving sleep
- Reducing appetite and aiding in weight reduction

Those who exercise are less likely to suffer from heart attack, stroke, osteoporosis and late onset diabetes, and even diseases such as Alzheimer's.

It is almost certain that the greatest barriers to exercise are habit and a failure to realise the many options which are available, particularly for older people. It is also true that access may be an issue, particularly in rural areas where the traffic environment renders walking uncomfortable if not downright dangerous. Breaking poor habits underlines the importance of starting early, so that exercise is incorporated into daily life in the same way as brushing your teeth or shaving.

Developing a routine and investing in rainwear that allows you to walk with comfort in our damp climate are other useful possible supports for ongoing exercise.

Health

Health is not a barrier to exercise for most people, including older people, who tend to be sensible about how they exert themselves. Those who suffer from heart disease (such as angina), lung disease (such as asthma) or active arthritis should talk to their doctor before undertaking vigorous exercise. As a general principle, those who are starting out for the first time should introduce themselves gradually to their exercise and should be alert for pain and discomfort. Again, while most people are quite sensible about not overdoing things, a good rule of thumb is that you should be able to talk while you are exercising. Another important precaution is to both warm up beforehand and cool down afterwards.

How Much and What Type of Exercise Should I Do?

The minimum that should be aimed for would be 30 minutes' exercise at least three times a week. There are several types of exercise which are recognised, and many common exercises involve a number of these types. The main types are:

- Endurance (aerobic)
- Strengthening
- Stretching
- Balance

Endurance exercise involves making the heart and lungs work harder, and usually means exercising for at least twenty minutes at a time. Walking, running, swimming, cycling and dancing are all aerobic exercises. Golf, while enjoyable and sociable, rarely develops the level of exertion needed to be truly aerobic.

Specific strengthening and stretching exercises are most likely to be recommended to you through an exercise class or by a physiotherapist, but all exercise involves some element of strengthening and stretching. Strengthening exercises, such as squats and exercises with weights, work on specific muscles.

Stretching, as the name suggests, stretches muscles and ligaments, and both improves flexibility and lessens the chance of injury. Examples of stretching exercises include shoulder rolls, back stretches and tricep stretches.

Balance exercises have been given a boost by the finding that tai chi reduces the risk of falls. Tai chi is a gentle and accessible programme and can be strongly recommended if there is a training programme near you.

That's All Very Well, But I'm Too Sick for All That!

It is very important to realise that exercise is for everyone, and the frailest might actually have the most significant benefit from exercise, as long as it is tailored to their capabilities. If everyday activities such as walking or swimming are not feasible, then you or your helper may have to search a bit to look for a physiotherapist or exercise class that is suited to your needs. Even in the nursing home it should be possible to find some activity that is suited to you.

My Mother Doesn't Want to Exercise

All older people have their own way of reacting to their situation. Those who were raising families in Ireland in the 1950s and 1960s were often so busy that the idea of exercise might seem foreign. Do discuss this openly if you have concerns, but again respect for an older parent's wishes should be your key aim. Also, do you have your own exercise programme? It is unrealistic to expect to influence people if you don't practice what you preach. In fact, perhaps just asking someone to go for a walk followed by a cup of tea might kill several birds with one stone, without a single formal discussion on exercise.

Mental Activity

The principle of 'use it or lose it' is less clearly established for mental as opposed to social activity, but it is relatively clear that mental stimulation is good in later life, just as it is at all ages. This can be provided at both formal and informal levels and it is important that older people feel comfortable with the level at which it is provided. Just as with exercise, it is never too late to start an adult education programme at any level. Local vocational education committees can give guidance on the wide range of courses available and a particularly helpful innovation is the University of the Third Age, an organisation that arranges courses specifically designed for the rhythm of life of older people.

Another helpful resource is the plethora of daytime activities arranged by libraries, museums and galleries. Reading, doing crosswords and playing games such as bridge are also useful ways of keeping the brain active.

Social Activity

Throughout this book, I emphasise that older people must be facilitated to do that which *they* want to do. Social activity, or the way in which we include ourselves in our community and surroundings, is a very personal activity, and will only be successful if we do it essentially on our own terms. Clearly, if we develop a habit in younger life that maximises our social contacts and stimulation it is more likely that we will continue it later in life. Social activity, on our own terms, is good, but those concerned about an older adult should also be mindful that it can be very stressful to be involved with something with which you have little sympathy.

This social activity can take many forms. For some, continuing to work after what is perceived to be the retirement age can provide a fulfilling way of socialising. For others, volunteerism is a useful way to combine social activity with a sense of giving back to society. All sorts of charities in Ireland are crying out for volunteers, and most will find some niche to accommodate those who may not be as nimble as previously thought. Ongoing participation in clubs and societies is clearly another form of activity, and choosing sports or activities with a wide range of opportunities for social interaction can be helpful.

Active retirement associations have a very valuable role and tend to develop a wide range of activities. As these are very much run by their members, you may or may not find that the range of options suits you.

Day clubs and day centres represent another option that is valuable for some people, particularly if transportation is feasible. However, there are also others for whom the idea is anathema for a whole host of reasons. In an ideal world, the participants can set the agenda for activities and services; if you wish to participate in a club you should look to see whether or not this is the case.

Organised religion is another focus for social activity, and indeed it may be one of the reasons why people who actively practise religion live longer. Getting involved in your church and its activities is a helpful form of social activity (as well as the other reasons for being involved), and adds a focus and structure to the week – religious ceremonies and contact and belonging to a community add a richness and ceremony to life.

Perhaps the most important advice is not to disengage from your social activities should you develop some disability and decide that you are a 'drag' on the group. The fact that you now have a walking stick, a hearing aid or impaired vision will loom larger in your mind than in that of the group. While you may not manage Croagh Patrick, trust in the flexibility of the group to bend to you in the way that you would bend to others. Also, consider whether or not you might be suffering from depression if you are beginning to withdraw from your social activities – you might discuss this with your family doctor.

My Mother Spends Too Much Time at Home

Again, remember that it is up to your mother to set her own social pace. Getting involved in something that doesn't suit her may be counterproductive for all concerned. While social interaction is in general a good thing, some people are intensely private. Remember also that as we advance into later life we begin to lose friends and colleagues to illness and death and this can change patterns of social activity hugely. So do not feel that you have failed your mother if she does not go out often – this may be her way of selecting, adapting and compensating. Support with transport for the things that she enjoys doing can be helpful; if not accepted, don't take umbrage. Also, home tends to be a more enriching and stimulating environment than casual consideration would suggest: all the artefacts and furniture are imbued with memories and emotions which reinforce the sense of a life course. Finally, do give some thought as to whether there might be depression or some other illness if a parent who has previously been socially active begins to withdraw from social activities without a clear cause. Discuss with your parent whether it might be good to have a check-up with their family doctor about this.

5

Healthy Ageing

Although the elements of Chapter 4, active ageing, are the main source of remaining healthy in later life, there are specific medical issues that also need to be taken into account, and older people and their relatives should be aware of the medical opportunities to keep them healthier in later life. If you have bought this book because of a specific health problem you may wish to go straight to that topic; however, it is helpful to have a wider view of health in later life.

The Good News

As population ageing became an ever-present reality, the 1950s and 1960s were marked by concerns that this would lead to a big increase in the numbers of people with disability and disease. A very perceptive doctor in California, James Fries, saw that there was another possibility. With access to population databases of a big healthcare provider, he proposed that people were ageing in a healthier way and that in fact we would see what he called 'the compression of morbidity'. By this he meant that rather than dying at 70, having suffered from a heart attack at 45 and a subsequent 25 years of ill health, a person would die at 75, but suffer major illnesses much nearer the time of death, say at 65, so with just 10 years of ill health.

The good news is that for the current generation of older people both life span and health in later life have improved. For example, in the United States, disability among older people has dropped by 1.5 per cent a year over the last decade. This pattern seems to be replicated around the developed world so that the amount of later life spent with a significant disability is dropping.

However, despite the good news, late life disability has not been abolished. Old age is the time when you are most likely to develop a disability. Naturally enough, all of us would like to know what we can do to prevent this happening or to reduce its impact should we become disabled.

There is very good evidence that a relatively simple range of measures will reduce our chances of disability in later life, and that these measures are still effective into advanced old age. Some of these we have discussed in Chapter 4, the rest will be discussed below, with an emphasis on how you can practically achieve your goals with your family doctor. However, with the best will in the world, and even when following all the best advice, disability and disease can occur, so you must not feel that you have failed yourself should they occur.

The Health Promotion Schedule

Everybody should follow the basic health promotion schedule:

- Ensure an adequate secure income (Chapter 6)
- Ensure adequate secure access to healthcare (Chapter 7)
- Exercise frequently (Chapter 4)
- Engage in mental activity (Chapter 4)
- Engage in social activity (Chapter 4)
- Control your weight and eat a healthy diet
- Check and control your blood pressure
- Get yearly influenza vaccinations
- Check your cholesterol levels
- Undergo cancer screening
- Quit smoking
- For diabetics, control their diabetes

Weight Control and Diet

Malnutrition is an interesting concept – it means 'badly nourished' rather than 'under-nourished'. This means that it also includes being overweight, sometimes known as obesity. Obesity is increasingly common in later life, and is probably the most common form of malnutrition in later life. It is worth tackling at almost any age. While the theory of keeping weight at an ideal level is simple – less food, 'better' food and more exercise – the practice can be difficult, especially if you are disabled or live on your own. Exercise has been dealt with in Chapter 4. While general guidelines on diet are outlined below, if you find that you cannot lose weight, or even are still putting it on, look for help. The best help is from people in the same situation, and Weightwatchers and other groups are probably the best form of peer support and positive peer pressure. Try to get over the embarrassment – this is your body and your future, don't worry about what others think.

We all can get into poor practices, whether from snacking, comfort foods or not exercising enough. There are also convenience and cost issues: in an era of supermarkets and convenience stores getting fresh fruit and vegetables that are ripe and affordable can be quite a challenge. Often purchasing small quantities is more expensive. However, it is worth persisting in trying to buy strategically so that you can buy fresh fruit and vegetables, and to consider cooking dishes that can be used over several days – a good soup can last several days, and bread, vegetables and fruit will all keep better in your fridge than outside of it.

Cooking can become more challenging when it is only for one person; a very good source of information for interesting meals for one person is Delia Smith's *One is Fun*, which provides a host of ideas for cooking for one person. Using a sequence of meals with one ingredient can be a good solution – the left-overs from a roast half-chicken could be made into a stew or curry the next day. Also, the use of the microwave for fresh cooking can be a winner on all fronts – it facilitates preparation of meals for one, keeps the goodness of vegetables, saves on electricity costs and cuts down on the washing-up. A particularly good book in this respect is *Microwave Gourmet* by Barbara Kafka.

While you are still independent, consider some changes to your routine that will allow for healthier eating, and try to plan for the week ahead.

- Start or develop the five portions habit – eating five portions of fruit or vegetable a day. Although that seems a lot, a potato and a serving of vegetables at dinner and prunes or half a grapefruit with breakfast already makes three. Adding to this is not as difficult as it might seem.
- Try to reduce the biscuits and cakes part of the shopping list; even apparently healthier-looking options such as digestive biscuits are loaded with sugar and fat. If you need a stock of goodies for entertaining consider buying them in smaller sealed portions so that you don't find yourself finishing off a whole cake or packet of biscuits by 'grazing' after the visitors have gone.
- Try to keep the habit of cooking rather than buying pre-prepared meals – much as I enjoy a good high-quality prepared meal, the salt and fat content of such meals is often higher than dishes which you prepare yourself.
- Increase fibre in your diet. Fibre works at a whole range of levels: it releases calories in a more controlled way, and it helps to reduce appetite and intake. Good sources of fibre include porridge, wholegrain bread, lentils and beans, fruit and vegetables.
- Cut down on saturated fats such as butter, red meat and in refined foods such as cakes, biscuits and fried foods.

- Maintain a reasonable intake of calcium to maintain strong bones. The main sources are in milk and dairy products such as cheese.
- Eat oily fish regularly. Oily fish (such as mackerel, sardines and salmon) provides the richest source of a particular type of polyunsaturated fat known as omega-3 fats, which can help to lower blood fat levels, prevent the blood from clotting and regulate the heart rhythm.
- Watch your alcohol intake. Not only is alcohol high in calories, but taken in excess it affects many organs and, in my experience as a doctor, our tolerance as a society of high levels of alcohol intake is too generous. Alcohol may also reduce your inhibitions about eating food, and those drinking alcohol with meals consume more food than those who don't. You may get away with higher levels of alcohol intake now, but behind the scenes you are reducing your reserves in your brain, liver, heart and bones, which will become more apparent when you develop an age-related disability. Two measures or units of alcohol a day is enough (a bottle of wine is six units, a pint of beer two units and a bottle of spirits 26 units).
- As the digestive process slows with age, it is well worth considering smaller, more frequent meals, including snacks, instead of two or three large meals a day.

If you should become more disabled, you may need to look for help with keeping the cooking going, especially from occupational therapy. A reconfiguration of your kitchen and dining area (counter-level oven, trolleys, etc.) and the use of aids (such as those which help in the opening of jars and cans) can make a big difference. Other possibilities include getting your meals made for you occasionally during the week, whether this is the local pub lunch, in a day centre, a pre-prepared meal from a family member or a supermarket, or else Meals-on-Wheels. Discuss these options with your family and friends.

If you are having difficulty eating, discuss this with your public health nurse or doctor; they will be able to check whether some illness is diminishing your appetite. Some medications can also affect the sense of taste and/or smell, or can give you a dry mouth, which makes eating more difficult. In addition, think about your teeth and/or dentures. Increasing numbers of older people have retained their own teeth, and if these teeth are in poor condition, or if dentures are loose and poorly fitting, then eating will be correspondingly more difficult. Your dentist can advise on these and treat you. New techniques are also appearing, such as dental implants, which may play a helpful role.

As a family member, try not to fret too much about your older relative's eating habits. Discuss some of the points in this book, but late life is a time of complexity and choice, and older people rightly need to feel that they are in control of their own life. Eating is a complex function, which is not only about nourishment but also about pleasure and social engagement. If you are concerned that they are not eating well, the very best way of improving this is to eat with them, either by having them over for a meal, or joining them for a meal.

In the later stages of some illnesses, older people seem to survive on what would be impossibly short commons for you and me, but this is a recognised phenomenon, and, again, may not improve with all the care in the world. In Chapter 14, we cover ways of supporting feeding, including the issue of tube-feeding.

With alcohol, too, do not fret. We all need to have the right to behave within a fairly wide band of behaviour, and keep at the forefront of your mind how you as, say, a 44-year-old would like your 21-year-old son or daughter trying to control what you consider to be reasonable drinking habits. The difficult area can be around purchasing alcohol for a house-bound older person with alcohol dependency. This is an area that requires some skill, and indeed may be only a continuation of a difficult problem over a life span. Discuss the issue with your older relative and other family members, but do not let it become a major rift between you and your older relative.

What about Vitamins and Supplements?

In general, the use of vitamin supplements is a complete distraction from the realities of nutrition and healthy ageing. It has led to a raft of useless books promoting them as virtual elixirs of youth, and less well-publicised literature on the possible harmful effects of large doses of vitamins in people with heart disease (which is common in later life). Some of these books might make you feel guilty for not taking multi-vitamins, folic acid, individual vitamins such as Vitamin E, gingko and what are often called antioxidants; this is completely untrue, and a distraction from all the other things you should be doing. It also medicalises normal old age.

If you have a healthy and balanced diet, following the five fruit and vegetables a day rule, you will have all the minerals and vitamins that you require. There are also benefits in terms of fibre and avoiding obesity from getting your vitamins through healthy eating rather than from a pill. It is really only the very small minority of frail people with inadequate nutrition who cannot manage to get the full nutrition they require, and, in these circumstances, they are best advised by a dietician. The same principles apply to nutritional supplements such as Ensure, Fortisip and Pro-Cal. So, in general, spend your money on fruit, or buy Supermilk!

Blood Pressure Control

High blood pressure is an important and common factor in causing heart disease and stroke in later life. Ideally you should arrange to get your blood pressure checked between the ages 40 and 50, and at least every few years after this. The normal blood pressure is usually taken to be about 120/80. As long as you don't have side effects from blood pressure medication your family doctor should aim for as near this figure as possible.

In the first instance, normal blood pressure should be achieved by lifestyle changes such as exercise (see Chapter 4), stopping smoking, weight reduction, drinking less alcohol and reducing your salt intake. These can all be effective, but may take a little time to work.

There are a range of medications for reducing your blood pressure, the most worrying side effect of which is 'postural hypotension' (also known as orthostatic hypotension), where your blood pressure drops when you stand up or bend over. In later life this can also occur quite a long time after standing up. This is a potentially worrying symptom as it may lead to falls and unsteadiness. Discuss this with your doctor, as it is important that they factor it into your treatment schedule. There may even come a time when it is no longer reasonable to treat high blood pressure due to this side effect, as you are at more risk from falling than from the effects of high blood pressure. A wide range of tablets are available, so if you find that you don't get on with one, there are many others that can be substituted, and most people can usually tolerate at least one of them. Most people do not feel any specific symptoms with high blood pressure (such as headaches or dizziness), so it can be a challenge to keep taking tablets for something which is only an abstract concept for you. However, it is worth persisting, as blood pressure control can protect you not only from stroke and heart disease, but also from other illnesses such as dementia (including Alzheimer's disease).

If high blood pressure has been found, your doctor will probably arrange to keep an eye on it regularly, and some may wish to also have a home monitor for blood pressure. These are quite inexpensive, and you should work with your family doctor, usually by using the blood pressure monitor to keep a diary of your blood pressure, which will help the doctor to adjust your medications as necessary.

Influenza Vaccination – The Flu Jab

Vaccination for influenza is one of the most extraordinarily effective simple interventions for preserving health among older people, and one which has been undersold. Part of the problem is that the wider benefits of vaccination – reduction in the incidence of stroke and heart attack – have not been widely advertised, and the other is that people might think the flu is a relatively mild illness, which it is not; most of those who die from the flu are older people, particularly those with chronic illnesses. Why does the flu jab work so well? Apart from its efficacy in preventing flu, the answer probably lies in the fact that it reduces inflammation in the blood stream, and this inflammation is a contributor to diseases of the blood vessels such as stroke and heart attacks.

Some may also be concerned by reports of mild flu-like symptoms after the injection. Be reassured that these occur in a minority of people, will pass and are significantly less than you would experience with the real flu. So each autumn, make an appointment with your family doctor and get the flu jab. This is usually given in October.

What about Cholesterol?

Cholesterol is a fatty substance which is found in the blood. It is mainly made in the body and actually plays an essential role in how every cell in the body works. However, too much cholesterol in the blood can increase your risk of heart problems. There are two main types of cholesterol, called lipoproteins:

LDL (low density lipoprotein) is the *harmful* type of cholesterol, and HDL (high density lipoprotein) is a *protective* type of cholesterol. Another important fat in the blood is *triglyceride,* which is found in foods such as dairy products, meat and cooking oils. People who are very overweight, eat a lot of fatty and sugary foods, or drink too much alcohol are more likely to have a high triglyceride level, and thus have a greater risk of developing cardiovascular disease than people with lower levels. Although part of the cause of high blood cholesterol levels is from eating too much saturated fat, there are also genetic and constitutional factors such as the way your body metabolises cholesterol, and some people have high blood cholesterol even though they eat a healthy diet.

There is much talk of getting cholesterol checked, but for otherwise healthy older people who do not smoke, we have little idea as yet of what to do if you are found to have a high cholesterol and no other significant illnesses, but exercise and a diet high in fibre and low in saturated fats is good for you anyway, and helps in lowering cholesterol.

However, for those with known diabetes, high blood pressure or diseases of the blood vessels (stroke, heart disease and peripheral vascular disease) there is quite good evidence that treatment of cholesterol reduces your chances of heart attack, stroke and death. So, if you have one of these conditions, if not already done, you should ask for your cholesterol to be checked. Discuss the results with your doctor and try to work out in which camp you lie.

If for one of the medical reasons outlined above you do need to control your cholesterol, then in general this will almost always involve one of the medications which lower cholesterol, as well as reviewing your diet and partaking in exercise, which increases your HDL levels (the 'good' cholesterol). The main type of cholesterol-lowering medication, a group of medications called statins, actually have many actions, and may actually provide a protective health effect by mechanisms other than lowering cholesterol, for example, by antioxidant action.

One urban myth which is worth demolishing is that the cholesterol which is found in foods such as eggs, liver, kidneys and some types of seafood, e.g. prawns, is a problem: these sources of cholesterol do *not* usually add to the level of cholesterol in your blood. What *is* recommended is a diet which is high in fibre, low in total fat and contains as much oily fish as possible. In fact, much the same diet as was recommended for all older people above. In general, it is good to get dietary advice for the condition that prompted the cholesterol control – diabetes or heart disease – and this advice will also be appropriate for your cholesterol.

What about 'cholesterol-lowering' margarines or spreads? These have a very modest effect on cholesterol, and have much less of a role than a good diet and exercise at tackling high cholesterol levels. They are not a magic cure.

What about Cancer Screening?

The most common form of cancer in later life is skin cancer in its various forms, which can usually be cured if caught early. The public's imagination has been caught by the idea of cancer screening, which is a somewhat contentious issue, and the cancers for which there is the most evidence of benefits of screening asymptomatic people are breast cancer and bowel cancer. In this section, we will deal with these two as whole population screening issues, and then with the type of vigilance you might consider for other forms of cancer, and what to do if these symptoms occur.

Breast Cancer

Screening for breast cancer has a small benefit at all ages, yet, bizarrely, the Irish government curtails access to breast cancer screening at the very age when you are most likely to get breast cancer. While older peoples' advocacy organisations and professionals make the case for removing the age barriers for breast cancer screening, what should you do? Regular breast examination is an important start, and you should discuss any change or new lump or lumpiness with your family doctor. In my experience some people feel embarrassed about breast masses, and delay reporting lumps to the family doctor. In fact, breast cancer in older people is often more treatable than for younger people; also the change may be benign, and speedy assessment will save you unnecessary worry. So, please discuss any change as soon as possible with your family doctor, who will refer you to a rapid access breast cancer assessment service.

Bowel Cancer

After the age of 50 there is increasing evidence of a benefit from screening for bowel cancer. It is likely in the near future that all people over the age of 50 will have a bowel motion checked every two years for tiny traces of blood that are not visible to the naked eye (called faecal occult blood). If this blood is present, they will then be referred for endoscopy, a process of inserting a flexible viewing tube into the back passage. In the interim, all older people should be concerned if they have any combination of:

- A change in how their bowels work – for example, new onset of constipation, new onset of persistent diarrhoea or a feeling of wanting to pass a bowel motion but a bowel motion not coming
- Bleeding from the back passage, or blood on the bowel motion (while this may be due to piles, it should still be discussed with your family doctor)
- Unexplained weight loss (not due to dieting or increased exercise)

Your family doctor will be able to put these changes in perspective, and refer you on as necessary to a gastroenterologist or surgeon for further assessment.

Prostate Cancer

Prostate cancer screening is a much more contentious issue. Men who have symptoms of difficulties with their prostate (having to go to the toilet more often, difficulties in starting and stopping urinating, a reduced stream, and having to get up more than once at night to go to the bathroom) should go to see their family doctor, who will assess them and usually perform a rectal examination (using a finger inserted in your back passage) to check the prostate. They may decide to refer you on to a urologist (kidney, bladder and prostate surgeon). The benefits of screening with a blood test called prostate-specific antigen (PSA) have not been established, and indeed a general screening with this test might be harmful due to the side effects of the investigations and treatment.

Skin Cancer

This is an area where older people and their families can make a difference to their future care by acting early on any spot, bump, mole or lump on the skin which appears, grows in size or appearance, or changes (for example, starting to bleed). Get in touch with your family doctor, who will assess you. In some cases they may remove the offending lump, or they may send you on to a specialist such as a dermatologist or a plastic surgeon. By acting early, most skin cancers can be completely cured by a simple removal while still small; if left to grow larger, removal might require major surgery, and may not result in a cure.

For Smokers

Stopping smoking is at once simple and difficult: simple in concept and difficult in execution. Like all addictions, most people need some help to stop smoking. The first barrier is thinking that it is too late. Do not be fooled by this. There is abundant evidence that stopping smoking helps at any age, and improves the outcome of many stroke-related diseases. A second barrier can be healthcare professionals who may be ageist about stopping smoking, and think (incorrectly) that it is not worthwhile. So, if you want to try to stop smoking, be prepared for a possible lack of interest from those around you, and push your case.

One support that can help you stop smoking is having a plan: it is a good idea to make a list of the settings and scenarios that are associated with smoking – after a meal, meeting friends at a pub – anticipating the craving that might come from these familiar surroundings and settings and figuring out how best to deal with them. Decide whether or not you will work best by sharing your plan with others – who could then support you – or whether you are a 'quiet quitter' who would find the inevitable questions annoying. If there are other smokers in the house or among your friends it makes a lot of sense to try to find common cause and all try to stop smoking together.

Smoking cessation classes are also available, as are a number of medications. The most common of these are nicotine replacements, such as chewing gum or nicotine patches.

You need to watch out for weight gain – smoking does suppress your appetite, and you need to be careful that you are not replacing one harmful influence (smoking) with another (over-eating).

For family members, do not fret if your older relative does not stop smoking; as with diet and alcohol, adults in our society are accorded a fairly wide range of freedom of behaviour, and your older relative must be given this freedom as well. If you are a smoker yourself, please consider giving up because a) you will provide encouragement and lessen occasions of temptation, and b) it is difficult to be taken seriously about smoking cessation if you yourself are still smoking.

For Those with Diabetes

To control your diabetes you should:

- Follow all of the advice discussed above
- Ensure you have a good diet
- Closely control your blood pressure, cholesterol and blood fat levels

Diabetes is a common illness in later life and, within the bounds of reason, as strict a control as possible of your diabetes will lessen your chance of developing complications. Diabetes is caused by your blood sugar (glucose) levels being too high (see Chapter 10 for more information about diabetes). You will need to discuss this with your doctor. Symptoms of diabetes include fatigue, weight loss, thirst and needing to pass urine more frequently, although older people with diabetes do not always have these symptoms. Your doctor will check your urine or blood for sugar levels, and will outline a plan, often in conjunction with a dietician, and also often with a diabetes specialist, also known as an endocrinologist. The vast majority of older people with diabetes control their sugar levels through altering their diet, with the addition of tablets for many. Only a very small number will need insulin injections.

Perhaps the most important ongoing responsibility will be an annual review, which will focus on sugar control, a check of how your kidneys are functioning, a review of your feet and an inspection of your eyes. A blood test, called the haemoglobin A1c test, is a helpful guide for your doctor as to how well your diabetes is being controlled.

In all other respects, it is important not to let diabetes become a barrier to continued normal living. You do need to let your insurance company know that you have diabetes if you are a driver, and, as information is power, it is well worth joining the Diabetes Federation of Ireland to access its helpful information.

An additional area of note is the need to control cholesterol for those with diabetes and this will in general be prompted by your family doctor or specialist; many patients will be recommended to take a medication to reduce the levels of certain types of cholesterol in their blood, and, for those with diabetes, it is worth taking these medications if at all possible as the failure to control cholesterol has more serious consequences for diabetics than non-diabetics. The most common side effects are usually minor impacts on your muscles and liver which you usually won't notice, and your doctor will need to monitor these with blood tests.

Are these Prevention Strategies just for Middle Age and Early Old Age?

All of the strategies outlined above are most effective when started as early as possible, but all continue to be important in the face of the illnesses that will inevitably develop as we age. Nearly all are effective right to the end – for example, the annual flu jab for those in nursing homes not only protects you, but also the nursing home staff. However, all of these good preventive strategies need sensible reconsideration and reprioritisation in the face of other needs that may arise – for example, you need to balance the benefits of high blood pressure treatment against the dangers of dizziness caused by postural hypotension should you develop a tendency to fall. Embarking on these strategies is also helpful in giving you a sense of control over what is happening in your life.

6

Finances and Ageing

One of the most important determinants of healthy ageing is access to a secure and adequate income. While this seems to be an obvious fact, one of the surprising features of ageing in modern Ireland is that this fact has not been addressed by society. This should be of major concern. There is a very major push towards changing the basis of pensions towards an investment model. This might work well for captains of industry who can put millions of euro into their pension funds, but it is almost impossible for ordinary workers to match their pension income by investment, and for 130 years pension payments have in general been intergenerational transfers (i.e. those who work transferring to older people on the basis of the same being provided to them, rather than being funded by investment).

A secure and adequate income is a key determinant of health and well-being at all ages, and the United Nations Declaration on Ageing promotes this concept, with a life-long approach to income adequacy and solidarity between generations (i.e. from child benefit to state pensions) as the fundamental basis for income adequacy in later life. It is striking that the philosophy of income support for older people in Ireland has been one of a very low safety level, with income levels predisposing to a relatively high level of poverty and the state pension pegged at one of the lowest levels in Europe. There has also been a sustained assault on defined benefit pension schemes over the last decade. This change is not only likely to lower the pension income of increasing numbers of current workers, but also reduce inter- and intragenerational solidarity between those in defined benefit and those in defined contribution schemes. If unchecked, current trends threaten to erode intergenerational solidarity and contribute to the myth that older people are unproductive, cost too much and cause intergenerational conflict.

A further change is the increases envisaged in the age at which you will be able to obtain a state pension, which rose from 66 to 67 in 2012 and will rise again to 68 in 2028. One concern about this is a potential poverty trap in late middle life, as should you lose your job at this time there is evidence of ageism in employment policies in Ireland, and you will not only find it hard to get a further job, but you may also be challenged in keeping up enough PRSI contributions to obtain your expected State (Contributory) Pension.

Thanks for the Speech, But What About Me Now?

The role of this chapter is to provide some advice on measures which will help you to manage money, discover extra sources of support, and provide some advice on future planning for you and those close to you when age-related illness may affect your ability to manage your affairs.

Managing Money

Although some older Irish people are wealthy, they are still in a minority, and even then there is usually a trend for even defined benefit pensions to fall behind in purchasing power; choices to pursue private health and social care options such private home care supports or a privately funded nursing home will quickly deplete what might have seemed quite a big fund of savings. For the rest, older Irish people have a high risk of relative poverty relative to those aged 16–64, so it really is worthwhile maximising your income sources, benefits and, for some, tax credits. At the very least, make use of your local Citizens Information Centre's information and advice, and for those at higher levels of income a session with your accountant will be helpful.

Pension Planning

For most older people reading this book it will be clearly too late to be adding to a pension. Do not get overly depressed by this. For most citizens of this state, the private pension system is circuitous and inefficient but almost the only way of adding to your resources in later life. While captains of industry who can invest millions of euro in such funds can benefit accordingly, workers on the average industrial wage can really only add modest amounts to such pension funds, which have fees taken twice – once in managing the fund and again when the funds are being disbursed. More importantly, during the last years of working life ensure that you have contributed the minimum amount of PRSI required for a State (Transition) or State (Contributory) Pension; if you retire early, you may need to continue to make PRSI contributions to ensure the highest level of payment.

You need to apply for your state pension *three months* ahead of your expected date of retirement, six months if you have paid contributions in more than one country. If you retire before the age of 66 you should ensure that you take the necessary steps to keep your social insurance record continuous until the end of the tax year prior to your 66th birthday. You should contact the Records Section of the Department of Social Protection to check whether or not you have enough contributions to qualify for the State (Contributory) Pension. They can tell you how many PRSI contributions you have already and how many more you need to qualify. You will then know if, and for how long, you should sign on for credits or remain a voluntary contributor, and whether you can claim for any credits towards a pension.

Maximising Your Sources of Support

One of the challenges of Irish society is that while there are a fairly wide range of supports available to you, depending on your age, income and/or discipline, they *never* arrive automatically, and one of the challenges of accessing them is to find out how and where to access them. A nearly full list is given below of the potential state or state agency supports, the names of which alter from time to time; some of these are benefits in kind, and some are of money. One of the most useful sources of advice is through the Citizens Information Centres, which have offices all over Ireland, and also the Citizens Information Call Centre (see Useful Resources at the end of this book). A further source is the constantly updated list of benefits for those over the age of 60, and for those with a disability.

Allowances

- State (Transition) Pension (formerly known as the Retirement Pension); this is being phased out from 1 January 2014
- State (Contributory) Pension (formerly known as the Contributory Old Age Pension)
- State (Non-Contributory) Pension (formerly known as the Old Age Non-Contributory Pension)
- Pre-Retirement Allowance (of limited applicability, scheme closed to new applications in 2007)
- Early Farm Retirement Scheme
- Living Alone Increase to state pensions
- Increase to state pensions for those aged 80 and over
- Island Allowance

The guide and website from the Citizens Information Centres (www.citizensinformation.ie and the advisory service) covers just about every eventuality, including what contributions you will have needed to make, what the means test involves and details on contributions or pensions from other countries.

Benefits

- Free Travel
- Companion Pass
- Household Benefits Package (Electricity or Natural Gas Allowance, and Free TV Licence and Telephone Allowance)
- Fuel Allowance
- Disabled Drivers and Passengers Tax Relief Scheme (very circumscribed conditions)
- Disabled Person's Parking Card
- Driving Licence (free for those over 70)
- Bereavement Grant (based on PRSI contributions)
- Diet Supplement Allowance (for diabetic or other special diets; you need a certificate from a hospital consultant or registrar verifying the medical condition and the nature and duration of the diet)

Payments and Benefits also Available for Carers

- Carer's Allowance (means tested)
- Carer's Benefit (based on PRSI contributions)
- Carer's Leave
- Respite Care Grant
- Credited PRSI Contributions
- Homemaker's Scheme (for pension contributions)

Tax and Tax Allowances Applicable in Later Life

Many social welfare payments, such as the State (Contributory) Pension and Widow's, Widower's or Surviving Civil Partner's Pensions, are taxable. On the other hand, many health and social care expenses can be claimed back against tax as tax credits, as well as DIRT (deposit interest retention tax) on savings if your income is below the taxable level.

Relevant Tax Credits for You as an Older Person and/ or Carer

- Age Tax Credit (over 65 years)
- Blind Person's Tax Credit
- Tax relief on the costs of employing a carer for an incapacitated person (one or more family members of the person being cared for can claim this allowance)
- Home Carer's Tax Credit
- Dependent Relative Tax Credit
- Tax credit for tenants
- Rent-a-Room Relief
- Bereavement allowances
- Tax relief on medical expenses
- Tax relief on nursing home fees (most nursing homes are eligible, but check)

Who Will Look after My Money if I Become Incapacitated?

Even though at age 95 you are more likely than not to retain all of your memory and faculties, there is an increasing risk as we get older of developing memory problems or illnesses such as dementia or stroke which can make it difficult to manage our own affairs.

One of the simplest ways of managing our affairs, particularly if we are living with our spouse or partner, is to hold a joint bank account. In this way,

a spouse or partner who is not affected by significant memory problems can continue to manage the
financial affairs.

If you open a joint account with someone other
than a spouse or partner it is important to discuss if
the approval of both yourself and the other account
holder is required before you can access your money
or what would happen to the account if one of the
account holders dies. Under the Financial Regulator's
Consumer Protection Code, your bank/post office/
credit union must warn you about the risks involved
in having a joint account and find out if there are any
limits you want to put on the account, for example
needing the signature of both account holders to
withdraw money, or setting a maximum withdrawal
amount for a single signatory. If setting up the account
with a family member who is not a spouse or a partner
this would be a good time to consider arranging for an
Enduring Power of Attorney (see below).

Another useful idea is to set up a direct debit or
standing order for your recurring household bills
such as telephone, electricity and gas so that these
services are not cut off should you go to hospital or
become unwell and miss paying a critical bill.

In the case of social welfare payments, you may
choose to nominate a friend or family member to be
your 'agent' to collect these payments. While you
still have the capability to manage your own money
you can appoint a 'Type 1' agent on a temporary
or permanent basis. This agent, usually a family
member or trusted friend, is empowered to collect
money on your behalf and is under a legal duty to
give it to you.

If, however, you are no longer have the capacity to manage your own money a community welfare officer can decide in consultation with your family and doctor to appoint an agent, now known as a 'Type 2' agent. This person is again usually a family member or may be the matron of a nursing home or hospital if you are in long-term care. Unfortunately, although a Type 2 agent is bound by law to ensure that the money is used for your benefit, there is no supervisory mechanism in place.

Enduring Power of Attorney

Another way of looking after your affairs is to make a formal legal agreement, through your solicitor, to say that somebody can act on your behalf. This arrangement is called 'Power of Attorney' while you still have the capability to manage your own affairs, and 'Enduring Power of Attorney' when you plan ahead for the time when you no longer have capacity and nominate someone who will look after your affairs then.

In practice the ordinary Power of Attorney is not so useful, as it is no longer valid when you no longer have the capacity to look after your own affairs. Probably the more useful agreement is the Enduring Power of Attorney. In this, you decide ahead of time that should you lose your memory or intellectual function to the point where you can no longer look after your money, that you want a certain person (usually a family member but it may be a friend) to look after your financial affairs. A document is drawn up, and you have to be assessed as fit to make the decision by a doctor, but *nothing is done* until the point arises where you no longer have capacity. At that stage, the Enduring Power of Attorney is registered with the Wards of Court Office, and you will be assessed by a doctor again to clarify that you no longer have the capability to manage your own affairs. The person you have nominated then takes over your financial and some other affairs. There is quite a significant cost associated with preparing an Enduring Power of Attorney, and you must ask for an estimate of the cost before progressing and bear this in mind in terms of the information outlined below before deciding whether to progress or not with it.

As the solicitor drawing up this document with you may not be involved with drawing up this type of document frequently, it is important to remember that the default option of the Enduring Power of Attorney has quite a lot of powers. These include:

- Where you should live
- With whom you should live
- Who you should and should not see
- What training and/or rehabilitation you should receive
- Your diet and the clothes you wear
- Who may inspect your personal papers
- What housing, social welfare and benefits you need

It is very important to remember that you can actually choose *not* to have all of these included in your Enduring Power of Attorney. Healthcare decisions are not included in the Enduring Power of Attorney, and this is not necessarily a bad thing. In general, evidence suggests that doctors in Ireland consult appropriately with your family members on important medical decisions should you have a significant memory problem.

As a precaution to ensure that you were not under undue pressure when you signed, you are obliged to notify two people who are not the person you wish to look after your affairs (the attorney) when you want to make an Enduring Power of Attorney. At least one of them is required to be either your spouse (if he or she is alive and living with you), a child if your spouse is no longer alive or does not live with you, or a relative if neither of the above are applicable.

It is very important that you have a significant level of trust in the person to whom you wish to give this power, because although the legislation says that the attorney is obliged to keep adequate accounts, in my experience there is *nobody* supervising this. The Wards of Court Office only checks the actions of the attorney if a family member or health professional tells them that they suspect you are being taken advantage of by the attorney, and even then my experience of reporting concerns over possible abuse of funds have not met with a positive response from the courts system. The Law Reform Commission has proposed changes to the monitoring of the Enduring Power of Attorney, and while awaiting this I would welcome their proposals, but emphasise that you must trust the person to whom you are giving these far-reaching powers. Indeed, you can insert into your Enduring Power of Attorney document a provision, that your accounts are reviewed yearly by some other person such as your family solicitor or a trusted other individual.

While awaiting new legislation, a route used by a *very small* number of people is a process called ward of court. This is where you reach a stage where you are no longer able to look after your affairs, you have significant assets, and almost anybody, but usually a member of your family, applies to the Wards of Court Office for a form of protection for yourself and your assets called wardship. A case is presented to a judge who will appoint someone to look after your affairs, called the 'committee' (even though it is usually only one person). In this instance accounts must be kept and presented to the Wards of Court Office on an annual basis. There is a fairly significant cost for this procedure, which is usually taken out of your assets. I would emphasise that this is a route that only a *minority* of older people and their next of kin will take, and in general the officials in the Wards of Court Office are helpful in discussing practical problems that may arise with the ward of court process. There is a very helpful booklet available on the ward of court process on the Irish Court Services website (www.courts.ie).

Making a Will

While you are thinking of financial affairs, whether as an older person or as an adult child or relative who is reading this book, this is a good point at which to consider making a will. It really is worth making a will because if you are married and die without making a will, leaving a spouse and children, your spouse inherits two-thirds of all you own; if the family home is solely in your name your children could ask for one-third of its value, leaving financial problems for the surviving spouse. The positive benefits of making a will include the fact that you can:

- Express your burial wishes
- Save your next of kin and other beneficiaries substantial inheritance tax
- Appoint guardians for any children under the age of 18 if both you and your spouse die
- Leave specific assets to specific children or beneficiaries
- Specify that certain beneficiaries can only inherit property on reaching the age of 21 or more
- Make precise provisions for beneficiaries who may have a drink, drug or gambling problem, are irresponsible with money or may suffer from mental disability – in this situation a will can set up a trust for the protection of such a beneficiary

Although it is not necessary to have legal advice, it is well worth the relatively small charge to ensure that the will is drawn up properly with a solicitor, as each person's case and family is so different. For a will to be valid, the following must apply:

- It must be in writing.
- You must be over eighteen (or exceptionally have been married before this age).
- You must be of sound mind.
- You must sign or mark the will or acknowledge the signature or mark in the presence of two witnesses.
- Your two witnesses must sign the will in your presence.

- Your two witnesses cannot be people who will gain from your will, and they must be present with you at the same time for their attestation to be valid. The witnesses' spouses/civil partners also cannot gain from your will.
- Your witnesses must see you sign the will but they do *not* have to see what is written in it.
- The signature or mark must be at the end of the will.

These are legal requirements and if any of them are not met, the will is not valid. If you want to change your will after you make it, you can add a codicil (amendment or change) to your will; this codicil must meet the same requirements as above.

Equity Release Schemes

Although there is a wide range of incomes among older people, some people ask me about equity release schemes. In general, these represent an unsavoury side of Irish financial life, and many are very intrusive into your personal life. For example, they may wish to alter your will so that they become preferred creditors, and the interest rates and charges are fixed in such a way that you and your estate can be quite severely disadvantaged. The Law Society has complained about the intrusive nature of some of the arrangements in terms of wills, and I would be very slow to suggest that anybody reading this book would consider this other than as an act of desperation, and you should get good legal and financial advice before embarking on this course of action.

Signing over Property

It may seem tempting, considering inheritance tax or trying to avoid a clawback on your estate for nursing home care under the so-called Fair Deal scheme for nursing home payment, to sign over your house, property or assets to a member of your family. While in a minority of cases this may work out, my experience as a geriatrician, and that of many of my colleagues, has been that this is often not a good idea. Sadly, the old adage 'eaten bread is soon forgotten' is too often the principle that comes into play here. Our resources in later life for combating adversity are who we are and what we own, and in terms of security, flexibility and the maintenance of a sense of self it really makes very little sense to hand over your major assets to another person.

In clinical practice I have relatively frequently encountered situations where an older person gave over their house to a relative on the expectation of ongoing care in the house and then found that when they became sick or disabled that this verbal agreement no longer held. In fairness to those involved, it may just be that the adult child or other relative did not realise the implications of this care, or the challenge of accessing support and services in the community. As with equity release, should you decide to go down this route again consider getting legal and financial advice before embarking on it, and any agreement with regard to your future care and support should be in writing.

7

Planning, Accessing and Coordinating Health and Social Care Services

When You Need Health and Social Care

There is a high likelihood that you or your relative will have bought this book because of the onset, or fear of the likelihood, of age-related disease and disability. This may have come all in a rush, such as with a stroke, or more usually in a gradual fashion. The key needs are for as thorough an assessment as possible, and to access the appropriate treatments, services and supports. As the system is quite fragmented, complex and often difficult to navigate, this chapter looks at how you access care, and the following chapters deal with some of the common conditions.

This is the beginning of a more complex stage of life, but there can be a danger of portraying it as an unrelieved misery. After the initial adjustments, or indeed shock, I find that older people and their families want to make a strong effort to keep their lives as normal as possible; many learn a lot about themselves and their families (good and bad), and there can be a deeper sense of co-dependency between generations.

However, almost universally, people feel let down by the lack of clarity and connectedness between the services, and how patchy experiences can be. Even those within the system can find it hard to navigate, so in the first instance we will look at the issues of who is responsible for your care, and how the services are set up; palliative care services will be dealt with in Chapter 22.

Who Is Responsible for My Care?

This is both simple and complex. The simple answer is that the main driver for responsibility for your health is you yourself, in conjunction with those services that you provide yourself, those provided by your family and those provided by the state.

The complex part arises when there is significant disability, particularly dementia, and you have either less ability to drive the process on your own, or the disability causes a burden which is greater than you might be expected to manage on your own. While there is a general, if vague, understanding of a duty of care by families and the state in this situation, the Irish system has never clearly articulated the extent of this care and the relative responsibilities of family and state, as have other countries. For example, Singapore and India have laws requiring adult children to care for their parents (under threat of prison) and the United Kingdom has laws clearly stating the requirement of health and social services to provide care on the basis of need.

This lack of clarity with regard to duty of care and entitlement to services is one of the most stressful areas for you and your carers when significant illness strikes. The so-called 'Fair Deal' policy for nursing homes in Ireland, while on the one hand offering an apparently clear and transparent system, continues this ambivalence by proposing a selective inheritance tax on those with complex illnesses and disability in later life, particularly stroke and dementia. Confusingly, there are also unstated flexibilities throughout the whole health and social care system, and your chances of making use of this flexibility are very much influenced by being as well-informed as possible and by forceful advocacy.

Even worse, while you might be eligible for services, these might be so under-staffed, or under such pressure, that it can be difficult if not impossible to access them in a timely way. Finally, pinning down the coordination of care can also be frustrating; you may be very fortunate and find that your GP and/or public health nurse (PHN) is very active in facilitating this care, or you might not.

One of the main aims of this book is to outline what is available and potentially available, and to suggest ways that you (and those caring for you) might promote your care.

Who Coordinates My Care?

Again, this is both simple and complex. The simple answer is that you and your chosen family helper are the coordinators of your own care, drawing on the advice of your GP, public health nurse and whatever resources you may find.

The more complex answer arises when there is a significant complexity, which is not helped by the very fragmented nature of the care providers. Apart from the relatively rare occasions where a local HSE office (or voluntary organisation) has either a social worker or what is known as a home care organiser, the responsibility still lies with you or a chosen carer/family member. However, the skills of a social worker can be very helpful in trying to see your way through the complex jigsaw of care and also reviewing how you and your family are approaching it. At the moment these do not exist at all in some areas of the country, and tend to be limited to departments of geriatric medicine or old age psychiatry in hospitals. As yet there is no clear idea of how the social workers in most other areas, including the new primary care teams (if there is one in your area), will work. Many (but not all) departments of geriatric medicine or old age psychiatry have a social worker on their team. Referral to one of these departments is therefore to be recommended for this (and many other reasons) if the care organisation is complex and particularly if it does not seem to be covering all the bases. If there is no social worker, I would suggest discussing the issue with the manager for services for older people for your local health area. If this is still not satisfactory, then the next senior level of management is the director of services for older people in the local health area, and above them, the local health manager. Much as we may find it personally distasteful, other options include lobbying TDs, councillors and Ministers. However, it may help, and there is no harm in them being reminded of the inadequacies of the system.

What if I/We Cannot Access Adequate Care?

One of the big challenges here is working out your best course of action for when you seem to have gone as far as you can and yet there are still gaps. While in an ideal world you might take a court case, this is exhausting, expensive, time-consuming and not open to most of us – and it might also fail, as occurred in the case of a 61-year-old who sued the former Northern Area Health Board to provide 24-hour cover at home. Your anger and frustration will eventually drain your resources. So you (and your family) will have to make pragmatic decision to work with what is available, and pointers here are:

- Ensure that you have a full hand of cards by getting maximum advice, assessment and treatment from:
  - Your GP
  - Public health nurse
  - Home care coordinator (if one exists for your area)
  - Primary care team (if one exists in your area)
  - Geriatric medicine or old age psychiatry team
  - Advocacy groups – Alzheimer Society of Ireland, Carers Association, etc.
- Mobilise resources available to you.
- Look at whether hiring in some extra help is feasible in terms of your resources.

- Discuss with your family carers whether or not there is a possibility of the family filling in the gaps.
- Join an advocacy organisation and channel your experience in a useful way to try to make the system more responsive to the needs of its older people (and to remind the general population that they are looking after their own futures as well).
- Let your elected representatives know about the shortcomings of the care system.

As pointed out in Chapter 3, health and social services are under-funded in Ireland, and it is important to keep this in mind when dealing with PHNs, home help managers and social workers; almost all wish to give of their best, but may be strapped for resources. The challenge is the appropriate channelling of your frustration if you do not believe you are getting the services you need. Do try to maintain a good relationship with the person on the ground, but go higher if necessary. In general, the system does bend somewhat to firm pressure, and discussion with higher levels of management of the services is strongly recommended.

Structure of Your Care

The first points of contact for you or your relative are the family doctor and the public health nurse. We will cover their roles and your relationship with them, then discuss the process of planning care, and finally describe the roles and possibilities of other professionals and services, as your GP and/or PHN may be able to help you to mobilise the following in your area:

- Home help
- Home care attendant
- Home Care Package
- Meals on wheels
- Chiropody
- Physiotherapy
- Occupational therapy
- Day centres
- Respite care

Some of these services may be channelled through the new primary care teams – a grouping of nurses, therapists and social workers who liaise with GPs – in some specific areas.

Your family doctor may also refer you to specialists who deal with specific medical issues in later life, including geriatricians or old age psychiatrists, or other specialties if appropriate. Their teams often (but not always) include:

- Physiotherapists
- Occupational therapists
- Social workers
- Speech and language therapists
- Clinical nutritionists

And in addition, if you/your family is able to afford it, you may be able to locate private services informally by employing someone yourself or through formal agencies that provide care assistants.

Your GP

The family doctor or general practitioner (GP) is the key figure in the health service. You cannot see a hospital specialist at a clinic without referral from a GP, and GPs are usually a fount of knowledge on local health service provision. Some GP practices are formally linked with a wider range of services (practice nurses, physiotherapists, etc.) and it is hoped that the new primary care strategy will be successful in its intent to increase the number of surgeries with these facilities. GPs are specialists in their own right, and their methodology is both sophisticated and deceptively simple. What may seem to be a simple conversational exchange in the surgery will usually involve a great deal of observation and clinical judgement. The better a GP knows you and your family, the more likely it is that they will be able to help you, as they are experts at finding patterns in how people present with problems over time. Also the development of a relationship is part of any consultation; the more opportunities this relationship has to develop the better.

In an ideal world, the same GP or practice will take you from middle adulthood into later life. However, the absence of a National Health Service type service in Ireland will perhaps mean that you may have had little contact with a GP up to the point of your first health problem, or indeed that you may have seen a range of GPs if you are under the age of 70. After the age of 70, many older people have the right to Medical Card care, which means signing up with a particular GP. This may mean that going to the GP can be quite novel and may require an extra effort.

There may also be an element of difficulty in finding a GP if you try signing up for the first time after the age of 70.

So, it may be worth considering the following when choosing a GP if you do not already have a Medical Card:

- Start developing a relationship with one GP/GP practice rather than several practices.
- Give consideration as to whether or not they take Medical Card patients (some GPs practice entirely in the private sector) so that they will be able to continue your care under this scheme after the age of 70. If your GP does not usually take Medical Card patients check to see whether they would be willing and able to take you under a special one-off deal with the Department of Health which provides for individual Medical Card contracts with the GP.
- Find out whether they are likely to do home visits for bed-bound patients.

Your Relationship

The relationship between GP and patient is a complex one and it is important that you are as happy with it as you can be. Fortunately, the vast majority of older people are happy overall with their relationship with their GP. However, in a minority of cases, you both may not seem to get on well (it does work both ways). As it is a professional relationship which is hugely influenced by how well you know each other, it is important to realise that changing a GP, particularly if you are in the middle of an illness, is not like changing a hairdresser or butcher, and, indeed, there is probably a limit to how much you can change in a relatively small country. It is therefore important to make a decision early if you do wish to change and virtually no doctor will take umbrage or cause difficulties. Indeed, this may well be by mutual agreement. Your notes should be passed on to your next doctor.

The Consultation

Perhaps the most common reflection a patient has after a visit to the doctor is, 'But I forgot to tell him/her about ....' It can be very helpful to have a brief written summary of your concerns to bring in with you. It is also very useful to bring your last prescription and/or your medications (in their packaging) with you, as review of medications is an important part of ongoing care of older people. If you are among the small minority of older people who do not wish to have bad news broken to them, please let your doctor know this. The doctor may also work with a practice nurse, who may do some assessments, or take blood, and this can be very helpful.

House Calls

House calls are for medical reasons, and not for social or personal ones. It is an area that is not openly discussed in many societies (including Ireland), and there has been somewhat of a shift in recent years, with the PHNs undertaking much of the 'look-in' role that people might associate with GPs in the past, such as in the TV series *Dr. Finlay's Casebook*. There would appear to be a highly variable degree to which GPs perform house visits, and PHNs seem to have a sense of how to work with this, as many of the referrals to my clinic are at the prompting of the PHN, and the GP may not have seen the patient for some time. If you are sufficiently disabled that you cannot leave home and are fortunate to have a GP who will visit, this is very helpful. If you have difficulties in accessing a home visit if you believe you really need it, discuss this with your family doctor. Use may be made of the locum or deputising service to respond to your needs.

Night and Weekend Cover

Many GPs now work in cooperatives whereby night and weekend cover is provided by one of the group on a rotating basis, sometimes in a local hospital, surgery or clinic or by a doctor coming to your house. Therefore there is less chance that your usual doctor will see you, and it is important that these visits are reserved for emergencies.

Which Is My Doctor – My GP or My Specialist?

As you get older, it is increasingly likely that your GP may refer you on to one or more specialists, such a geriatrician for an overview, a diabetologist or a heart specialist. These are there to provide support to your GP, and your GP remains your primary doctor. This can be confusing for some patients, particularly if the specialist provides a specific course of treatment; however, the underlying convention is that they are doing this as an extension of the GP's role, and will keep in communication with the GP (although the restrictions on the health service may mean a delay in sending letters). If something goes wrong between specialist visits or treatments, the GP is the first person you should contact.

One significant change, should you go into a nursing home, as covered in Chapter 20, is that unless you go to a nursing home in your locality which your GP is happy to visit, most residents need to change to the doctor or doctors providing medical care in the nursing home. This is something you and your family should clarify ahead of any move to a nursing home.

Your Relative's Doctor

We must stress here that the older person's relationship with their own family doctor must be allowed to run at the pace dictated by the older person. It is common for me to find that adult children will complain about what they perceive as inactivity on the part of their parent's GP. There may be a range of reasons why this might appear to be the case, but actually it may have as much to do with your parent's position as anything else. If you have these concerns, the first person to discuss it with is your relative. If you have significant concerns still, you might suggest a number of options, such as getting a second opinion or the possibility of accompanying your parent to the GP. Some may try ringing the GP but this should only be done after clearing it with your older relative. Firstly, the GP cannot discuss your parent without their consent and, secondly, just stand back and think: if you were the 42-year-old parent of a 19 year old, would you like the GP to discuss you with your adult child without your consent?

If significant memory problems or dementia is an issue, it is likely that you and your relative will form a loose coalition together in your dealings with the health service, and in particular with the GP. Still, it is important that you give priority to your relative's own wishes in terms of the shape and emphasis of the consultation.

'Please don't tell my mother that she has cancer.' It is also common for doctors to be asked not to disclose bad news by a family member of a patient. This is usually well-meaning but in practice it raises some big problems. It diminishes your relative's control over their life, and makes management difficult – how is your relative's doctor going to arrange chemotherapy and radiotherapy without telling them that they have cancer? Most older people want to know difficult diagnoses, and the majority want to be told on their own or in a way of their own choosing. Please try to respect this, and remember that most doctors will have some training in breaking bad news.

If you live in the United States, you will have become accustomed to a situation where people may not have a family doctor, and where they can go directly to a specialist without being referred by a GP, and people therefore have a multitude of 'my doctors'. While this might make sense for one single condition, this can actually lead to confusion in later life, with a too-many-cooks situation. If your parent is agreeable, the GP is the best person to ask about your parent's condition.

The Public Health Nurse

Public health nurses (PHN) are assigned to every local health area and each has their own patch, so that everyone has a PHN in their area. PHNs cover a wide range of issues, literally from cradle to grave, from looking in on newly delivered babies to helping with terminal care. The number of PHNs in an area and the services they provide vary considerably from one area to another, so it is difficult to give an exact summary of what you can expect to receive.

PHNs are nurses who have postgraduate training in public health nursing. They know the facilities available in your area, and in particular can trigger the provision of services such as home help, home care attendants, meals on wheels, chiropody, physiotherapy and occupational therapy. Direct hands-on services include dressings of wounds, and in some areas they will help with administration of medications, provision of equipment and continence care.

How Do I Contact My PHN?

PHNs are based in health centres run by the HSE's local health areas and a telephone call will usually do to arrange a visit. In the case of chronic illness, they will usually keep the older person 'on their books'. Also, after discharge from hospital, the hospital team may ask the PHN to visit. If you, or a loved one, are going home from hospital after a significant illness, ask the nursing staff on the ward to confirm that the PHN has been alerted to the discharge.

I Don't Seem to See Enough of My PHN

Just as there may be a range of types of relationships that exist between older people and their doctors, so too there is a variety of relationships between older people and their PHNs. Also, PHNs tend to be organised by catchment area and often there are shortages in the numbers employed. This may be at the heart of your perception that you don't see enough of your PHN. Remember that, apart from some clear tasks such as the dressing of wounds, their role is one of assessment, coordination of other care services and regular review. If your care needs are complex, it may help to try to coordinate their visit with a time when a member of your family (of your choice) can meet them as well.

Therapists and Primary Care Teams

The HSE is currently undertaking a major expansion of therapist and social work services in the community, through primary care teams. There is still a lack of clarity as to the core services provided by these teams, and it is a little worrying that the first major publicity about the teams showed a huge range of initiatives and projects, but little by way of a simple description of access, core services, conditions treated and eligibility. There is also no clear sign that there would be an imperative to ensure that these teams would have specific training in the complex needs of older people. However, this initiative is just beginning, and hopefully input from older peoples' advocacy organisations and professional organisations will help to shape their activities. Links with GPs are variable between teams, and it is too early to say yet to what extent the primary care team will meet the needs of older people requiring assessment, rehabilitation and support in the community. The key workers in the primary care teams are likely to be physiotherapists, occupational therapists, social workers, dieticians, and speech and language therapists, but their challenge will also be one of meeting the needs of the full age spectrum from babies to older people. I will give a brief description below of what each discipline does, particularly in terms of meeting the needs of older people.

Physiotherapy

Physiotherapy is a therapy that works mostly on your balance, walking and limb function. It is probably the therapy that most people understand most easily. In the community, physiotherapists tend to provide different treatments for a range of conditions, including treatment for *musculoskeletal* conditions – arthritis, back pain and sports injuries – and *neurological physiotherapy*, which is the treatment of muscles weakened by neurological diseases such as stroke and Parkinson's disease – this includes strengthening weakened muscles, and improving walking ability and arm function. In the hospital and outpatient services, you will find specialist physiotherapists who have a deeper knowledge and experience of these different areas of practice. The Irish Society of Chartered Physiotherapists has a specialist section for neurological diseases and illnesses of older people.

Access to physiotherapy is usually by one of three ways. Firstly, through community services, which may be by way of the primary care team or through a standard community physiotherapist; the best person to ask about accessing this is your public health nurse. While there is no legal obligation for the HSE to provide such services, it is available in most areas. Secondly, you may access physiotherapy through a specialist service, such as geriatric medicine (whose outpatient physiotherapy service may be provided in a day hospital), rheumatology or neurology. Access to the service is nearly always only by way of referral from a consultant in the hospital. Finally, for ease of access and convenience, you may choose to use a private physiotherapist, and there is a list of these available on the website of the Irish Society of Chartered Physiotherapists (www.iscp.ie). You may wonder whether or not it is good to use more than one physiotherapy service. In practice it is best to use one service at a time, as too many cooks can spoil the broth, and professional guidelines from physiotherapists back this up.

The question that patients and their families often ask me is whether they should have ongoing physiotherapy if they have problems with gait and balance. What I usually say to them is that rehabilitation is not done to people but with them and physiotherapists nearly always will give you, and your family if you require, a series of exercises to carry out yourself at home, and it is really these exercises which will make you stronger and safer on your feet. It is probably more important for you to do these exercises and just touch base with your doctor or

physiotherapist again if your gait or balance deterio-
rates. However some people do find it reassuring to
have a more regular check-up, and it may be helpful
to consider investing in some top-up physiotherapy
from a private therapist, perhaps on a monthly basis.

Occupational Therapy

Occupational therapy is a therapy which works with
people who have a disability and aims to return
them to as full a function as possible. Occupational
therapists will assess you by testing those personal
qualities needed for living life to its fullest (such as
memory, perception and function), as well as looking
at your environment. An occupational therapist will
assess how well you can manage what are called your
'activities of daily living', which include dressing,
feeding, managing the toilet, washing, shaving, and,
in addition, what is known as 'instrumental activities of daily living', which include cooking, cleaning,
managing finances, driving, and so on.

If the occupational therapist finds areas where you
have problems as a result of your illness they then
devise a plan which will include rehabilitation, review
and change of your home environment as necessary,
and adaptations and aids which might be helpful
(see Appendix B for more information on aids and
appliances). An occupational therapy assessment
is often very useful upon leaving hospital, particularly if you have developed a new disability. Should
you begin to have a problem with unsteadiness or
falls an occupational therapy assessment is also
very helpful. An assessment fulfils two purposes: the

therapist imparts useful information and education, and they may help in adapting your environment to your new circumstances.

Occupational therapists will propose solutions which may include direct therapy to retrain you in a skill that you may have lost, as well as adaptation of your home or other environment. It is the sum total of advice which represents the benefit of their intervention. If you are having difficulty, for example, in managing your continence they may review your clothes (for example, using elasticated waistbands and avoiding buttons), and review your routines and equipment, as well as eliminating unnecessary hazards such as trailing wires or loose rugs.

Occupational therapists are important in terms of advising on any aids that might help you should you find yourself with a disability after an illness such as stroke. These include hand rails, stair rails, grab bars in the bathroom, and many other possible adaptations such as raised toilet seats, tilting kettles or equipment to help you dress yourself. An assessment by an occupational therapist is also needed for the Housing Adaptation Grant for People with a Disability Scheme and you should not make any significant investment in aids or make major adaptations to your house without first discussing it with an occupational therapist.

Access to occupational therapy is usually by one of three ways. Firstly, through community services, which may be through the primary care team or else with a standard community occupational therapist, and the best person to ask about accessing this is your PHN. Unfortunately, in many parts of the country there are very long waiting lists for occupational therapy, and you will be put on a waiting list and prioritised by condition. Sadly, this can mean being on a list for several years. Secondly, you may access occupational therapy through a specialist service, such as geriatric medicine (where the occupational therapy may be provided in a day hospital) rheumatology or neurology. Finally, while there is little by way of private occupational therapy available, the Association of Occupational Therapists of Ireland (www.aoti.ie) maintains a list of private occupational therapists on its website. You will need an occupational therapy assessment for a grant for house alterations for disability from your county council.

If you are unhappy about the delay in accessing occupational therapy, as with all other services, contact the general manager for services for older people in your local health office, or the local health manager. The prioritisation of cases tends to be done on a historical basis, prioritising cancer ahead of other illnesses, and this may not always be fair or appropriate for all the people who have equally serious disabilities as a result of stroke or dementia. The occupational therapy assessment is a key part of the application process for the Disabled Persons Grant, and you or your family may need to exert some pressure and persuasion to ensure that you get this assessment in a timely fashion.

It is hoped that the developing primary care teams will improve access to occupational therapy and it is very much to be hoped that they will be attuned to the needs of older people and their particular needs and concerns. Access to public occupational therapy services at the moment is without charge but the situation regarding the provision of aids, while generally covered by the HSE in conjunction with the public health nurse and local occupational therapist, is not always clear, especially for more expensive items of equipment.

Social Work

Social workers are professionals who aim to maximise your psychological and social health. They are experts in counselling, assessment of family dynamics, and the psychological and social impact of illness, and are the profession most aware of possible services available to you and your family. In a more specialist role, they are the main group of professionals involved in the assessment of suspected elder abuse.

There is limited access to social work in the community, usually through primary care teams, and, more often than not, older people and their families will access social work services through the social workers attached to geriatric medicine and other specialties in hospital practice, or through social workers who work with departments of psychiatry of old age and general psychiatry.

Department of Social Protection Representatives (formerly Community Welfare Officers)

Department of Social Protection representatives (formerly known as community welfare officers) are employed throughout Ireland by the Department of

Social Protection. They are based in health centres and are responsible for the day-to-day administration of community welfare services. These include schemes such as the Supplementary Welfare Allowance and Medical Cards. They are involved in supervising the nomination of someone to collect your pension should you begin to have significant problems with memory. They also assist with types of payments which are relevant to older people, including rent supplement, and diet and heating supplements.

Planning Care in the Community

If you or your relative finds that there are problems with living independently in the community then you need a structure to plan for this. One possible list of priorities might be:

- Diagnosis and assessment
- Listing of care needs
- Matching needs with community-based services
- Filling the gaps

Diagnosis and Assessment

One of the most important issues to be dealt with before we discuss community services is the underlying question: Do I have a diagnosis for my problem? This might seem obvious but it is not a bit obvious. As described in the health section, disability in later life is caused by age-related disease; it is important that this disease is diagnosed and treated rather than compensated for. The classic example is poor mobility – rather than just provide a home help and meals on wheels wouldn't it be better to be able to walk better and do the things for yourself? In practice, both approaches might be good, but a diagnostic/therapeutic approach is the first priority. Another is continence – rather than launching straight into incontinence pads and pants, surely it is better to see if it can be treated so that you may not need such assistance.

So, if you find that you need help don't just ascribe it to old age; ask your GP why this is happening. If you do not get a clear answer, a second opinion from a geriatrician or old age psychiatrist may be very helpful. A period of assessment, treatment and rehabilitation may be required, and support from community services may be required simultaneously.

Listing of Care Needs

This might seem obvious, but in my experience you might be surprised how some families overestimate the care needs of older people. The most typical is concern that the older relative needs someone to stay overnight with them. While this may arise from a desire to protect the older person, in fact it may be intrusive and use up stores of energy and goodwill that would be better saved for a later date when the person does need more support.

Come with Questions as well as Answers

Rather than saying I need (or my mother needs) meals on wheels, it is better to think what aspects of meal preparation are compromised and to see can they be put right, or, if not, which part of the process can be improved. For example, it may be that alteration of the kitchen or adaptation of utensils (with the help of an occupational therapist), such as placing the oven at chest height so you don't have to bend down to access it, may allow cooking to take place. Also, it is worth remembering that time may not be an issue, and it doesn't matter how long making the meal takes. Finally, remember that eating in company will not only improve your intake of food but also provide an opportunity for social contact with family or friends.

In general, you, the older person, must set the pace for identifying and filling these needs, unless you are affected by dementia, which doesn't allow you to prioritise yourself. The involvement of family or strangers in the provision of care needs is a major step, and the least possible amount is best for all concerned.

What Type of Care Needs Are Required?

A helpful way to start can be to look at the different levels of care needs, starting with the least personal, and see can different solutions be reached for each:

- Strenuous gardening/heavy housework – this may be an area where getting in help is perhaps the easiest, as the tasks are clearly defined and not as immediately personal as self-care.
- Transportation – health, social, leisure, worship
- Shopping

- Meal provision
- Laundry
- Light housework
- Personal hygiene – washing and shaving
- Personal hygiene – bathing/showering
- Dressing
- Continence care – this is clearly one of the most intensely private areas, and for the older person requires someone they can trust and relate to.

For each of these levels of care, you need to think how often a day/week/month the service is needed, and then, with the help of your family, see what is available from within your and your family's resources and from community-based services.

Include the older person when planning for someone to come into the home to help. Issues of self-care and problems in living are highly personal and involve routines and rituals of daily life that are well established. The older person is likely to have strong preferences for details of how and when help is provided. Older people will feel loss of control when strangers are involved with their intimate daily lives. Even the arrival in the home of what seems to be a relatively straightforward service to someone else – a home help – represents a huge change for most older people. The best way to avoid a severe sense of helplessness is for the older person to retain as much control as possible. If the older person has not been involved in the plan, they are much more likely to refuse the help or to work against its effectiveness. Of course, if you are caring for someone who has lost the ability to make decisions, you will need to provide more guidance. You might also need to evaluate your own ability to provide the needed help compared to making arrangements for outside help. Regardless of the situation, it is important to involve the older person as much as possible in planning the care.

A commitment to the least possible intrusion is useful and if the older person is resistant to new people, it often helps to suggest starting slowly by arranging for one person to come in for a limited time. If outside help is needed to take some of the burden off your shoulders, be open with the older person about this. They need to understand that outside help is important to you and for your health.

The employment of private carers, whether informally or through an agency, and whether funded by a Home Care Package or by private funds, can be challenging, and in general is best done by you and the older person together. If not done through an agency, it is best to ensure that you have written references, and you need to consider whether or not to get liability insurance; while most people are decent, the last thing you and your relative need is a law suit from a care assistant who has put out their back while working with an older person.

Matching Needs with Community-Based Services

There are considerable differences around the country in how other community services are provided (and their availability). They are described below as comprehensively as possible, and we also signpost the way to negotiation of services.

Home Help Services

Home help services can be very helpful to you or an older relative but vary enormously in their availability and what they offer around the country. Home helps usually assist people with normal household tasks and although they may also help with personal care, this is not strictly within their job description. The home help is expected to provide a set number of hours of assistance each day or each week. The sort of work that a home help is normally required to do includes light cleaning. It is discretionary, and less usual, for them to assist with shopping, cooking and laundry, but it depends on your individual needs. Cooking and sharing a meal with an older person may be a much better way of ensuring adequate intake and social interaction than a meal from meals on wheels eaten alone. Home helps are not expected to provide nursing or medical care.

Home help services tend to be run by voluntary organisations funded by the HSE or run directly by the HSE. In each area, they will be coordinated by a home help organiser and you usually access them through your local PHN. You or your relative will be assessed in your home and a determination made of your needs and often some assessment of your means, and an offer is made of so many sessions a week. The HSE may take a number of factors into account, including income, other family support available, remoteness from services and availability of suitable people to provide the service.

The big issues for you or your carer are likely to be: i) availability, ii) affordability and iii) acceptability.

Home Help Availability

Availability may be limited by several factors. The first is lack of available people to perform the duties. As home helps are paid modest salaries (not far from the minimum wage), this availability may be particularly short in areas of high employment or affluence. The home help service may accept someone nominated by you who agrees to carry out the function and this is worth discussing with the home help organiser.

A second and more difficult problem can relate to lack of funding of the service in your local health area, and you might be offered nothing, be put on a waiting list (not much help if you need it now) or given insufficient home help support to match your needs. In this case you should discuss the situation with the home help organiser and your local PHN. Do remember that the financial constraints are not their fault and reflect a deeper problem with the system; politeness and firmness rather than antagonism will be the most helpful strategy. If you still do not feel that you have made sufficient progress, a discussion with the manager for services for older people in your local health area is the next step, and following that the director of services for older people or local health manager in your local health area.

Home Help Affordability

The service is generally free to holders of Medical Cards. Other people may be asked to make a contribution to the cost of the service. If you get a home help, you may have to make a contribution towards the cost, even if you hold a Medical Card. In some cases, you may have to pay all the costs involved. If you are in a position to pay the costs involved, you can approach the local health area for an arrangement whereby the local health area has the responsibilities of an employer while you pay the costs.

Home Help Acceptability

Most older people get on well with their home helps, but the prospect may be daunting for those who are unused to having outsiders in their home; common lore often relates the story of the frail older person who tidies up the home ahead of the arrival of the home help. It is generally a very useful service but, as ever, the wishes and preferences of the older person must be given priority. Occasionally, you might not get on with your home help. The home help organiser usually keeps an eye on the situation to ensure a reasonable match; if you have concerns, he or she should the first person to discuss this with. Should any serious concerns arise, do discuss this with your PHN or GP also.

Home Care Attendants

Home care attendants provide assistance and support to people with physical disabilities in their own homes, and provide elements of personal care, particularly bathing and showering. My own clinical experience would suggest that most older people access this service about once or twice a week, but should you (or your relative(s)) consider that you need more input from this service, again discuss this with your PHN or local manager of services for older people. In general, there is not a charge for this service

Home Care Grants/Packages

Since 2005, a system has been in place to provide care in the community – the Home Care Grant/ Package system. This works either by giving cash to the older person and their family to arrange care, or else providing hours from a commercial agency that employs care workers. In the presence of significant disability, you should check with the PHN or manager of services for older people in your local health area as to whether or not this scheme exists in your area. The scheme is usually arranged by a PHN or sometimes a Home Care Package coordinator, and is usually accessed either following a hospital stay where increased care is needed at home, or else through contact with the Home Care Package coordinator through your PHN.

The system was means tested up to 2011, but this has been challenged and for the time being is not means tested. In general the maximum amount given is equivalent to about twenty hours of care, to which might be added time from home helps, home care attendants and care that might be received from the Carers Association or the Alzheimer Society of Ireland. There is also generally a fixed budget for this service, and you may find yourself faced with a situation where you are told that there are no more packages until someone receiving a current Home Care Package dies, or improves to a point where they no longer need it. Also, the scheme tends to give preference to those with a disability who are discharged from hospital. Although this may be frustrating to you, there is a certain logic to this from a health administrator's point of view: it is in effect a form of rationing, and those discharged from hospital are on average more disabled than those in the community. However, it does highlight the unsystematic approach to needs in the Irish health service.

There has been little research into how this system works, and while the vast majority of those working in the system are hard-working and caring, there is no system of regulation and inspection comparable to that provided for care in nursing homes. If you are unhappy with the care provided you should discuss this with the PHN or Home Care Package coordinator, and if you or your relative has concerns about the possibility of abuse, then you can also consider contacting the elder abuse senior case worker in your area. Under no circumstances should you consider any requests for loans or financial assistance from a care assistant, and any such request should be discussed with the PHN or Home Care Package coordinator.

After assessment by a Home Care Package coordinator (accessed through your PHN or hospital team), a grant will be decided, with which you and your family can purchase care. This grant may be increased on appeal (through the PHN/Home Care Package coordinator or manager of services for older people), and while in my experience this figure is usually about €200–€500 a week, some cases have received over €1,000 per week for a complex care package upon discharge from hospital. A rule of thumb is that €20 buys one hour of care, so that a call-in three times a day of one care assistant is what the higher level of usual grant would cover.

An increasing number of providers are through companies and agencies, and this is a new experience for older Irish people, their carers and these agencies and companies. There is considerable variability between such agencies, and there is currently no regulation of either the companies or the services they provide, unlike nursing homes.

The coordinator of Home Care Packages may give you, or your relatives, the names of these companies and agencies, and you or your relative will then negotiate with them.

Private Services

An increasing number of private agencies have developed to provide care for older people in their own home. You, or your family, may choose to use this type of service, or you may be directed to these services as part of a Home Care Package, as outlined above. In general, these agencies provide training to their care assistants, and will also have insurance for any injury or other untoward event that might occur to the care assistant while they are in your home. If the service is provided over seven days, you may find that more than one care assistant may be catering to your needs. This can be challenging, and will be an important area of discussion between you (and your family if they are involved) and the private carers or carer agency.

The task of becoming effectively an employer, as well as navigating new or worsening disabilities, is a challenging one, and I would give a strong recommendation to undertaking the task in conjunction with a trusted family member. In addition, if you are using this agency in conjunction with a Home Care Package, you and/or your relative should keep in touch with the Home Care Package coordinator, particularly if there are any aspects of the care that you are unhappy with.

The care agencies are not regulated by the state (to be fair, many of the care agencies themselves have been asking for this), and there are concerns about the potential for abuse. The HSE seems confused about this, and persists in allowing agencies to use the HSE logo and called themselves 'HSE Preferred Providers' without any clear basis for this, which may give false reassurance to you, the older person, or your family.

Filling in the Gaps

In an ideal system, the care provided will match the needs of the person. Sadly, this is the exception rather than the rule. It may not even be over hours of service that the problem occurs; a simple item like ensuring that you get your medications might be a stumbling block. In some areas, neither home helps nor PHNs will help with the supervision of medications. You and your family will need to discuss how you can get around this. If discussion with the PHN and GP does not significantly improve your situation, a discussion with the local manager for services for older people is the next best option. It may be possible within the family to make up these gaps; if not you and your family will be left with an imperfect solution.

This is an area where you and your family may need support and referral to a geriatrician or a psychiatrist of old age (depending on the nature of the illness causing the disability and care need) may help all concerned to see where they might be able to help out. It can be difficult to see clearly at such times and, in my experience, families sometimes under- or overestimate care needs at such times. A full assessment can guide all concerned. It is perhaps most important in helping everyone adapt to a new situation and accepting compromises.

Other Services

Meals on Wheels

Meals on wheels are usually provided by voluntary organisations funded by the HSE. There is no set assessment, and the service is usually accessed through the PHN. There may be a fee for Medical Card holders or there may be a charge based on an assessment of your means. There are areas of the country where this service does not exist at all. In this case, you might be able to use a company which provides frozen meals for reheating (such as Wiltshire Farm Foods), or make some arrangement among your family to provide a stock of frozen meals.

Podiatry (formerly known as Chiropody)

The care of feet and nails becomes increasingly important in later life, particularly when we become less supple when bending over, and less dexterous in terms of managing nail scissors. It is particularly important for those with diabetes, and you may find that you can get your podiatry/chiropody done through your local hospital diabetic service. The availability of the service is quite variable, and where it is available it can be provided either through your local health office or else by a voluntary organisation that provides the care on behalf of the HSE. The service is free to Medical Card holders. If you do not have a Medical Card you will be able to claim tax relief on podiatry/chiropody if you are required to attend as part of medical treatment, i.e. you have a significant disability or serious illness and your doctor directs that you attend a podiatrist. Your public health nurse is probably the best guide to podiatry/chiropody services in your area.

Respite Care

Respite care is fairly widely distributed through Ireland. It is a scheme whereby you, the older person, would go into a public or private nursing home for a week or two so that a carer who is required to be present with you at home can take a holiday, receive health treatment themselves or undertake some necessary project. In general, most of the older people and their families I deal with are happy to work with this service, but it is very important that your family and the respite service should pay due attention to your consent to go into respite care. Respite care is usually arranged through your PHN, and it is good practice that you would be seen beforehand by a geriatrician to make sure that the disability that is the root cause of you requiring respite care is not something that could be improved by treatment or rehabilitation.

For carers it is important to be reasonably upfront in discussing your needs with the older person you care for. It can be quite a big change to go into a nursing home for one or two weeks, and have patience if the older person does not like it. Should the older person suffer from dementia, be prepared that they may be a bit more disoriented during the first day or two in respite care, as well as being a bit more disoriented on the first day or so after coming back home. However, a break for you, the carer, can mean that you can provide care in a more consistent way over the course of the year, and this should form a part of your discussion if necessary.

An alternative short-term arrangement is for respite care at home, and there are several ways of doing this. One of the most simple is for a member of the family who doesn't usually provide the care to come and spend a week or two living with you. A more short-term but helpful form of respite in the home is having another carer spending a morning or after-noon in the home, as with the scheme run by the Carers Association.

Geriatric Medicine and Old Age Psychiatry

You may ask to be referred, or you may find yourself being referred, to a specialist in geriatric medicine or old age psychiatry by a family doctor, sometimes because you wish it, sometimes at the request of the public health nurse, and sometimes at the urging of your relatives.

Geriatric medicine is a medical specialty whereby a doctor is trained in four areas in addition to general medicine: gerontology (the science of ageing), reha-bilitation, disability sciences and palliative care. The geriatrician works from a base in a hospital, usually with a multidisciplinary team consisting ideally of nurses, physiotherapists, occupational therapists, speech and language therapists, clinical nutrition-ists and social workers. In the larger hospitals they may have day hospitals and clinical assessment units where they may specialise in the assessment and treatment of the complex conditions of later life including falls, and gait and balance problems. It is an unfortunate fact, however, that the HSE has not always provided full teams for geriatricians, and if it appears that there is a therapy service that would be helpful to you but is not available, have a discussion about this with the geriatrician.

One small area of potential confusion is that while geriatricians are quite happy with the title 'geriatri-cian', older people and their families are not very happy with the adjective 'geriatric', and don't like the idea of going to a Department of Geriatric Medicine. So, many of the departments have slightly different names such as Age-Related Healthcare, Medicine for the Elderly, and Medicine for Older People; however, they all do the same job of providing specialist health-care for older people.

In the first instance, you will usually be referred to an outpatients' clinic. There the doctor and some-times nurses will undertake some assessments which revolve around asking you a series of ques-tions (the history), asking your next of kin a series of questions (the collateral history), particularly if you have memory problems, and giving you a thorough examination. They will also undertake some blood tests, and often a chest X-ray or ECG. Further tests will depend on your possible diagnosis. For example, if the geriatrician is concerned about a diagnosis of stroke they may ask for a special scan of your brain (either a CT scan or an MRI scan). If possible, and available, they may try to make an appointment for assessment by an occupational therapist or physio-therapist, or refer you for these assessments at their day hospital if they have one.

In general, these services will take place in public hospitals, but private services are also beginning to develop. However, these are predominantly of a once-off assessment nature, and should you require a day hospital or other services, they will refer you back to the public geriatric medical services. Few, if any, of the private hospitals and clinics have geriat-ric medicine services and cannot be recommended for the assessment of problems related to frailty or multiple illnesses. Indeed, you may only be delaying an assessment by a geriatrician in the public system, as the private system either refers such patients on to the public system, or their GPs will.

Another way of seeing the geriatrician or old age psychiatrist can arise if you are admitted to hospital with something else, and you, your family or the hospital doctor thinks that it is worthwhile getting it checked out by a geriatrician or old age psychiatrist. A consultation can be arranged, and this is certainly worthwhile if you or your family are concerned that you have lost some of your ability to think clearly, walk with agility or manage your continence. Ask your specialist in hospital for a consultation with a geriatrician or old age psychiatrist if you feel that any of the above applies to you or your relative.

Plans are in place to develop geriatrician posts with responsibility for liaising with the family doctor looking after those in nursing homes; this should become a useful extra resource for you and your family in the future should you enter a nursing home.

Old age psychiatry is a most useful support for older people and the health service and is relatively widely available throughout the country, but not everywhere, and in some areas is very understaffed. This service has a strong focus on how you or your relative is managing a psychiatric illness that is affecting you at home, and very often will arrange for assessment and treatment in your own home. In properly staffed services, the consultant will have the support of a team which includes community psychiatric nurses, therapists, psychologists and social workers. Referral is through your family doctor, and in particular is helpful if you or your relative is suffering from low mood, depression, memory problems or dementia with behavioural problems. The community-based nature of the service is particularly helpful for families and patients, and the Alzheimer Society of Ireland has strongly recommended further development of this home assessment service as a model of support for those with Alzheimer's disease and dementia.

And Back to Coordination

What a range of services! Some of my patients and their families can find themselves dealing with more than twenty individual professionals and agencies. It would clearly be better for all concerned if the range of services needed by an older person could be organised in a focused and coordinated manner. This occurs for a relatively small number of older people in a formal way, either after assessment by a geriatrician or old age psychiatrist, or by the intervention of some of the more organised teams, some primary care teams and some specialist teams for older people. You or your carer should ask whether such teams exist in your area. If not, maximise your chances by arranging for as comprehensive an assessment as possible, and asking your GP, PHN or specialist whether or not you would benefit from the services outlined in this chapter. Do discuss this with your family members, as outlined in the next chapter, and liaise with the appropriate voluntary advocacy groups that have experience in the area, such as the Carers Association or the Alzheimer Society of Ireland.

8

Developing into the Carer Role:
Ageing and Families

When an older person becomes frail, roles will inevitably change. The biggest adjustment will be for your spouse or partner. This can occur in many different ways, and it is always a wonder to me as a geriatrician that people cope and adapt to this as well as they do. I do not mean to minimise the difficulties that might be involved, but in general most relationships have an in-built contract that implies mutual support. During the course of this chapter we will explore some of the ways in which the burdensome side of caring can be alleviated. It is important to emphasise that most partners, adult children and others involved in the care of an older person do not wish to see this care portrayed exclusively as a burden. There is a wider aspect to caring but, as you will see, the structure and support for relieving the burdensome aspects of caring are poorly developed.

Adult children may have the most difficulty in adapting to this role. In addition to whatever form of relationship you may have had with your parents, you now have to try to forge a new relationship which tries to support them in their chosen way of dealing with their frailty. In many ways, this new style of relationship will test both your bonds and the difficulties that you both simultaneously experience as part of the parent–child relationship. You cannot change the way that your parent is, and a large part of the skill of caring lies in changing *your* reactions so that you ease the inevitable tensions that may arise. It is most important that you recognise that your primary role is as a *collaborator* rather than a director. Even if your role becomes more prominent as your parent's frailty develops, maintaining the sense of your role as collaborator rather than the main driver is important.

Getting a Clear Perspective

Several issues are worth clearing up at this early stage. *It is very important to avoid any sense that this role is akin to parenting.* Your parent is and will always be your parent and you will always be their child. It is very dehumanising for an older person to be treated or spoken to as a child. No matter how much disease and age may have changed your parent's body or mind, no matter how much or how little they can do or think for themselves, and no matter how much you're doing for them, they are adults and need to be treated as adults. Your parent has a lifetime of experience and skills and will find their own ways of dealing with their frailty. You may not agree with these or even think that they are foolish, but your parent must be let do their thing in their own way to the greatest extent possible. You will only give yourself grief and aggravate the tensions and downsides of the parent–child relationship by not recognising their adulthood and life experience.

This brings us to the next step, which is the realisation that once you and your parent have ensured appropriate assessment, treatment and services, there are in essence only two things which can potentially change in the parent–child relationship. Either they can change, or you can change. In my experience of looking after older people, much grief comes from an undue expectation that the older person will change. Even though you may be providing a lot of your time, energy and love, it is vital to emphasise that is less likely that the older person will want to, or even can, change their way of doing things. You need to put yourself into your parent's shoes here: they are still your parent in their mind, and this will not change unless they see a clear reason that suits them. It is you who will need to change your style and way of thinking and doing things, and this is one of the keys to reducing the burdensome elements of caring. When you are under pressure with your own workplace, young family and other commitments, it is very tempting to try to bargain with or change your parent's way of doing things. Difficult as it may be, now is the time to realise that you need to come to terms with a situation that is not quite as you would wish it, and that has many imperfections, but which represents how your parent sees it.

A third point is the importance of *maintaining independence* for your older relative or parent. It is tempting to step in and help people when they have difficulties carrying out a function such as cooking or cleaning or going to Mass. Unless called upon, stand back! While at all times it is worth discussing whether an assessment might be necessary for any difficulties with everyday life, maintaining independence, even if the task is done slowly and seems to be burdensome, is critical to maintaining quality of life in later life. This independence is important at several levels. The sense of having control over your life is an important factor in psychological well-being. The very activity in itself, even if done more slowly and clumsily than previously, maintains physical function, fitness and capabilities. Intervening and removing these tasks, usually with the best of intentions, may unfortunately add to your older parent's sense of helplessness and dependency. If your parent seems to be suffering distress while carrying out these activities, discuss and negotiate with them whether they might consider some aid or help. In general, do not step in and assume responsibility for the task without discussion, negotiation and agreement.

It is only when there is a significant safety issue, or when dementia is so advanced that your parent loses the capacity to make rational decisions or understand their options, that you might need to step in and make decisions for a parent, such as bringing them to the doctor when they are very ill, ensuring that gas and electricity bills are paid or have a car immobilised when they can no longer drive safely. However, these are exceptional, although not uncommon, circumstances and in general you will help yourself and your older parent by trying to make sure that you are not acting in isolation when this happens.

Help from family, assessment and advice from your family doctor or a geriatrician, and support from a clergyman or clergywoman can help you to gain insight and perspective. Involvement with a carer support group, which we will discuss later, can also be very valuable in framing your mindset to understand the situation and get the balance right between your parent's priorities of independence and risk over your priorities of health and safety. Don't forget that your parent is usually more interested in living fully than in living longer.

Tenacity allied with *tact* is important. As you will learn, the squeaking wheel gets the most oil, and the response of the system varies enormously. For all that you may have a superb response from the public health nurse, you may also find the health and social care response melting away when they discern a caring family (the same phenomenon can happen with siblings). Firm and tactful pressure is important, and will need to be ongoing.

Not for the Thanks

Finally, caring is one of those tasks and activities which is often not openly recognised by the person being cared for. Indeed, you may find that the frail older person may vent their frustration and anger over the disability and frailty on you, the carer. In a perverse way, there is an element of this that is a sign of love and trust. In the general run of things, we usually put on a brave face with health and social care workers, and as well as with acquaintances. It is only with those we love and trust that we can let our guard down. This can be distressing for you as the spouse and carer, or for an adult child. You will, in time, find a balance between allowing the older person to vent their frustration and the very important task of setting boundaries for what is and is not acceptable behaviour between you both.

The task of caring is one that we often assume unconsciously and gradually; the exception arises from a significant stroke or from the death of a spouse who had been caring up to that point. We come to it with a range of attitudes, previous experiences and all the complexity of relationships between adults, and between adults and their adult children. For most people, the caring role is something that we assumed would happen at some stage, but it is always a surprise when it does. In my experience, most carers wish to undertake their care, but may feel under-supported by some of the rest of the family or by society. It is this element of compulsory altruism which can compound the difficult side of caring. As we have previously discussed in Chapter 3, Irish society has not clarified its duty of care to those with disability and frailty. Part of the frustration of caring can be a sense of failure of solidarity from society and community. For you as the carer, in the immediate future, all you can do is maximise your support, reflect on and reshape your role, and adapt your philosophy. In the longer term, get involved and try to change the system. Join an advocacy group, and make your community and society aware of what it needs to do to ensure that your parent's care can be carried out with adequate support and dignity.

Prodigal Son Syndrome

One particular situation which can rankle is a variant of the prodigal son syndrome, where the contribution of the most significant carers seems to be very much taken for granted, and yet the child who appears twice yearly from afar with a bouquet of flowers is given praise and celebrated. There is no easy answer or solution here, but awareness that this is not uncommon may at least make you feel that you are not alone if this is happening to you. It is rarely intentional, and raising this with a frail parent may seem challenging or churlish; it is probably best to develop a thicker skin and concentrate on practical ways of dealing with the situation. Family discussion on sharing care tasks may help to ease the burdensome aspects and involve more family members. Often those who understand the caring task assume their siblings have a similar insight, yet they will learn little from suppressed anger and gritted teeth, and it is important to either engage with all potential carers or else take a decision to write them out of the equation and move on. The strategies outlined below may be of some assistance.

A Time of Growth Too

You will learn many things about yourself and the older person being cared for during your time spent caring. Many carers have reported to me that they have learned about their parents and themselves, and that despite the difficulties, hard work and bad patches they themselves have grown during this part of their life. They have learned the strengths and weaknesses of their families and perhaps have had time to reflect on what life will be like for themselves should they develop a disability in later life. As mentioned above, one area which often affects people emotionally is a sense that the older parent may not recognise or be grateful for the care provided. This may be most notable with dementia, where the older person may have no awareness, or even actively resist the help provided. Not only can you be the object of abuse in this situation, but you may find yourself unfavourably compared to a brother or sister who lives many miles away and is either unable to or does not contribute to the care in the way that you do. While this is personally hurtful to you, it is important to realise that in most cases the older person does not mean this and if they were not suffering from dementia they would not be likely to behave in this way.

Dementia

Dementia is a common cause for triggering care, and is perhaps the illness that most tests carers. However the situation is not universally gloomy and the dementia experience is enormously different from one family to another. It is important to try to maximise your chances of success by accentuating the positive and building on retained skills. Repeated questioning, failure to acknowledge your support and help, and repetitive behaviour can all be challenging. In this setting it is important to seek out assistance, whether this is purely information or increased support from professional care services, such as respite care or home help.

Although you as a carer may continue to see the person who is your relative, much of the negativity around dementia arises from negative social reactions by others. We will cover these in Chapter 14 on dementia, as well as ways of breaking out of this negative cycle of 'malignant social psychology'.

Strategies for Caring

There are a few strategies which will help you to navigate the caring process without extra stress.

Information

The first is to gain the maximum amount of information possible about the condition, or conditions, which have caused the older person to need care. You'll also need to learn about the resources and facilities that are available, and some awareness of how society responds to frailty in later life is also helpful. Hopefully you will gain some of this knowledge from this book, but you will need more specific knowledge for specific conditions, and there is little which can replace a personalised assessment. Another way of gaining the maximum amount of information and also giving support is through carer training sessions, which are run by a number of voluntary organisations and healthcare services. These groups can be very helpful for emotional support, developing a sense that you're not alone, and also seeing glimpses of the lighter side.

Share the Caring

The second strategy is to share the caring in whatever way seems most reasonable to you and your family. Accepting and enlisting help should be done sooner rather than later. Avoid trying to feel possessive around the care of an older person, no matter how special your relationship with them. Bearing in mind that most causes of frailty in later life are not only chronic but progressive, it is better to enrol your brothers and sisters early in the process when the tasks are smaller. It will then be easier to adjust later on when the situation requires more effort. The web of care may indeed be wider than you think. The older person's friends, neighbours and other networks may be willing to help but may need to be asked. Again, remember to try to ensure the older person's preferences are at the centre of this network of care. Getting brothers and sisters and other family involved can look like a daunting task. A useful way of getting people involved may revolve around the older person's consultation with the doctor or a first assessment at a hospital clinic. You may also want to organise a family meeting.

The rest of your family usually want to help, but may not get involved because they feel that they would be interfering with your role, because they don't take directions from you or because they don't agree with the way you are handling things. Sometimes, they may not even agree that your parent has a problem.

A family meeting can be helpful but it is also a novel and often difficult experience for most people. It may be helpful to either have this with a meal in a social setting in one of the family houses or else try to have a family meeting with your parent's specialist or a social worker. Given the often large size of Irish families, is important to try to keep the number at such a meeting as small and manageable as possible. While the concerns of the older person must be central, for your first meeting you may wish to meet among yourselves. The following guidelines might be helpful. You may or may not be able to get people to agree to them in advance – try showing them this book.

- Keep cool, and if you find something that some-body has said to be hurtful, count to ten and trying not to pour oil on the fire.
- List out the care needs the older person has in terms of the time involved and the nature of the task.
- Listening is important, and if possible ensure that all participants listen without interrupting. The care of your parent can be a very emotional subject and may bring up all sorts of emotions from childhood, adolescence and young adult-hood. However, you should try to clearly stick to the issue of care for your parent and avoid other issues.
- Identify a link person. In many families there is often one person who can be clearly identified as either the primary care-giver or else as someone who would be a good spokesperson. Clearly agreeing on who this should be sets up two respon-sibilities. Each side needs to listen to the other, but the spokesperson needs to give a commit-ment of clearly communicating information from

the doctor and other healthcare providers. For the other members of the family, some patience is required, as getting used to somebody else asking questions and liaising for you may leave you feeling that there is some information you still do not fully appreciate. In general, and particularly with larger Irish families, your doctor and the health service will appreciate knowing that there is a clearly identifiable person helping with the care of the older person. Don't forget that for most of us our spouse is our next of kin. Adult children *must* ensure that their older parent's spouse has a key role.

Setting Limits

The third element of the strategy revolves around a setting of limits. In the middle of a first crisis of severe illness most of us will invest heavily in the care issues of an older relative. However, as many of these conditions are chronic you will need to stand back and reflect in more depth as to what you can reasonably do for a parent or relative, and what things you cannot realistically do. This is perhaps one of the most difficult things for you to do, and can clearly be helped by having the maximum information and maximum use of available services. Once done, however, you will find that this is a very valuable exercise which will allow you to discuss your plans more realistically with the rest of your family and your older relative. You need to combat a sense of guilt at this stage – there is no point in burning out early or in putting in levels of time and effort that are not sustainable in the longer term. In sporting terms, the medical emergency is the 100 metre sprint but the longer-term caring is the 10,000 metre race and you need to pace yourself accordingly.

Look after Yourself as Well

The fourth element of strategy is to look after yourself as well. This extends to your spouse and family and may seem a tall order. However, the analogy of the 10,000 metre race is appropriate here and if you fall into difficulties also then both you and your older parent will suffer. You need to make sure that you are carving out some space every week for your own social pursuits, keeping up with friends, and doing some activity or exercise. To do these things you may need to get somebody to sit with your parent or call in help. You must not feel guilty about this, as the healthier and happier you are, the longer your parent will manage to stay at home.

Channel Your Anger and Frustration into More Useful and Constructive Pathways

If you have a brother or sister who does not seem to be pulling their weight, despite family meetings and discussion, you will need to find ways to lose this anger. You will not change their input by your anger, and it will only eat away at your peace of mind. Attending a carer support group may help by showing that you are not alone in this predicament and sharing your feelings about this may be helpful. Equally, use your anger about inadequate services to write letters to elected representatives and join advocacy groups.

Develop Personal Strategies for Dealing with the Negative Emotions You Will Experience while Caring for Someone

Just as with the last recommendation, dealing with anger and resentment is an important (if difficult!) part of surviving the care experience. Anger and resentment can be a common part of your experience and indeed they may arise partly from the reactivation of old patterns from childhood and early adulthood. Our parents are among the only adults we know who may still criticise our dress, our lifestyle and the way we raise our children. The intrusiveness of these comments may become all the more marked with the onset of dementia. As one carer said to me, there is no one who can cut the legs from under you like your own mother. If dementia is not present do not overreact, but think of ways in which you can remind your mother or father you too are an adult. Gentle humour is usually more effective than snapping back. Even if dementia is present, gentle humour and some reminding of boundaries may help both of you.

Adapt to the Pace

One challenge I find from busy middle-aged children of frail parents is that they want the situation 'sorted' with speed. While not in any way detracting from the need to have responsive, focused services for older people, you will experience heartbreak if you come to the caring situation thinking that there is a slick, client-centred service that will look after mum or dad, and set your worries at ease. Even allowing for the many great people in various community services, managing the expectations and needs of older people, who may find a procession of different carers through their house very difficult, and stewarding a complex care package, will require vigilance, tolerance, strength and patience.

Professional Help

A range of professionals can help to mediate the process of caring (see Chapter 7). Many families and children find it quite difficult to be certain how best to engage with professional mediation. In some ways this can occur informally during the process of consultation with a public health nurse, family doctor or hospital consultant. A more formal way is through a session or sessions with a social worker. Your older relative may have a primary care team with a social worker in their area; if not, you may be able to access a social worker attached to the geriatric medicine or old age psychiatry services in your local health area.

Learning from Others

It can be very helpful to share the experiences of others who have cared. The Carers Association is the longest standing and biggest organisation for looking after those who care in Ireland. It has a network of carers' centres, a library of documents, a useful website and also helps in delivering a range of services. A particularly helpful service, if it is available in your area, is a carer who will visit regularly to provide in-home respite for an afternoon or a morning in your house. In addition, the association provides care information packs and training to carers. It also gives background information on the Carer's Allowance and the Carer's Benefit. The association's freephone telephone care line (1800 240724) is a useful fallback where you can talk to trained and supportive staff. Finally, it really is important that those who care for older people and suffer from the inadequacies and poor information of the Irish health and social care services should group together and lobby the government so that things can be improved now and into the future for all of us as we age.

For those caring for a relative with Alzheimer's disease or a similar dementia, the Alzheimer Society of Ireland offers a range of supports as well, including a carer support telephone line, day centres, some in-home respite, carer information packs, and carer and patient support groups. In some areas, it also has a liaison worker who will help with the coordination of care. It also fulfils a useful advocacy role, and it is important for many of us to continue with important advocacy and lobby initiatives.

Similar groups exist for stroke – the Volunteer Stroke Scheme (www.strokescheme.ie) – and the Parkinson's Association of Ireland (www.parkinsons. ie). Each has something to offer that may be unique to the illness. For example, the Volunteer Stroke

Scheme has an innovative scheme to provide psychological support and counselling to those who have had a stroke, a need which is poorly provided by both hospital and community services.

Becoming an Employer

The new system of Home Care Packages means that you, or your older relative, will become an employer or contractor. Although in many cases the public health nurse will provide some support and input, you or your relative will inevitably assume significant responsibilities. The Home Care Package generally allows up to twenty hours a week of paid care in addition to possible input from the public health nurse, a home help and the home care attendant. While technically the home care agency may do the nuts and bolts of employing the home care worker, it really is you or your relative who will be determining the rightness of fit and the adequacy and punctuality of the service, and who will first notice if things are not going right, and who will have to deal with this in the first instance.

It helps greatly if you, other family members and your older relative can agree that a single person will act as the link person between the older person, and the various agencies and people who come into their house. Increasingly, the home carers will come from a commercial agency, which in general undertakes some training and supervision of the home care worker. When dealing with these agencies it is helpful where possible to ensure that the discussion about service providers is done in conjunction with the public health nurse or the local HSE Home Care Package coordinator, if one exists. It is also helpful to ask that as few changes in personnel as possible occur as this is more complicated for the older person and also for the carer in terms of providing consistent care.

The standards of care to be provided should be clearly detailed, and the commercial provider should outline how it will supervise punctuality, adherence to standards and quality of care. It should also clarify what arrangements it has should a worker cancel or not show up. Ideally, the agency should be part of the trade association, the Irish Private Home Care Association, and it is likely that in the near future the HSE will provide some form of recognition or recommendation for some of the home care agencies. There is currently no official regulation of care provided at home, and, to be fair, the home care agencies have requested that there should be.

Ideally, encourage your older relative to ask you or another family member to meet the home care worker together and assess how the interaction goes. Is this person respectful, courteous and well groomed?

You or your older relative may find yourself thinking of hiring people yourself, and again think about issues such as qualifications, training, experience and certification. Does the person have experience working with the particular problems that affect your relative, for example dementia, incontinence and stroke? Finally are they physically able to meet the older person's care needs, for example can they support the older person so that they can move from a bed and chair?

You and your older relative then need to keep a fairly close eye to ensure punctuality and appropriateness of care. Among the examples of concern I have heard from friends, patients and their carers are lack of punctuality, failure to carry out tasks appropriately, the paid carer bringing their children along with them to the house as a highly inappropriate form of childcare, and touching the older person for loans. None of these behaviours should be acceptable to the agencies, but older people and their families often find themselves in a delicate position, despite the fact that they are effectively the employers of these carers. It is important to try to catch any of these problems early, and to discuss them with the agency as soon as possible.

In addition, you must be very cautious that the care agency representative does not try to sell more care on the basis of their assessment, as they clearly have a vested interest in providing more of their care. I am aware of one case where this occurred, and where the relative, upon declining the care, was threatened with being reported to the elder abuse services. Any increase in care should be determined by you, or you and your relative in conjunction with the public health nurse.

Elder Abuse and Home Care Services

We hope that serious problems are rare but they do happen, and abuse can occur from family carers or with home care services. Prevention is better than cure so try to avoid having money and jewellery in sight, and never let the care worker have access to your older relative's bank account or finances. If there is any unexplained deterioration in the older person's well-being, or any signs of new or unexplained bruises or wounds, then you need to think about the possibility of elder abuse. One challenging area is where an older person with memory problems loses something, such as money, and then thinks that somebody has taken it, and a family member or home carer may be the nearest target. You need to check this out quite carefully, and provide reassurance if it seems that the accusations are untrue as this is hard for a home care worker. If there is any suggestion that there may be abuse occurring, you should mention this to the supervisor, and give strong consideration to reporting it to the elder abuse senior caseworker either through the HSE helpline (1850 241850) or to your PHN.

Without in any way condoning poor practice or shoddy care, it is also important to remember that no one is going to look after your relative in exactly the way that you think they should be cared for. There may be some compromises, such as the aide watching television perhaps with your parent or relative, but if the older person likes their home carer and they are doing a reasonably good job try to achieve a balance. Also, do try to develop a good relationship with the carers, who are not enormously well paid as the agency takes a considerable portion of the fee. Showing appreciation by way of a 'thank you', or by giving appropriate praise to the agency representative can be helpful, as can giving them an appropriate gift at Christmas.

If you are thinking of employing somebody as a completely private venture, all the above advice applies, but think hard about issues such as insurance, as if the carer falls in the house or becomes injured lifting the older person they may decide to sue. Also, it is not only illegal but also a false economy to not pay PRSI, and remember that the expense of hiring a carer is allowable against tax.

Aftercare

When the episode of care is over, do think of giving some thought to helping build up support for other people who might be in the same situation. Joining the Carers Association or the Alzheimer Society of Ireland as active or passive members is one good way of both helping others with your experience and also trying to build an Ireland where we will be more confident of better care for all of us as we age.

9

Transport and Driving

Transport, and in particular driving, tends to be a very under-recognised part of the fabric of our lives which we tend to take for granted. Access to a private car is now the predominant mode of travel, and the longer you as an older person can continue to drive, the longer you will maintain important levels of social access and independence. Driving extends independent living as it allows people to shop, go to healthcare appointments and maintain social contacts, and whatever illnesses or disabilities lead to driving cessation usually also preclude you from using public transport.

Older drivers are in general the safest group of drivers on the road, despite the accumulated physical deficits of later life – arthritis, reduced vision, etc. This is because the wisdom of later life allows them to manage the task of driving better and more strategically, and to avoid situations that might be threatening.

However, the greatest barriers you will find to continued driving are likely to arise from popular, and ill-informed, prejudice about older drivers, as well as financial costs. The prejudice against older drivers is manifest in the Irish licensing system's demand that those over 70 require a medical certificate once they turn 70, and every one to three years after that. Drivers over the age of 60 can only get a three-year licence or a licence up to their 70th birthday, and those over 70 can only get a driving licence for either one or three years (rather than ten years for younger drivers). After a driver turns 70 they require a fresh medical certificate every time they renew their licence. There is no scientific or medical basis to this demand, which may deter some drivers from continued driving. There is also no basis for increased rates of motor insurance, or difficulties with getting car hire, in later life.

In addition, the costs of continued driving are steep, particularly those for purchasing a newer car, with the result that older drivers are probably more likely than their younger counterparts to require NCT testing for their cars, with the attendant costs. However, the costs of not driving are also significant in terms of loss of independence and social connections, so it is very much to be encouraged.

Illness and Driving

If you are affected by certain illnesses, however, you do need to ask your family doctor or specialist about whether you can continue to drive, and clarify whether you need to inform your insurance company (if in doubt, the answer is yes – failure to do so may invalidate your insurance). These conditions include:

- *Stroke* – the deficits associated with stroke can be varied, and there may be no impact on driving or there may be a significant impact. Your stroke specialist will give some guidance, and you may, in addition, need an assessment by an occupational therapist or a specialised driving test on the road. This assessment will tell whether or not you are fit to drive, and whether or not your car might benefit from adaptations, or you might benefit from some rehabilitation lessons.
- *Parkinson's disease* – this can affect your body, your speed of thinking and your mood. Your specialist again will give some first indications (in mild cases no further assessment is needed), and may again call on an occupational therapist or specialist driver assessment. As this condition is progressive, you will need ongoing assessment perhaps every six to twelve months.
- *Alzheimer's disease* and other *dementias* – it often surprises the public, but those in the early stages of dementia can often drive with a safety record equivalent to those without the illness. However, it is not really possible to tell in the clinic whether or not your driving skills are maintained, so in general the specialist will recommend a specialised driving test at first contact, and every six months after that. You will also need to plan eventual withdrawal from driving as the illness progresses.
- *Diabetes* – in general, the type of diabetes that starts in later life does not cause significant problems for driving, but do check with your GP or specialist.

- *Vision problems* – the regulations for these are the most clear-cut of all, and your eye doctor or optician should be able to advise you on this. With your sight corrected if necessary by glasses or contact lenses, you need to have a visual acuity of 6/12, or, in decimal terms, 0.5. In addition, any impairment in your field of vision (for example, after stroke or with eye diseases such as glaucoma) needs to be assessed by your eye doctor or optometrist to see whether or not it impairs your ability to drive. Early treatment of cataracts is recommended.

Medications and Illness

There is a significant medical literature on the possible impact of medications on driving, but relatively little hard evidence of actual negative impacts of medications on driving once the underlying illness is taken into account. However, do tell your doctor if you find yourself at all drowsy or slower in thinking with any new medication.

On the other hand, many medications probably make it easier and safer to drive, such as those for Parkinson's disease, depression and arthritis because they counteract symptoms which may make driving difficult; so do keep taking these medications.

Making the Driving Task Easier

A number of small adjustments can make driving easier, including a swivelling car seat to allow easier entry and exit (a black plastic bag to help you turn is a cheaper, if sweatier, alternative), built-up keys for those with arthritis of the hands, and panoramic rear-view mirrors for those who have limited neck movement. Some of these items can be sourced through the Assist Ireland website (www.assistireland.ie). For more significant alterations, contact your local driver assessment centre.

When You Can No Longer Drive

Between you, your family and your doctor(s), most older people with progressive illnesses or disabilities eventually agree a point where driving is no longer possible. It may be a little more complex for those with memory problems or dementia, but at this point the sourcing of other transport is a priority.

Most people get support with transport from their families, and while a natural reluctance to be seen to impose on others is common, it makes sense to accept their offers – you probably supported them with transport in your time! The options outside of private arrangements are relatively limited in Ireland, and a cause of concern for successful ageing. In a number of rural areas there are rural transport schemes which provide a variety of services, depending on the area, from disability-friendly buses to more individualised transport; ask your public health nurse or local welfare officer for details. In Dublin, a not-for-profit organisation called Vantastic can provide door-to-door transport for those who can no longer drive, as well as dedicated health and shopping routes in north central Dublin.

I'm Worried about My Mother's Driving

If you are concerned about the driving skills of a parent or older relative the best person to discuss this with is the older person in the first instance. However, do bear in mind that this is a discussion between two adults, and think how you might feel if you are approached about your driving by your adult child. Research shows that a majority of older drivers would prefer that such discussions are with their spouse in the first instance, followed by another family member, followed by their doctor.

It will help therefore to keep the focus on the driving task, and not your older relative's disabilities, for which they are usually making compensation. Are there new scratches or bumps on the car? Any reports of erratic driving? Have they gotten lost when driving on a relatively familiar route?

If yes, then try to raise your concerns in this light, and suggest a discussion with the family doctor. Have some thought as to what transportation alternatives there are for the older person before starting any discussions. This may take several discussions, with men more likely to be resistant than women. Don't be dissuaded by initial negative reactions, and remain supportive.

It is helpful that the assessment of choice for drivers with neurodegenerative diseases such as Alzheimer's is a specialised driving test – in effect a neutral party, although still threatening for someone who may not have sat a driving test in over 60 years.

If your relative is suffering from a dementia and seems to be unable to engage with the discussion, it is worth signalling the problem to their doctor. I find that in general most of these cases do resolve themselves, particularly if transport needs and alternatives are explored. The 'nuclear option'

– discussion with the Gardaí over concerns about unsafe driving – is a manoeuvre best reserved as an absolute last resort, and I have not needed to use it in over twenty years of practice, although the potential threat has been helpful.

Public Transport

While there have been some significant developments in public transport (for example, 'kneeling' buses in Dublin to facilitate those with mobility problems and wheelchair users), some challenges remain for older people who have problems with personal mobility. In particular, the acceleration and deceleration of buses and trams at stops and in traffic can be sudden, leading to an unsteady ride and a risk of falling and injury for those who suffer from problems with gait and balance.

On the other hand, free public transport over longer distances can be invaluable for keeping in contact with friends and relatives, and significant improvements have been made in the train system for people with disabilities. However, do ask about such access ahead of a planned journey, and arrive with plenty of time to spare.

Section II

Common Health Problems

10

Diabetes

Diabetes is one of the more common medical conditions of later life, but with appropriate care should allow for a full and normal lifestyle. This chapter will provide a brief overview of some of the points relevant to diabetes in later life, and in particular to the issue of diabetes occurring with other illnesses, the relationship with frailty, and diabetes in those in nursing homes. There is also a wealth of good information available for those with diabetes from the Diabetes Federation of Ireland. Diabetes is also one of the few illnesses of later life which is covered by the Long-Term Illness Scheme; if you do not have a Medical Card, the cost of medication for diabetes and related conditions, as well as of the reagent strips for testing glucose, will be covered by the scheme.

Diabetes is one of the chronic illnesses which would lend itself well to a shared care programme between primary and specialist (hospital) care. Unfortunately, the planned integration by the HSE of GP and specialist care into a national programme of shared care has not yet happened. This is a pity, because the planned programme would give a clearly defined plan of how your diabetes care is shared between your family doctor and the specialist (an endocrinologist or diabetologist). It also includes the setting up of a network of diabetic community nurses, which would be an invaluable support. This chapter will try to outline what sort of care you should be getting, whether managed by your family doctor or specialist.

What Is Diabetes?

Diabetes is an illness where the cells in your body cannot process the sugar in your bloodstream, because either your pancreas is not producing enough insulin, a hormone for processing sugar (this usually leads to type 1 diabetes), or else your body cells lose their sensitivity to insulin (type 2 diabetes, in general). Type 2 diabetes is the most common form of diabetes in later life, frequently, but not always, related to obesity. For most older people, type 2 diabetes can be managed with diet, lifestyle management and tablets. Type 1 diabetes is managed with regular injections of insulin. A smaller number of older people will require insulin for type 2 diabetes, and many of those with type 1 diabetes will enter old age while continuing their insulin treatment. Virtually all those with insulin-dependent diabetes will attend a diabetes specialist clinic, and although many with type 2 diabetes also attend these clinics, very many are not insulin dependent.

The classics symptoms of type 1 diabetes – weight loss, thirst and frequent urination – are not so common in type 2 diabetes, and many with type 2 diabetes are diagnosed as a result of a general health screening, or when they become unwell with some other illness.

The two big challenges with diabetes in later life are a) keeping a balance between careful control and not letting it dominate your life, and b) an awareness that if you become frail or have problems with memory then very strict control of diabetes might be counterproductive.

Who Will Look After My Diabetes?

You may be looked after by either your GP or a diabetes specialist in a hospital. The key elements of your care are:

- To become educated about your diabetes and its complications
- To review your diet
- To set agreed levels of control of your diabetes
- To establish how this control is measured
- To arrange for yearly check-ups of the body systems potentially affected by diabetes, particularly your eyes, feet, nervous system and kidneys

You should discuss with your GP how this package can best be achieved for you; your GP and/or public health nurse may have access to some services, such as dietetics and podiatry, but, if not, you should ask how you can access these.

The diabetes specialist team, led by a specialist doctor, termed an endocrinologist, or sometimes a diabetologist, usually includes doctors, diabetes specialist nurses and dieticians (also called clinical

nutritionists). In addition, you will encounter eye specialists to check the back of your eye (the retina) for diabetic
eye disease, and other specialists as requested.

Education, Diet and Exercise

Your role relates very much to taking ownership of
the condition, and education is key here. This may
happen in a number of ways. A number of education
programmes are run by the Diabetes Federation of
Ireland, known as Community Orientated Diabetes
Education (CODE). In addition, there are a number of
services run by other educational groups, known as
the DESMOND and X-PERT programmes. If you are
referred to a specialist service, the diabetes specialist
nurse will also provide education and you can avail
of these courses as well. If not referred to a specialist
service, ask your GP or public health nurse for the
best way to get this education, and/or contact the
Diabetes Federation of Ireland.

The best way to keep healthy is by learning about
diabetes, and adopting healthy eating habits and
regular physical exercise. Ideally you should get a
dietician to review your diet soon after diagnosis,
and you will hopefully find that the recommended
changes are not too drastic. The recommended diet
may fulfill other goals, such as helping to reduce
weight and preventing heart disease and stroke. You
should avoid foods labeled as 'diabetic' products
as they are expensive and unnecessary if you are
already following the dietician's advice.

The exercise recommendations are similar to
those in Chapter 4 and, combined with diet, can

contribute to better overall health, reduced weight, better diabetic control and less likelihood of diabetic complications.

How Often Should I Be Checked Up?

In general, a review every three months or so is considered a reasonable standard; your visit may be with the practice nurse or your GP. A review with the hospital team is usually at longer intervals; this may be more frequent if controlling your glucose levels, or the complications of diabetes, is problematic.

One of the key areas to be discussed with your family doctor and specialist is an agreed target for controlling the levels of blood sugar in your body, commonly called glucose. Often a measure is used called HbA1c; this tracks your glucose levels over a longer period. If you are generally otherwise well, and are paying attention to your diabetes care, it is good to get this level below 6.5 per cent. However, if you are frail, have a lot of other medical conditions, or are variable in your attention to your diabetes, then trying to keep your blood sugar too low might not be good for you. Your doctors will discuss what seems to be the most appropriate level with you, and with your family as well, if you wish.

There is quite a degree of variability in Ireland as to whether or not those with type 2 diabetes are asked to engage in regular monitoring of glucose. This is done by performing a finger prick, applying the resulting drop of blood to a special reagent strip and reading the glucose level with a glucose meter. If other medical conditions do not interfere with your control, and you are able to manage your diet, exercise and medication regime, your doctor may not think regular monitoring is required. Glucose monitoring may be recommended, after discussion with your doctor, if control is difficult and during illness, and will always be recommended should your diabetes require the addition of insulin therapy.

If your control is such that you are likely to find your sugars levels are high, the doctor and nurses might recommend that you test your urine for ketones with special strips which you dip into your urine.

Medications and Diabetes

There is a range of tablets that your doctors can add if diet and exercise do not keep your glucose levels under control. The choice of tablet depends on any other health conditions you may have, and if you are likely through forgetfulness or other illness to omit eating, or take a tablet too many. Some classes of medications may be avoided, particularly those which can cause your blood sugar to drop too low (hypoglycaemia).

During acute illness or at times of poor control your blood sugar may rise, either from not taking your medication or stress to the body due to infection, illness or surgery. At this stage you may become dehydrated, confused or drowsy, or have seizures, and, in the worst incidents, have a type of coma. Should any of these symptoms appear you should arrange for an urgent check of your glucose levels with your family doctor or the practice nurse, or by yourself/a family member if you are monitoring your own glucose.

The management of insulin is quite a specialised area, and is beyond the scope of this general guide to ageing, but many general principles apply. In particular, tight control of glucose is indicated if you are reasonably well regarding other illnesses, but a more loose control is indicated if you are frail, suffer from a number of illnesses, or may have difficulties in managing your insulin and glucose monitoring.

The main type of medication that can cause you to have low blood sugar, other than insulin, is a group of medications called sulphonylureas. Common symptoms of low blood sugar levels include sweating, nausea, warmth, anxiety, shakiness, palpitations, hunger, headache, blurred or double vision, confusion and difficulty speaking. In the worst cases, persistant low blood sugar can cause coma, permanent brain damage and even death. Should you find yourself getting spells of low blood sugar levels then you need to take a sugary drink (not a diet or sugar-free version) followed by some longer-acting carbohydrate such as biscuits or a cereal bar and arrange for an urgent review with your family doctor and/or the specialist team.

Complications of Diabetes

You also need to control your risk factors for diseases of the heart and stroke. As well as embracing a healthy diet and an exercise regime, smoking should be avoided at all costs, and alcohol should only be used in moderation. It is important that attention is paid to high blood pressure, and most older people with diabetes should also be on cholesterol-lowering medication, if tolerated, to reduce their risk of heart disease. Your doctor may also recommend aspirin in a small dose if you are considered at moderate to high risk for heart disease or stroke.

You should also get annual checks of your kidney function, by way of a blood test, and a urine test which looks for a specific protein, microalbumin, which suggests kidney damage.

Attention to foot care is also important as patients with diabetes may develop what is known as a neuropathy, a reduction of sensation in the feet in particular so that you are less aware of injuries, and can develop foot ulcers which may prove slow to heal and possibly get infected. Early referral to a podiatrist is of utmost importance here and advice on appropriate footwear will also help.

One form of neuropathy which can be troubling is that which causes pain. Your specialist may try a range of options, including medications which alter the perception of pain, improving the control of your glucose levels, specialist foot care by a podiatrist and reviewing the circulation in your legs. Depending on the source of pain, medications may be helpful and may be either pain relievers or medications such as gabapentin and pregabalin, which act on the transmission of pain to the brain; some antidepressants, such as amitryptiline, may also be helpful. Your specialist may also involve a specialist in pain medicine.

You should be offered annual eye checks for the two main types of illness which can affect your eyes if you have diabetes: diabetic eye disease of the retina at the back of the eye and cataracts, which is clouding of the lens of the eye. Treatment is usually through the use of laser therapy by an eye surgeon for disease of the retina, and the removal of the cataract(s) in the case of cataracts.

Sexual function can also be affected by diabetes, including impotence in men and vaginal dryness in women. If you are troubled by these, do not hesitate to discuss the issue with your doctor, as a range of possible solutions are available.

Driving and Holidays

Once your control of your diabetes is satisfactory, there should be little problem with continuing to drive. You need to let your insurance company know you have diabetes and when renewing your driving licence you will need to ask your doctor to provide a report to the National Driver Licence Service. Your GP/specialist will base this on your overall health as well as on your diabetes. In general, type 2 diabetes is not associated with any significant increased risk on its own, and your insurance company should not load your insurance.

The main concerns relate to your blood sugar dropping low (hypoglycaemia) because it reduces brain functioning and concentration so you will be less able to manage the car, and indeed may lose consciousness. If this occurs you need to discuss it with your doctor, and stop driving until the problem is resolved.

In the Nursing Home

In the nursing home, much the same degree of monitoring and attention to diet and exercise as feasible is also indicated. As generally those who are residents of nursing homes are affected by frailty and multiple medical conditions, and are more likely to have memory problems, it is likely that the imperative for tighter control is less, but the need for an individualised care plan is no less.

Each resident should have a care plan for diabetes agreed between the patient, their family if wished, the general practitioner/medical officer and the nursing home staff. Each resident with diabetes should undergo an annual review, preferably conducted in the nursing home. This should include a detailed clinical examination including nutritional assessment, functional assessment (physical and mental), visual acuity measurement, examination of the back of the eye if possible and assessment of your glucose control and kidney function.

The provision of insulin treatment should be done in conjunction with a specialist service as well as the family doctor, and an assessment by a dietician should be made available. Foot care, eye care and mobility should all be promoted and, where possible, ongoing preventive care for heart disease should be maintained.

If your older relative or friend seems to have difficulty in understanding the process of shared care between their family doctor and the specialist, it is important that you or a nominated family member joins in with the education and monitoring programme set up between the GP and the specialist. It is particularly important that you let the GP know if any of the symptoms of low blood glucose arise, particularly if the older person is on a sulphonylurea medication.

In terms of diet management, as with many of the recommendations in this book, we doctors may propose but the patient will dispose, and beyond gentle encouragement we need to keep reminding ourselves that we all have a right to behave in inconsistent and not always sensible ways. While you may be concerned that your older relative will suffer in the future if their blood sugar is not brought to as normal a level as possible, bear in mind that over-tight control for those with multiple illnesses, memory problems and less ability to manage their illness may also lead to difficulties. In the nursing home, you should ask about the diabetes care plan, and particularly about the desired level of glucose control, as well as access to dietician support for managing their diet, and podiatrist support for foot care.

11

Mobility Problems and Falls

In the next few chapters, we will outline some of the more common problems which affect older people. Nearly all can be improved to some extent by appropriate diagnosis, treatment, rehabilitation and adaptation, and it is important that you get appropriate advice on this. Although these problems are discussed in isolation they may also occur together, and in general the more problems that occur together, the more you should think of a specialist assessment.

Mobility and Balance Problems

A significant number of older people, between 10 and 20 per cent, report balance and mobility problems. Usually, these are of gradual onset, but may arise after a specific illness such as stroke or inflammation of the inner ear. For many people, these problems will be as a result of more than one illness process – for example, they may have some arthritis, some degree of problem with maintaining blood pressure when standing upright and some loss of the brain's ability to fine-tune the complex task of walking.

Not only are problems with mobility and balance a considerable inconvenience, but also once you get them, you are now in a higher risk category for falling. This is therefore a signal to get something done by way of assessment and treatment before this should happen, as falls in later life are a significant concern. The risk of significant injury from a fall is high and it is a further deterrent to mobility and independence. So try to take action if you are developing mobility and balance problems.

Below we will outline the systems involved in walking (as you have not had to think of this so far in life), discuss the major illnesses that cause mobility and balance problems, and try to outline what you can do to stave them off.

Walking and maintaining balance is an incredibly complex act that we are accustomed to performing without the slightest thought as to how it is done. If you think about walking from the point of view of a robot, you need:

The structure	Your bones and joints
The power to get it moving	Your muscles
A network to send the signals from the ground and gravity and relay these signals to the brain, and in turn relay them from the brain to the muscles	Your nerves
A gravity sensor	Your middle ear
A central processor to coordinate	Your brain
Sufficient continuous energy for the coordinating centre	The blood supply to the brain

The key elements most commonly affected (and checked out during the assessment by the doctor) are:

- The joints – arthritis
- The muscles – weakness, known medically as myopathy
- The brain – stroke disease, both subtle and unrecognised, as well as overt stroke
- The energy – insufficient blood to the brain when standing up, known as postural (or sometimes orthostatic) hypotension

But while these are common causes, other causes will occur, and you should ask your doctor for their diagnosis or diagnoses of this.

Arthritis

You will nearly always be aware when arthritis is present. Pain, stiffness and difficulty moving your limbs usually signal themselves well. The most common form is osteoarthritis, followed by rheumatoid arthritis. The treatment and management of each has significant differences and it is important that you get a proper diagnosis from your GP.

Osteoarthritis

Osteoarthritis is often described as wear-and-tear arthritis, but there are other factors involved, such as a disposition in your family to osteoarthritis. It particularly affects your knees and hips, but also can affect your spine, shoulders and hands.

It is not just a matter of pain: because the pain reduces your movements, the muscles bracing your joints, in particular the knee, can become weaker, making the joint less stable, thus increasing the pain and reducing your ability to mobilise easily still further.

Treatment is by way of exercise, physiotherapy and pain-relieving medication in the first instance. It is important to realise that exercise and physiotherapy can make as much of an impact on your pain as powerful pain tablets. This puts the responsibility back to you in terms of keeping up with any exercises recommended by your physiotherapist.

Of course, in time, the arthritis will progress, and for a significant number of sufferers joint replacement may bring significant relief. Hip replacements, and increasingly knee replacements, can give good pain relief and, with enough therapy, a good return of mobility. Judging the right time to do this is a skilful and personalised choice, as you don't want to do it too early (they have a finite life span, and may need to be replaced) or too late, when your muscles have become very weak and you are out of condition. You need to discuss this with your doctor and possibly see a specialist, such as a rheumatologist, orthopaedic surgeon or geriatrician.

Rheumatoid Arthritis

Rheumatoid arthritis is related to an inflammation of your joints (and other tissues) and can affect a wider range of joints but in more varied ways than osteoarthritis. It is important to get a diagnosis as a) some medications may slow the course of the disease and b) the exercise pattern is different to that of osteoarthritis. Rheumatoid arthritis can be difficult to diagnose in its early stages for several reasons. Firstly, symptoms differ from person to person and can be more severe in some people than in others. Secondly, symptoms of rheumatoid arthritis can be similar to those of other types of arthritis and joint conditions, and it may take some time to rule out other conditions. Finally, the full range of symptoms develops over time, and only a few symptoms may be present in the early stages. Your doctor may arrange for X-rays and some blood tests to confirm the diagnosis.

Most people who have rheumatoid arthritis take medications. Some drugs only provide relief for pain (such as paracetamol); others reduce inflammation (called anti-inflammatory drugs). Still others, called disease-modifying anti-rheumatic drugs or DMARDs, can often slow the course of the disease. Your GP may prescribe these or refer you on to a rheumatologist. DMARDs include methotrexate, leflunomide, sulfasalazine and cyclosporine. Steroids, which are also called corticosteroids, are another type of drug used to reduce inflammation for people with rheumatoid arthritis. Prednisolone is the most commonly used steroid in Ireland. People with rheumatoid arthritis need a good balance between rest and exercise; they should rest more when the disease is active and exercise more when it is not.

New types of drugs called biological response modifiers can also help reduce joint damage. Early treatment with powerful drugs and drug combinations – including biological response modifiers and DMARDs – instead of single drugs may help prevent the disease from progressing and greatly reduce joint damage.

In some cases, a doctor will recommend surgery to restore function or relieve pain in a damaged joint. Surgery may also improve a person's ability to perform daily activities. Joint replacement and tendon reconstruction are two types of surgery available to patients with severe joint damage.

Muscle Weakness

Muscle weakness can occur for a range of reasons. One of the most common is disuse, whether due to a sedentary lifestyle or other illnesses (such as arthritis) limiting your mobility. Sometimes specific illnesses (e.g. polymyalgia rheumatica), vitamin deficiencies (vitamin D deficiency) or drugs (especially steroids) can affect the muscles directly. A particularly virulent form of muscle fatigue can set in after a significant illness if you have been bedbound for a while, called critical care myopathy/neuropathy.

Rising out of a chair without using your arms is a test for good function of your muscles (assuming that you don't have other problems such as significant arthritis). While this is the counsel of perfection, if you do have significant difficulties rising out of a chair you should talk to your family doctor.

Treatment depends on the diagnosis. If it is drug related, the doctor will try to see if you can do without the drug. Missing vitamins should be replaced, and muscle inflammation, such as polymyalgia, will be treated appropriately. For all of these conditions, and particularly for muscle weakness due to disuse, physiotherapy and exercise are very important, and a review of your nutrition might also be needed.

Problems with the Brain

The coordination of all the sensory inputs from your body and your gravity sensors is a complex task; even more complex is processing that information into the necessary instructions to the body to initiate walking. This is carried out by the brain in many separate sections working as a network. Diseases such as stroke and Parkinson's disease can affect many components of this system. A stroke can make you weak on one side, make you fail to appreciate sensation or gravity on one side, or affect your balance. Parkinson's disease affects the smoothness and ease of movement, which in turn gives rise to gait and balance difficulties.

A more subtle, but common illness, is a relatively newly described entity called *vascular gait dyspraxia*. This is a subtle form of stroke disease that can happen without you knowing it; you may have no weakness or sudden onset of walking difficulties. It is a diagnosis that is clinical, and is diagnosed when you have walking difficulties which are much more considerable than would be expected from the neurological examination that your doctor carries out.

For all of these brain-related issues causing disturbance of balance and walking disorders, the first priority is diagnosis by your doctor, who may send you on to a specialist. The good news is that a rehabilitation programme with physiotherapy is effective for most people. Also, your doctor may wish to make sure that you have touched all the bases for stroke prevention (see Chapter 16).

Reduced Blood Supply to the Brain

The brain is a highly complex and demanding organ (but still flexible). It requires a constant supply of blood (for oxygen and nutrients) at an appropriate blood pressure (so as to pump it around in sufficient quantities). If it is not getting enough blood and oxygen this affects its function and you will feel this either as dizziness or, if more severe, by a loss of consciousness. This is actually a protective mechanism – if you are dizzy you will generally sit or lie down, improving your chances of better blood flow to the brain, and if you fall you will maximise your flow of blood to the brain (although at a potentially significant cost).

One of the many miracles of our body's self-regulation (and one that you are not aware of until you have a problem with it) is how well the heart copes keeping a steady pressure for blood going to the brain when you change posture, from lying to sitting to standing.

Dizziness is one of the common features of people with balance and mobility problems, and in most cases it is due to a failure of the heart to keep a constant blood pressure available to the brain when you change position. This is called *postural hypotension* or *orthostatic hypotension*. You may notice this as a dizziness or light-headedness which occurs when (or shortly after) going from lying to sitting, or from sitting to standing. It may also occur when straightening up after bending down. Occasionally it can occur some time (several minutes perhaps) after standing up, and this may require specialist investigation.

Many things cause postural hypotension, but a common thread is previous (or indeed present) high blood pressure or disease of the blood vessels. The effect of these diseases is to impair the self-regulating mechanism of the heart and blood vessels so that your blood pressure can drop quickly when you stand up or bend down. This is one of the many ironies of later life: you may have simultaneously high blood pressure and yet also transient low blood pressure when you stand up.

Some things make postural hypotension worse, in particular medications. This includes those for high blood pressure, low blood pressure, Parkinson's disease and depression, and some sedatives. As you may still have these conditions, the biggest challenge for your doctor is trying to ensure an appropriate trade-off between the medication for your high blood pressure (protecting you from heart attack, stroke and many other things) and also its contribution to postural hypotension (which may make you unsteady, and can cause serious damage if you fall).

Measuring postural hypotension is difficult: the usual method (taking your blood pressure when lying down and again after standing up) often misses the diagnosis, and in general the geriatrician's rule of thumb is that if you have symptoms of light-headedness or dizziness on standing up, or find yourself sitting on the edge of the bed for a few minutes on getting up in the morning, then you have postural hypotension.

The treatment for postural hypotension is to try to reduce the use of other medications to a minimum and encourage exercise. You can also consider using support stockings to prevent blood pooling in your legs and the possible use of two medications which can increase your blood pressure – midodrine and fludrocortisone. However, they cannot be used if you have high blood pressure or heart failure.

A less common cause of loss of blood pressure to the brain is carotid sinus hypersensitivity. This is when the blood pressure sensors in the neck become ineffective and volatile. With this condition you may get sudden disabling attacks of dizziness and loss of consciousness, usually spontaneously. You will need specialist assessment for this, usually with a geri-atrician or cardiologist, who will need to assess these sensors by placing you on a tilting table, connecting you to some monitors, and then altering the tilt of the table and applying pressure to a specific blood vessel in your neck. If you have this condition confirmed, the treatment may be either a medication called fludrocortisone or a pacemaker, or sometimes both.

The Middle Ear

The middle ear is an important part of the body for balance, but tends to be an infrequent main cause for mobility disorders of older people. In three little canals, tiny stones attached to little hairs float in a fluid. The effect of gravity on them is transmitted to the brain and tells you where you are in space.

If you have an illness which affects the middle ear or its connections you can develop a balance problem where you will often have vertigo. Irish people sometimes say 'vertigo' for all dizziness, but in fact vertigo means a particular type of dizziness which is accompanied by an unpleasant sense of the room or your surroundings spinning around you. This may occur if you move your head in particular ways, a condition called benign positional vertigo (although sufferers may not consider it benign). Other causes include viral infections, a particular form of migraine, and a disease of the inner ear called Ménière's disease. Ménière's disease is a disorder that causes a person to experience:

- Vertigo
- Hearing loss that comes and goes
- Tinnitus, which is a ringing or roaring in the ears
- A feeling of fullness in the ear

It can affect adults of any age and the cause is unknown.

There are many ways to treat balance disorders. Treatments will vary depending on the cause. See your doctor if you are experiencing dizziness, vertigo or other problems with your balance.

If you have a balance problem caused by inner ear problems your GP may treat you as is or may refer you to an ear, nose and throat (ENT) specialist. This is of possible benefit, as there is a particular manoeuvre which ENT doctors and some other specialists perform which can free up the little stones in the middle ear if they become stuck.

The Action Plan

Prevention

Exercise will maintain both stamina and balance. In particular, tai chi and balance exercises can be recommended. As mentioned in Chapter 4, one of the barriers here is the newness of the idea of going to an exercise class, or embarrassment about your potential performance. You must try to move beyond these. Maybe you can find a friend or family member who might go with you or share lifts. Prevention of subtle stroke disease is a priority, and stopping smoking and controlling your blood pressure are again key elements. Ensuring a balanced diet with emphasis on getting enough vitamin D is also important. You should ask your doctor whether or not you are at risk for osteoporosis, and if so take appropriate measures.

Diagnosis

The conditions mentioned above are only the major causes, and assessment by your doctor is very important. You may be referred on to therapy, or to a specialist for further assessment and advice on treatment.

Treatment

The treatment will obviously depend on the causes, but physiotherapy is likely to figure if you have any significant loss of mobility or balance problems. You may be recommended an aid to help with both your stability and mobility, for example a walking stick (see Appendix B for more information). Try to engage with this; some older Irish people feel embarrassed about using walking sticks, but if it is recommended by a physiotherapist it is definitely worth using.

You again have significant responsibility here, and you should think of how you are going to keep up your exercise programmes, such as doing them with a friend. You should also think about arranging for, or possibly paying for, a regular review with a physiotherapist to supervise the maintenance programme.

If your balance and mobility are significantly affected it would be reasonable to have an occupational therapy assessment to look at your house.

The Ultimate Balance and Mobility Problem – Falls

Falls are unfortunately common in later life, and are of major consequence to older people. Because the word 'fall' is so common and conversational, the general public (and some doctors) may not take them very seriously. However, it is important to take them seriously, because much can be done to reduce your risk of falls, and to help protect you should you have further falls. Once you have had one fall, you are more at risk of further falls from then on in, so you should take this seriously and seek medical advice.

The assessment and treatment for falls is similar to that for balance and mobility problems, with some extra features and a greater sense of urgency.

As most falls involve a drop in blood pressure, it is important not to follow the understandable human instinct to sit up quickly and get off the floor as soon as possible, as this would drop your blood pressure further. In the first instance, roll over onto your side, bend your legs and stay there for a little while until your head seems clear. Then the easiest way to get up is what is known as *backward chaining*. In this you move onto your hands and knees, moving slowly all the time and direct yourself to a firm surface which you can use to support yourself, such as the arm of a sofa or chair. Facing the chair, raise yourself into a standing position and then turn and sit down.

If you are unable to get up or to get help try to avoid lying completely still as this will increase your chances of getting a pressure sore or a clot in the leg. Keep moving, even though you're on the floor. If a part of your body hurts significantly you should not move that part, but move other parts instead, for example on the non-injured side of your body. Do what you can to keep warm so as to reduce the risk of hypothermia by putting a blanket or rug over yourself if possible.

Fractures

It is important to treat any injuries that arise from a fall so as to get you back to mobility and exercise. As fractures are relatively common after falls in older people, a high state of vigilance is important. Older people can present with fractures in different ways, and the fracture may not turn up on the first X-ray. It may take a repeat X-ray a few days later, or specialised X-rays such as bone scans or a CT scan of the bone, to rule out a fracture. *An important rule of thumb is that if you cannot walk or bear your weight when standing after a fall, then you have a fracture until proven otherwise.* You will have to take a stand on this (metaphorically), and should immediately contact your doctor or the emergency services.

The most common fracture is that of the hip, also known as a fractured neck of femur. However, other common fractures that will prevent you weight-bearing are those of the pelvis or of the sacrum, a large bone between the base of the spine and the pelvis. A fracture of the hip is a serious condition and the most important element of care is that the fracture repair should be carried out if at all possible within 24 hours of admission by experienced staff. You or your family should ask the surgeon about any delay after 24 hours, which may be due to correcting any other medical illnesses you might have. If there is a delay it is important that you should get fluids and possibly food. After the operation it is important that you begin to stand and start to walk as soon as possible (the surgeon, nurses and therapists will guide you on this); with many type of hip repairs this will be within 48 hours. It is not uncommon for older people to suffer delirium, sometimes known as an acute confusional state, after an operation. This is a cause of medical concern, and your family should discuss this with the medical team, as it is important to remove any possible causes such as medication, infection or stroke.

Following the operation you will almost certainly require a period of rehabilitation. If your problems are mostly confined to difficulties with walking and mobilising this will predominantly be undertaken by physiotherapists within the team, but you may also need input from clinical nutritionists, occupational therapists, social workers, and speech and language therapists. You or your family can discuss your rehabilitation needs with the surgeon, possibly in consultation with the geriatrician. In the United Kingdom, services for those with broken hips are increasingly being run as a joint operation between geriatricians and orthopaedic surgeons. In Ireland, you may be offered a space in a rehabilitation unit in the hospital, in a dedicated rehabilitation hospital or in a nursing home. The most important issue to raise in discussions about rehabilitation is that of your specific needs, and from which therapists you require input. For example, one unit in Dublin has strong physiotherapy input, but much less occupational therapy and social work; this works fine for those who have predominantly mobility problems only, but less well for those who have complex needs. Do not hesitate to discuss your needs, or those of your relative, with the surgeon or his/her team.

After a fall which causes a fracture, or indeed after any fall, two main questions must be asked. The first is why you have fallen, and the second is whether or not your bones are sufficiently strong. The reasons for falling are generally those outlined above for problems with gait and mobility, as well as factors relating to the environment in which you fell.

Consider Your Bone Strength

After one fall, you may have no further problems, but statistically you are now in a group which is at higher risk of further falls. It therefore makes sense for your doctor to consider whether or not you have osteoporosis, and whether or not you should have further assessment (blood tests and a scan of bone density called a DEXA scan) and treatment. If you broke a bone with your fall, then you almost certainly have osteoporosis and should be actively considered for treatment. This usually consists of vitamin D, calcium and medications, the most common of which is a group called bisphosphonates.

Ensure that You Know How to Get Up After a Fall

This may seem painfully obvious, but some people may not be able to this without training. For those with significant disability, it may be a case of training a carer to learn how to lift without straining their back or causing other injury. Talk to your physiotherapist about this, and see the section above on getting up from falls.

The Extra Emphasis

Physiotherapy

As well as gaining strength and balance, physiotherapy can help with relieving pain arising from osteoarthritis, and ongoing review with a physiotherapist is recommended for all those with gait and balance problems.

Review of Your Environment

Although mentioned under balance and mobility problems, a review of your environment takes on a certain urgency after a fall to ensure that there are no hazards in the home that will make things worse. Again, you as an older person may be very reluctant to change the layout of your house, but do consider it strongly. An occupational therapy assessment might look at issues such as stair rails, non-slip mats, better lighting or a stair lift. Even more importantly, we now understand that occupational therapists transfer a significant amount of information to you and your family during these home visits, above and beyond the practical advice.

Fear of Falling

After a fall, some will find it so traumatic that they will be afflicted by a nervousness and fear of falling. If you are affected by this fear it is particularly important to get an assessment by a physiotherapist and/ or doctor to make sure this is not an unnecessary burden on you. However, the counterpoint of this is that you are often quite correct in having some fear of falling, given the medical conditions you will have, but in any event it is important to discuss this with a physiotherapist and/or doctor. In my experience, a course of physiotherapy is often the best way to overcome a fear of falling that is disproportionate to your risk of falling.

Review of Your Activity and Transport

With gait and balance problems, outdoor mobility can become more of a problem, particularly with public transport – the acceleration and deceleration of buses and trains can be difficult to manage, and older people are more likely to suffer injury than younger people from falls on public transport. In my experience, most older people adapt and avoid public transport when their mobility problems are severe. For this reason, continued car driving may be the most sensible solution. Older people's advocacy groups should take up the issue of ensuring that older people have access to adequate transport, particularly the private car. It is of some concern to experts on ageing that the Irish government asks for a medical screen for older drivers. Although lay people might think that this is a good idea, studies from other countries show that screening seems to prevent older people from driving, but does not reduce the number of older people who die or are injured on the roads. See Chapter 9 for more on driving and other forms of transport as we get older.

For adult children: watching an older relative's mobility deteriorate is troubling. While your advice may be ignored, the most important contribution that you can make is to discuss the possibility of clarifying the reasons why the gait or balance problem is occurring, and trying to access the services that are available.

Severe Gait and Balance Disturbance

Although for most older people the key to improving balance and gait involves ongoing walking, a time will come for a minority when they are so immobile that attempts to mobilise may actually be unwelcome, both subjectively and objectively. This is something that occasionally we will see when an older person takes to their bed. As long as there has been a good assessment to ensure that there is no illness or disability that can be treated, it may well be that the older person has made the right decision. While this does not absolve carers or nursing homes from providing stimulation and activity for older people, this final stage of mobility failure needs to be managed with some sensitivity and tact. Careful nursing is key for those who are immobile or bedbound, and the advice of the PHN in terms of avoiding pressure sores and dealing with continence issues is critical. He or she may also involve occupational therapy in terms of specialised mattresses, hoists, chair cushions and other equipment that will assist care at this stage.

12

Sight Problems

Although later life is associated with reduced vision, the wisdom of later life often adapts and accommodates without us thinking about it. We may limit our driving at night and in poor weather, unconsciously move our reading place to somewhere with brighter light, or drop some activities, such as sewing, which require very good eyesight.

This unconscious adaptation is both good and bad: good because we continue to cope, bad because we may not seek help early enough for eye conditions which could be improved with attention, or cause permanent damage or even blindness if not addressed in time.

In this chapter, I will emphasise the importance of seeking help as early as possible, and yet not despairing if you have left it late – remember, start early but it's never too late!

If you experience a sudden loss of all or part of your vision, do not in any way dally. This is a medical emergency, and may represent a serious illness such as the blockage of a blood vessel, a possible stroke or a bleed into the eye, and any delay in attending either Accident & Emergency or your family doctor can reduce your chances of salvaging the most sight possible out of this situation. This urgency also applies to pain in your eye, a discharge or pus in the eye, or flashes or streaks of lightning in the eye (this may be the first sign of a retinal tear).

For most people, visual problems will arrive gradually. If you find you have difficulty in reading with ease or viewing television, or have any other sense that your vision is not as good as it was, get checked out, in the first instance by an optician, who, although not a doctor, is trained to check for a number of conditions (glaucoma, cataracts, diabetic eye disease and macular degeneration) for which they will refer you on to an ophthalmologist, a medical doctor who specialises in diseases of the eye.

If none of these are the issue, then you will hopefully be able to manage with a change in spectacles, and you should consider a regular review with the optician every two to three years.

What about Eye Diseases?

As with most illnesses in later life, the response may be in part medical (including surgery) and in part by way of compensation (i.e. low vision visual aids). The common eye diseases are discussed below, and afterwards there is a section on adapting your home and lifestyle to low vision.

Cataracts

Cataracts are one of the most common reasons for reduced vision in later years, and occur when the lens of the eye, which is transparent at birth and in younger years, becomes cloudy. This cloudiness reduces the amount of light that gets through the lens and therefore less visual information gets to the back of the eye and so to the brain.

Removing the lens of the eye (by breaking it up with ultrasound waves and taking it out through a needle) and replacing it with a clear plastic lens implant is a safe and effective operation that can be done as an outpatient procedure. Normal activities can be resumed as early as the day following the procedure. You will usually be aware of a sudden improvement in vision, but it takes about a month for the eye to heal completely. The procedure can be performed on almost anyone regardless of frailty (both physical and mental) or age. In the public health system, you can be listed to have treatment under the National Treatment Purchase Fund if your treatment is likely to be delayed by more than three months.

Age-Related Macular Degeneration

Macular degeneration, which is the degeneration of an important part of the back of the eye, is another common cause of visual loss in later life. There are two main types: 'dry' in 85 per cent of cases and 'wet' in the other 15 per cent. It is associated with loss of vision in the centre of the eye, or seeing straight ahead, and particularly affects reading. However, you may also be able to adapt and compensate with the vision from the edge of your eyes.

The medical treatment options are limited for the dry form of macular degeneration, with the use of a particular combination of vitamins (which tend to slow progression, but some caution is advised if you are or have been a smoker) and sometimes laser treatment. For the wet form, an injection into the eyeball of medication can slow down the process and make a significant difference. It is important to stop smoking if you are a smoker.

As the illness progresses you will find yourself needing to adapt and compensate as discussed in the section below.

Glaucoma

Glaucoma is a process whereby the pressure inside the eyeball increases due to a failure of the drainage mechanism of the eye. This pressure presses on the main nerve relaying visual signals back to the brain, with a resulting loss of vision. If untreated, glaucoma can lead to irreversible blindness, and the earlier it is treated the better. As part of the optician's regular assessment they check out the pressure within the eye, and this is the most common way that glaucoma is detected.

Treatment is usually by way of eye drops or tablets, and less commonly by surgery. The treatments are aimed at preventing further loss of vision, but they cannot reverse the damage already caused.

Although usually a chronic disease (of insidious onset and gradual progression), in rare cases glaucoma may present as an acute illness, with pain in the eye, sometimes accompanied by any combination of redness, headache, nausea, vomiting, blurring of vision and seeing haloes around lights. As mentioned above, this is a condition which requires urgent assessment and treatment, and you should go to your family doctor or local Accident & Emergency department.

Diabetic Eye Disease

The leading cause of blindness is diabetic eye disease, usually through blocked or leaking blood vessels at the back of the eye. It is good practice for all those with diabetes to get a yearly assessment of the back of their eye, and this is often arranged through their diabetes service.

The better the control of your blood sugar levels the better your chances of not getting, or delaying, the progression of diabetic eye disease. The most common form of treatment for diabetic eye disease is laser treatment of the back of the eye, and this can be very effective.

Adapting to Poor Vision

Many of those with poor eye vision adapt automatically to their reduced acuity. However, the following tips may be helpful in terms of adapting to life with less sight. The National Council for the Blind in Ireland (NCBI) is also a very useful resource. The NCBI stocks an impressive range of aids and appliances, but, more importantly, also has community resource workers and peer support for those who have visual problems. The organisation is not just for the 'blind' but also for those with significant vision problems. Contact with the NCBI is strongly recommended for all those who would like to find ways of minimising the burden of poor sight.

Increase the Brightness of Your Lighting

When younger, we do not often appreciate how much increasing the brightness of a light makes reading easier. Increasing that 60 watt lamp to 75 watts or 100 watts can make a big difference for ease of viewing and reading, and the new long-life bulbs means that this can be done without a major increase in your electricity bill. Add extra lights around the house, and particularly in areas where you undertake activities, such as the kitchen.

Nightlights

With your reduced vision, you will probably find that your night vision is even worse. The use of nightlights, or else of lights which turn on with a motion sensor, will help to make you feel more secure if you have to get up during the night, and reduce your risk of falling.

Remove Hazards

If you have poor vision your risk of falling increases, so now is a good time to review trailing wires, loose rugs or small items of furniture which can be tripping hazards in your home and to tidy away or remove them.

Avoid Patterns

It can be more difficult for a visually impaired person to pick out objects on a table or a bedspread which has a pattern, so rethink tablecloths, counters and bedspreads, and where possible replace with plain-featured linens.

Visual Aids

From the simplest magnifying glass through accessible mobile phones to computerised magnification systems, a wide range of aids can be purchased to improve your vision when affected by eye disease. The NCBI has a large range of aids and appliances in stock, so it should be your first port of call.

Registering as Blind

This step is worth considering if your vision is impaired to a significant degree – a best corrected visual acuity of 6/60 or less in the better eye; your eye doctor or optometrist can advise you on this. You will then be entitled to a range of benefits including a Free Travel Companion Pass (which entitles you and any adult accompanying you to free travel on public transport), a disabled person's parking card and Eircom's free directory enquiry service, as well as a number of benefits from the Department of Social Protection. Your eye doctor/optometrist will fill out a form, which they or you send to the NCBI, who manage registration and will send you a further certificate which you can send in to the Department of Social Protection.

National Council for the Blind of Ireland
Whitworth Road
Drumcondra
Dublin 9
1850 334353
www.ncbi.ie

13

Hearing Difficulties

As we get older, increasing numbers of us will suffer from hearing problems, with older men affected more commonly than older women. The good news is that there is much that can be done to improve hearing problems. The bad news is that, unless you hold a Medical Card, the services are either reliable and expensive, or less expensive and of uncertain quality (I choose my words carefully here).

However, early assessment and use of modern hearing aids can make a huge difference to your quality of life and social interactions, and where possible you should seek help earlier rather than later. In addition, simple aids such as amplifying headphones for television and radio can make life easier for you (and those living with you), and appliances such as doorbells which link to a flashing light can be a great help.[2] In addition, many theatres, cinemas and concert halls have amplifying loops to

---

[2] These aids can be bought from DeafHear.ie, based at a number of centres in Ireland, and with headquarters at 35 North Frederick Street, Dublin 1.

feed in to hearing aids so that you can enjoy these leisure pursuits once more.

The challenge to this is that hearing loss occurs gradually in most cases, and through the process of adjustment that we all make we may not be conscious of it until quite late in its course. Your relatives might notice it by the way you begin to turn up the volume on the television or ask them to repeat questions – indeed if they repeat it in a louder voice, you may paradoxically ask them to stop shouting. This is because the problem is more one of distinctness rather than loudness; with deafness, high-pitched tones are harder to hear, and certain consonants ('s', 'f' and 't') are not clearly understood. Indeed, speaking more slowly and more distinctly, and not necessarily more loudly, is the key to better communication with those with hearing problems.

Assessment

In general, hearing loss in later life is due to age-related changes in the ear and/or lifetime exposure to loud noise, with a very small number of cases due to medications or illness. You need to be checked by either an audiologist or ear, nose and throat (ENT) surgeon; you can be referred to either of these by your family doctor or you can make contact directly with a HSE hearing centre if you have a Medical Card.

After ensuring that you do not have some relatively simple cause for your hearing difficulties (such as earwax occluding the ear channel), you will get a hearing test which clarifies the nature of the hearing loss, and which sets the scene for a possible hearing aid fitting.

Hearing Aids

The earlier you go, the better, as new hearing aids are not 'fire and forget' aids like walking sticks, but require some getting used to and regular review to ensure they are adjusted correctly for you. In general, there have been great advances in the technology of hearing aids, particularly with digital hearing aids, which can be programmed to lessen the impact of distracting noises. However, the fitting and subsequent sessions of training and adjustment are all important, as otherwise the wrong noises might be amplified, or the hearing aid appears not to work. It is this part of the process which is the most critical, and helps to avoid the syndrome of expensive hearing aids sitting in the drawer. Particular areas which need attention are a whistling sound when using the telephone and inappropriate adjustment between background noise and the sound you need to hear; proper choice and adjustment should help with both of these.

Some hearing aids are very small, and fitting the batteries can be challenging if you are less nimble than previously, so perhaps consider enlisting the help of nimble-fingered younger relatives.

For those with poor sight and dexterity, on-body aids – somewhat like an updated version of the old hearing aids – have the control and amplifier in a box that you clip to your clothes, with a lead to the earphone, and allow for easier adjustment and management.

Cost

The newer digital hearing aids are relatively expensive, and made more so by a relatively high mark-up in the Irish market. If you have a Medical Card, the assessment, hearing aid, and the fitting and follow-up are free of charge, although there may be a waiting list for the service.

If you do not have a Medical Card, the situation is more complicated and less transparent. Either you may be referred to a private audiologist, who will provide the same service (usually more expensive but standards are clearer), or you may consider one of the chains of proprietary hearing aid providers. However, these are not regulated as yet in Ireland in terms of who is providing the fitting and after service, and there have been complaints in the public domain about some but, in fairness, not all of these providers. Recently Specsavers, the optician chain, has started a hearing aid service as well. Be sure to do some research and shop around before using any of these services.

If you have been paying your PRSI contributions over a sufficient length of time in the appropriate categories (A, E, P or H), you (and/or a dependent spouse, civil partner or cohabitant) will be eligible for a grant of up to half the cost of a hearing aids up to a maximum of €500 for each hearing aid every four years.

For relatives

As with many issues discussed in this book, if your older relative does not want either assessment or a hearing aid there is no point in making life difficult for you both in a futile campaign of persuasion. Charm and adult discussion are the best ways forward, and as hearing aids require a reasonable amount of adaptation and commitment on the part of the person using them there is not much point in forcing the issue.

If the older person is not willing to be assessed, the following tips may make for better communication:

- *Don't shout* – as mentioned above, speaking more slowly and distinctly is more important than talking loudly, and the deeper you can pitch your voice the better.
- *Turn off the radio and TV* – any background noise makes communication more difficult with deaf people.
- *Move to a quieter room* – just as with the TV/radio, moving away from background noise will maximise your chances of effective communication.
- *Look directly at one another's faces* – We all rely on visual expression, possibly some subliminal lip-reading, when talking, but this becomes more important for deaf people and those who are hard of hearing.

It is not uncommon for family members to be concerned that their older relative will not wear their hearing aid. It may be that they are uncomfortable or not fitted correctly, and it is worth checking this out with the audiologist. However, many older people find the type of amplification provided not completely to their taste (a phenomenon which may be more marked with memory loss), and may prefer not to wear them. A compromise may be to encourage use for social occasions, and allow a rest from use between times.

14

Memory Problems and Dementia

You may have turned to this book because you yourself have problems with memory, or it may well be that you are a carer who finds that the person you are concerned about has problems anywhere on the spectrum from mild memory problems to marked Alzheimer's disease. In this chapter we will start at the beginning, try to develop a sense that the majority of people with memory problems continue to lead happy and fulfilled lives, but also realise that for the more severe end of the spectrum this book is a map rather than an encyclopaedia.

A big challenge is to break some of the stigma that such memory problems have, and the positive examples given by former US President Ronald Reagan and the author Terry Pratchett in disclosing their Alzheimer's disease is a good start in realising that having a memory problem does not in any way diminish our worth as human beings, and, in the earlier and middle stages, the ability to react to and interact with other people.

In our busy lives we all forget things, and we are much more aware of this as we get older. It is quite routine after the age of 40 to have a sense that we do not remember names as easily, and may forget items when shopping or going from room to room. What we don't realise is that we have gained in other ways, for example through wisdom or better strategic thinking. However, if this memory problem is more marked and sustained, it may be one of three major conditions, one of which does not affect your ability to carry out everyday tasks, and two which do:

- Memory problems which *do not* affect your ability to carry out everyday tasks
  - Mild cognitive impairment
- Memory problems which *do* affect your ability to carry out everyday tasks
  - Delirium
  - Dementia

Memory Problems which Do Not Affect Your Ability to Carry Out Everyday Tasks

Mild Cognitive Impairment

The first is a condition called mild cognitive impairment. This is relatively common, and in general means that you have a memory problem that is a nuisance, but does not cause you difficulties in managing your everyday affairs. Most commonly, short-term memory is affected. This is the memory we used for everyday activities, organising our lives and dealing with current events and activities. It is the most sensitive to change or damage by subtle disease processes. It is common in both this disorder and other memory problems that long-term memories, i.e. what happened when you were young adult or a child, remain quite vivid. It is short-tem memory, therefore, that the doctor will test in most instances, often with a simple memory test. In addition, they should ask a relative or friend who knows you well about how they perceive your memory, and whether or not you have difficulty with carrying out your usual functions – this is called a witness or collateral history.

You may need some further memory tests, which the doctor may conduct, or they may ask an occupational therapist to perform them. In the small number of units that have access to a psychologist, a psychological assessment may be helpful. In addition, a number of simple blood tests and possibly a brain scan may take place – these are to exclude other conditions, as there are no blood or X-ray tests to definitely confirm any of the memory disorders. If the doctor thinks that the mild cognitive impairment is caused by overt or covert stroke disease, it is sometimes called vascular cognitive impairment.

Once the diagnosis is established the doctor will generally keep an eye on you through regular check-ups. We still don't know for certain the natural history of this condition; many will maintain the state for a considerable length of time without deterioration, but some will progress to a mild Alzheimer's disease.

However I would emphasise that this condition should not become a barrier to living a full life, and there should be no difficulties with travel, taking a holiday or carrying out life's usual activities. Many people with this condition find it helpful to use memory aids, such as alarms or timers, diaries or Post-It notes.

Two cautions are worth mentioning. The first is that now might be a good time to consider advance planning, such as finally getting around to making your will, or considering whether or not you would be interested in an Enduring Power of Attorney (see Chapter 6). The second is that if you happen to be in a post or job that requires a full and sustained higher level of concentration and skill, such as being a director of a company, surgeon or architect, you should discuss the issue with your colleagues and a professional organisation if you have one. In most cases, your doctor will support ongoing activity as long as you have had a full assessment and you have disclosed your problem appropriately.

Memory Disorders which *Do* Affect Your Ability to Carry Out Everyday Tasks

Memory disorders which impact on your ability to manage your activities of daily living, to do your job, to manage your finances, or to deal with the complexity of everyday life are more serious and require careful assessment. The two most important syndromes causing memory problems which affect function are *delirium* (acute brain disturbance) and *dementia* (a longer-term brain disturbance).

Delirium

A relatively small number of people will present with a delirium. This is a dramatic change in your memory, and lay people would call this acute confusion. It is nearly always caused by an illness such as an infection, pneumonia, heart attack or stroke, or an adverse reaction to medication, and requires urgent assessment by a doctor. You, or your carer, may notice that you have trouble paying attention, are not orientated to place and time and are having trouble in carrying on a logical conversation. You may see this or notice it after a serious illness or a big operation – 10 per cent of people over the age of 60 have some memory problems after major surgery – and again this requires *urgent assessment* by a doctor. For most people this will settle with appropriate treatment, but for some this may represent some permanent loss of memory function. It is important that your family doctor is aware of any episode of delirium which passes, as what a delirium really means is that your brain and memory reserve is reduced, and those who have delirium are more likely to develop a memory problem in the years that follow.

In the Accident & Emergency department sometimes junior doctors may not recognise the importance of a delirium, and it is important that your relative is not discharged until a relatively senior doctor has assessed them, looked for reversible causes and provided appropriate support and guidance, including an assessment of whether it is safe for your relative to return home. You should discuss this by saying something like: 'I understand that delirium is an acute medical emergency and I would like to discuss the cause(s) and treatment with a senior doctor.'

Dementia

The more common serious form of memory loss is the syndrome of dementia. This is where your everyday functioning is affected by problems with memory and other aspects of brain function, such as orientation, language and reasoning. This syndrome is caused by a range of illnesses, of which the most common are Alzheimer's disease, vascular dementia, Lewy body dementia and frontotemporal dementia. In the past, blanket terms such as 'senile dementia' were used with this condition, but this is not a helpful phrase and many patients and carers will naturally be repelled by the word 'senile'. The phrase also suggests that there is nothing to be done, but in reality patients and carers can find a significant amount of help from information and support, as well as expert assessment and treatment. There is actually an enormous range of other conditions that can more rarely cause dementia, but your doctor will assess you to examine if this is the case. Depending on the stage of illness, your doctor may consider blood and X-ray tests and referral to a specialist.

One of the biggest challenges is trying to emphasise that the individual and family experience of dementia varies enormously from one person to another. One person can have a very mild form that progresses very slowly, with no behavioural disturbance, and another can have a rapid course with a major change in personality. In my experience this is not the only variability, because the other is that of how families interact – what will appear as a major burden to one family may not appear to be such a big burden to another.

Getting Help

In the past there was some debate as to whether early assessment of those with memory problems was worth doing, as there seemed to be little that could be done for them, and that perhaps all that was being achieved was to create worry. However, now we are aware that there are generic things that can help everybody with dementia (for example, information, advice, advance care planning, treating depression if it exists, removing medications that affect memory and planning for driving) as well as specific medications (even if not hugely effective) for Alzheimer's disease.

You and your family are therefore well advised to seek medical advice earlier rather than later for this condition. The assessment centres on defining a clinical pattern rather than on any specific blood tests or brain scans. Your doctor, or the specialist, will take a history from you, the patient, discuss the pattern of memory and function loss with a relative and undertake an examination which will focus on your memory, neurological system and cardiovascular system.

One of the big changes over the last twenty years has been an increasing awareness of involving the person with dementia in the choices implicit in this form of assessment. In general, our practice is to see the person with a suspected memory problem on their own first. Some families are concerned that the patient will not be able to tell us enough, but actually we also learn a lot from how the patient interacts with us, and in what they are unable to tell us.

A thornier issue is how to get the history from a relative or carer. I tend to say to the patient that I need an account of their memory and function from a relative or a carer, and that this can be with the patient present or not present. I explain that the benefits of doing this with the patient present are that they are aware of what it is that people are concerned about, and can clarify concerns over areas such as driving. On the other hand, an adult daughter or son may feel very inhibited about talking about their mother's or father's memory problems in front of their parent, particularly if, as is quite common, the parent has relatively little insight into their memory problem.

More often than not, I currently see the relative and patient together, but sometimes I will negotiate a separate interview with the carer. Practices will differ, but probably the most important point for you as a patient or a carer to remember is that this is rarely a single once-off visit – assessment is as much about developing a relationship as gathering elements of knowledge, and much is picked up from body language and what is not said.

Removing Things which Make It Worse

One of the first tasks of the doctor is to make sure that there is nothing making the dementia worse; particular culprits here are depression, medications and alcohol. Depression is important because nearly every negative symptom in life, whether it is pain, anxiety or memory problems, is worse with depression, and depression is treatable. As we will discuss Chapter 15, the biggest barrier to the treatment of depression is an unfortunate habit of the Irish people to see depression as some form of moral failure rather than a treatable illness. However, the fact is that depression is an illness that can be treated. Doing so can improve the symptoms of dementia and lead to a better quality of life.

Some medications can make your memory worse, in particular any sedatives or sleeping tablets. Your doctor may try to gradually withdraw these if this is the case and you are agreeable. Alternatively, they may try to switch you to new medications that would treat the problem being medicated, without the same side effects.

Treating a high alcohol intake or alcohol dependency is more problematic, as this treatment tends to need a reasonable level of insight that the alcohol intake is a problem, and this insight may be one of the first things to go with dementia. This is probably one of the most intractable problems in my own practice as a geriatrician, although sometimes, as the dementia progresses, the urge for alcohol may lessen. Liaising with community and specialist services is recommended, but their input will largely be supportive and compensatory.

There are a range of other less common causes which can exacerbate dementia and the doctor or specialist will check for these during your assessment.

Making a List

A good piece of advice before going to the doctor when there is a memory problem is for you, the patient, or your carer to make a list of the things that concern you. Seeing a specialist about something as personal as a memory problem can cause you sometimes to get a bit flustered or to forget some of the things you wanted to say. It is also quite helpful for the doctor to know the following things:

- When did the memory problem start?
- Was the start sudden or insidious in nature?
- Has the memory problem become worse over time?
- If it has become worse, was this in fits and starts or is it slowly progressive?
- Is there any change in personality?
- Is there a change in sleeping and waking patterns?
- Are there difficulties with managing money, house-keeping or self-care?
- Does the person with the memory problem drive?
- What supports are currently available?

As the Memory Condition Progresses

This book cannot cover all the conditions that might arise as a dementia progresses. For those affected, I would advise that they should be reasonably open with other people that they have a memory problem. This would mean that rather than being inhibited from attending a social event because you might forget the names of people, go to it and tell those you meet that you have a memory problem and remembering names is difficult for you. It may well be helpful at this stage to seek help in the form of home help or other personal visits so that you become familiar and accustomed with the idea of getting support at home.

It is useful to review how you take your medications if you have a memory problem, perhaps by using a dossette box (pill organiser), or asking whether your chemist will prepare calendar blister packs. You might consider whether or not you would sign up to a local day centre and in time your family or carers might consider two further care options. One is a day centre especially for people with Alzheimer's disease and similar disorders, called an Alzheimer's day centre, and the other is that of respite care. Respite care as it is currently configured usually means booking into a nursing home, private or public, for one to two weeks while your main carer takes a holiday.

Family members, remember the advice from preceding chapters about listening to your parents or relatives, particularly about what they want to do or don't want to do. It may well be that with the memory loss it now becomes quite threatening to go to a large social gathering. It is very common for families to say that their relative seems to have lost interest in life. Once it has been established that this is not due to depression, this usually means there is a disturbance of functioning of the frontal lobe of the brain. The frontal lobe is that part of the brain which acts as a conductor and director of your brain for everyday life. It plans and coordinates, and when this part of the brain is affected, as it commonly is with dementia, older people lose insight into the value of social events or occasions and hobbies. Do not worry overly that your older relative seems to spend a lot of time at home; home may well be the least threatening environment possible, and is very much enriched by familiar pictures, furniture and memories.

I would strongly recommend that you use the carer information pack from the Alzheimer Society of Ireland, books such as *The 36-Hour Day*, and other resources to get a fuller picture of the best way to support people with dementia, as well as looking after yourself.

One or two points are worth mentioning. I am often asked whether or not to correct somebody with Alzheimer's disease when they say something that is incorrect. Families often worry that by not correcting the error they are in some way contributing to the decline of the disease. This is not at all the case and indeed by constantly correcting a person with dementia you may only be giving yourself grief. If the error is not serious the best thing to do is to pass it over, and remember that it is probably quite isolating and disorientating to lose the security of a normally functioning memory, and the best response to repeated questioning and constant errors is a good hug, a kind word or a shared cup of tea.

The second concern is whether or not the person with dementia is getting enough stimulation. In general, I would say that as much (or more) distress may arise from dragging someone to what may be for them a threatening social encounter, or a day centre that doesn't agree with their way of being, than arises from them being in their own home environment. In fact, home is a much enriched environment, with constant feedback from pictures, mementoes and furniture which evokes memories, as well as radio, TV, occasional callers and a view of the neighbourhood. In general, older people tend to be good at working out what suits them and what doesn't, and gentle encouragement is the best working method, with graceful acquiescence when they don't wish to carry out an activity.

So what can I as a relative or carer do that is positive?

- *Be supportive* – try to help the older person see the humour in situations and assure them that being forgetful is normal and that your love and support have not changed. In the case of Alzheimer's disease or other forms of dementia, it can be difficult to work with the older person, so discuss coping strategies with your public health nurse and/or doctor, or in a carer support group such as those run by the Alzheimer Society of Ireland.
- *Be patient* – memory loss is frustrating for everyone. If the older person is trying to explain something to you and forgets a word, help them if you know the word. If the person loses something, look for it rather than asking them to remember where they left it. If there is a little memory slip-up, show the humour in it. Keep in mind that the problem isn't that older people won't remember to do things; they can't remember.
- *Avoid arguments* – when people with memory loss make mistakes such as calling someone the wrong name, or confusing places and dates, unless it is absolutely necessary do not argue or repeatedly correct them. They are not able to learn to get it right, and arguing with or correcting them only creates more anxiety and distress.
- *Avoid long activities, too much commotion and unfamiliar settings* – be sensitive that changes in surroundings are confusing to the person with memory loss, and they can tire easily. This can lead to irritability and behaviour problems when they are over-stressed. Short outings to familiar settings are best; avoid long trips, large groups and loud, chaotic settings.
- *Use reminding strategies* – when memory loss is obvious, try these reminding techniques:

- ○ Encourage them to a memo book in their shirt pocket or handbag to write down significant events or people's names.
- ○ Use neck chains for glasses or keys.
- ○ Keep the person active with 'over-learned' tasks. There are many activities that an individual might have over-learned through repetition during their lifetime. These might include playing an instrument, doing puzzles, and crocheting or other handicrafts that their hands can almost 'do by themselves'. These activities, especially those involving music, can be especially therapeutic. A very helpful book is *Failure-Free Activities for the Alzheimer's Patient* by Carmel Sheridan.
- ○ Encourage regular routines. Important activities, such as eating, exercising or washing, should be tied to a particular time of day and place to be remembered more easily.
- Make your instructions simple and break tasks down into simple steps.

Adult Children

If one of your parents suffers from dementia, try not to let their needs obscure the emotional and physical needs of the other parent. Although in popular imagination issues like wandering and behavioural disturbance may appear to be the most stressful elements of the carer experience, in fact the change in the nature of the relationship is a very stressful experience. Ensure that you provide support for the unaffected parent, such as by visiting the affected parent to allow the care-giving parent to go shopping or visit friends.

Deterioration

Most dementias will progress, so keep in touch with your family doctor (and eventually specialist services) as this occurs. Although dementia can fluctuate from day to day, one important point is that any sudden and significant deterioration should be considered a delirium until proven otherwise, and needs checking up with your doctor.

What Is My Future?

Patients and family may or may not ask this question directly, but it is one they usually wish to ask. The answer, without appearing to sit on the fence, is that it varies hugely from any one individual to another, and is hugely influenced by family and other supports. Also, as this is an illness that tends to occur in later life, a completely different illness might come from left-field and become the dominant issue. So, there are many paths, and just as we know that those with cancer cannot let go of the question but try not to obsess and let it dominate their life, so too those with dementia should try not to let this topic obsess them.

Behavioural and Psychological Symptoms of Dementia

This a term for the complications of a dementia which can make life difficult for family and carers, and includes wandering, agitation, delusions and hallucinations. The most important advice in this area is not to deal with this alone, and to get expert assessment, either from your family doctor, a specialist such as a psychiatrist of old age and his/her team, or a geriatrician and his/her team. All human behaviour has a reason, even in dementia, but it can be difficult to tease this out sometimes. It may be that the older person wants to go 'home', no longer recognising their own home, or wishes to go for a walk when they cannot be adequately watched. They may also suffer from other illnesses which make them irritable, such as depression, pain or constipation. So a full assessment and advice is your best way forward, as well as arming yourself with *The 36-Hour Day*.

In the Nursing Home

Most people with dementia will continue to live in their own homes for the majority of the course of their illness. However, a significant minority will be admitted to nursing homes, and this is covered in Chapter 20. In my experience, it will be your family or close friends who will negotiate this on your behalf, but should you wish to have some say in this, do think in the early stages whether or not there are specific nursing homes in your area that you might be either agreeable to, or unhappy about.

15

Loneliness, Bereavement and Depression

Loneliness

Loneliness affects a minority of people throughout their life, and is at its highest in adolescence and young adulthood. It is important to understand this in order to appreciate that although older age is often caricatured as a time of great loneliness, there may be elements of loneliness that relate to your personality and your background as much as your age. It is also separate from social isolation – you can be lonely in the midst of company, or with frequent visitors. Loneliness is generally defined as an unpleasant sense that your social relationships are not living up to your expectations. Even so, it is a cause of suffering in later life, and may be aggravated by the deaths of a spouse, friends and relatives, or the constrictions in opportunity that you may suffer through age-related disease and disability or reduced income in retirement. While there are no quick-fix answers for loneliness, unless you are suffering from depression (see below), the answer lies very much with you and your own resources, and your ability to master your own life. Try to focus on what you have, how you might help others and how you can get involved, in any way, in your parish, community or family; it will not necessarily remove all the pain, but may alleviate your condition. Think hard about whether expressing your loneliness repeatedly to family and friends helps; while no one expects emotion to be completely bottled up, repeated exposure to this type of suffering may in time deter social contact. Talking to the Senior Help Line (1850 440 444), or indeed the Samaritans (1850 609 090), might be helpful. In the evolution of time, could you even consider yourself helping out with these activities?

For carers, finding the best ways to respond to loneliness in an older parent or relative can be one of the most challenging aspects of being an adult child for those in this situation. From phone calls which start with 'Ah sure, I'm just looking at the four walls all day' (when several visitors may have passed through) to prolonged and painful leave-takings, these are the ways in which love can be truly tested – and, as previously discussed, those who provide the most attention are the most likely to be presented with these loneliness difficulties. Again, there are no easy routes out, but a couple of approaches might be helpful:

- See beyond the verbal – we all crave belonging and affection, and actions and humour speak louder than words.
- Try to find the fun and positive in encounters – get out of the house, bring grandchildren with you to visit, focus on tasks, such as buying new clothes, visiting the hairdresser or barber, and gardening.
- Develop a little thicker skin and a little deafer ear.

- Shared mealtimes can alleviate loneliness perhaps more effectively than visiting at other times.
- See can you involve your older relative (without abusing them) in tasks which are useful (and make them feel wanted and useful) – from ironing to episodic babysitting.
- Learn that phoning several times a day may actually develop a pattern of increased dependency.
- Watch out for depression or prolonged bereavement (see below).
- Try to share social inputs with your siblings and the wider family.
- Keep remembering that your older relative is an adult, may have had these tendencies for some considerable time, and rather than them changing, it is you who needs to change in most instances.
- Ensure that you don't get so absorbed that you miss out on your own social circle and activities; you too are a future older person.

Bereavement

As the only certainties in life are death and taxes, as we age we and our loved ones come nearer to death, and one of the defining characteristics of this age is the attrition among your friends and loved ones of your age. The death of a spouse or partner is particularly difficult, and it is not easy to give specific advice within the confines of a book. However, perhaps two common misconceptions can hinder coming to terms with these huge events.

The first is that it that there is some form of progression through stages of grief which leave one at some form of accommodation with pain and loss. While Elisabeth Kübler-Ross's stages of reaction in the face of death – denial, anger, bargaining, depression and acceptance – provide some form of framework to think through how we deal with these situations, they are too simplistic to fit the bill for describing your experience. The word 'acceptance' also over-simplifies the ongoing hole in your life and those resurgences of emotions at unexpected moments. So, no one should expect life to return to the same equilibrium, but people do find new levels of accommodation, which will always have that tender spot.

Equally, there is a popular concept that it is good to 'get it all out' and talk about it, and your adult children or relatives may worry that you are 'not talking enough about it all'. In fact, grieving is still a largely private process, and we are a private people – and not just us. More than twenty years ago, the US National Widows' Study showed that those who expressed their emotions the least counter-intuitively seemed actually to do better in the long run.

So, the important message is to feel secure enough to carve your own way through the process of grieving, adaptation and loss that accompany the loss of a spouse, partner or friends. If, however, after six to twelve months you are persistently unable to feel any pleasure in life, consider strongly whether or not you might need some help (your family doctor or public health nurse can guide you towards bereavement counselling), or whether or not you might at this stage be suffering from a depression that requires medical attention (see below).

Depression

Although depression is arguably no more common in later life than at younger ages, there are several reasons why it is important to have some focus on it in this book. It tends to occur at the same time as major illnesses and other significant life changes, which are more likely to occur in later life, and tends to worsen the suffering of these events. As well as this, older people, their carers and family doctors often have a fatalistic approach to depression, rather than seeing it as a treatable illness which can be cured or managed. It can also impact in a negative way on your relationship with your family, and can be an important element of carer stress, which can be alleviated with proper treatment.

Depression may be caused by many of the changes of old age. These include the physical changes that affect your eyesight, hearing or ability to move your body as you once did, or the changes in your health or new medical conditions that require you to take a number of different medicines. Other factors may be lifestyle changes, such as retirement or assuming the role of a carer. Finally, most older people experience the loss of friends or family members who die. Indeed, several of these changes may occur at the same time.

Some mood changes are clearly understandable as a reaction to any or a combination of these, and it is unrealistic, and unhelpful, to expect older people to be cheerful all the time. We all have periods of anxiety, feeling down or having the blues; what makes depression different is, firstly, the fact that it does not improve after several weeks or months, so is *prolonged*, and, secondly, it is clearly causing *suffering* and a reduced quality of life. So, when a person is sad, discouraged, pessimistic or despairing for several weeks or months, and when these feelings interfere with being able to manage day-to-day affairs, it is likely that they are suffering from depression. Depression can last a long time if the person does not do something to stop it.

Other markers of depression, which may not be so notable for older people, include loss of appetite, problems with sleeping, low energy, poor attention and concentration, and less enjoyment of favourite activities. There may also be vague physical complaints such as headaches, constipation or aches and pains in several parts of the body with no clear cause. *Anxiety* is a common element of depression, and may be quite disabling; it is important that there is a medical review to screen for depression in all patients with marked anxiety. New or worsening *drinking* may also be a sign, especially if the change has occurred since the person has experienced a significant life event.

If untreated, an older person with depression will have problems coping with the changes that are happening in their life. This then can become a vicious cycle, with the older person less able to put energy into solving problems. The depression magnifies the perception of pain and discomfort, and the person feels worse. In severe cases, older people may think suicidal thoughts, and these are certainly a cause of concern. The challenge is to intervene at the appropriate moment, not medicalising every reasonable reactive sadness on the one hand, but not allowing a depression to continue on a downwards cycle either.

One of the most important barriers among Irish people, which needs to be vigorously countered, is the perception that depression is somehow a sign of weakness or a failing. I am constantly astonished at how Irish people (not just older people) seem to be ready to take tranquilisers such as diazepam (Valium) or alprazolam (Xanax) (which are only licensed for use for short periods, and commonly cause dependency) but hesitate before taking antidepressants. Thanks to the great work of charities such as AWARE this is improving, but we need to keep putting across the message that prolonged depression is an illness which causes much unnecessary suffering, and that the treatment needs to be fully followed.

Getting Help

The first step is accepting that you need help, and listening carefully to your family if they express concern that you might have depression – it is not an easy thing to bring up, so it usually means that you should be checked out for it. Your GP is the first port of call. A full check-up is needed, as depression may accompany any of a large variety of other illnesses or can be a side effect of some medicines. Usually, a twin-track approach is needed, with a review of the other illnesses and medications as well as treatment of the depression. For example, someone with severe pain after suffering shingles who gets depression will benefit from treatment for both, as each will interact with the other.

The two main forms of treatment are psychotherapy and antidepressants, and in practice you will get some of both. Psychotherapy is often inflated in the popular mind to psychoanalysis on Sigmund Freud's couch. In fact, what it means is the therapeutic use of the relationship between the doctor, nurse or psychologist and you, the patient. It may occur in what seems to be a relatively informal way in your encounters in the GP surgery or psychiatry clinic, in session with a psychologist, or during a visit to your home by the community psychiatric nurse. Or it may be more formalised as counselling, cognitive behavioural therapy, brief therapy or, rarely, a full psychoanalysis.

Antidepressants are effective medications, but have different ways of working to other medications. The biggest difference is that it can take several weeks or even months before the medicine is fully effective, so you need to be encouraged strongly to keep taking it until the medication starts to work. The second is that the side effects at the beginning of treatment may be poorly tolerated, so talk to your doctor if you wish to stop taking the medication because of them. The good news is that there are a few types of antidepressants, and your doctor can consider a different tablet which may not have the same troubling side effects for you. Another point is that you will need to take them for a fairly prolonged period of time, usually at least six months, and possibly longer, so you must not stop taking them because you feel better; if stopped too early, you can suffer a relapse. Discuss with your doctor when is the best time to stop taking the tablets.

Specialist Referral

If the depression does not seem to be lifting, your GP may refer you (or you should consider asking for a referral) to a specialist in psychiatry of older people (old age psychiatry), or a general psychiatrist if there is not an old age psychiatry service in your area. If you have private health insurance you may also be referred to one of the private psychiatric hospitals, some of which now have old age psychiatrists attached to them. In my experience these are hugely valuable services, and it is most important not to let any fears or prejudice stand in your way. Depression is a truly wretched experience, and this is no time for worrying what others might think.

Old age psychiatry services have a range of supports, and may assess you in your own home or in a hospital clinic, but will often follow up with a home visit. As well as the psychiatrist's own assessment, a key member of the team is the community psychiatric nurse, who plays an important role in supporting you and monitoring your treatment. You might also be offered a period of treatment in a day hospital. This is where you will attend once a week at a day hospital where the full team, including nurses, occupational therapists, psychologists and social workers, can provide fuller support for you.

Most people will respond to these treatments, but in *very* rare cases of severe resistance to treatment electroconvulsive treatment (ECT) may be indicated. This will only occur in conjunction with a decision to bring you into hospital. There are a lot of false myths about this very effective treatment, and, if it is suggested, do debate its benefit with your psychiatrist.

For carers, your help is invaluable to a person who is feeling depressed, but it can also be challenging for you – you may find yourself dealing with more phone calls, more complaints and less get-up-and-go. If the depression seems to have the features of both persistence and suffering do try to discuss this with the older person, and encourage them to seek help. If they are on antidepressant medication your help can be invaluable in ensuring that the medicine is taken as directed. It might take several weeks or even months before the medicine is fully effective and it may be continued for a significant time after the depression subsides.

With the older person's tacit or overt consent, the doctor who is prescribing the medicine will need feedback on how the older person is responding and you might need to help here as well. It is also extremely important that the doctor who prescribes the antidepressant medication is fully aware of all the medicines the person you care for is currently taking, regardless of the reasons why they were originally prescribed.

Be sure to give the doctor a list of all prescription medicines, over-the-counter medicines bought at the pharmacy, and any herbal or other alternative therapies, as well as the dosage levels and the times they should be taken. Preventing negative drug interactions is very important.

An area of particular concern is where the older person presents with ideas of suicide or self-harm. This suggests a severe depression, and the older person needs urgent attention as suicide in later life is a genuine area of concern. Try to engage with your older relative's family doctor, who may not have been aware of these ideas, ideally with the consent of your older relative. This will usually be the trigger for intensifying treatment, either by the GP or by referral to a specialist.

Living with or spending large amounts of time with a person who is depressed can be stressful and can even lead to you becoming depressed yourself. It is important to pay attention to your own emotional health so that you can do your best as a caregiver.

16

Stroke, Heart Failure and Atrial Fibrillation

Stroke is one of the more common illnesses of later life, and this relatively brief chapter can only be an overview of what is a complex disease. There are two main forms of the illness: acute stroke (including transient ischaemic attack, a stroke whose symptoms last less than 24 hours) and chronic stroke disease. After decades of neglect, services for stroke are slowly being developed, and you should know how to access and deal with these services.

Acute Stroke

Acute stroke happens when the blood supply to the brain is interrupted, either by a clot blocking an artery or, less commonly, a bleed from a leaking blood vessel. Among the common symptoms are sudden onset of weakness of the face and limbs, slurring of speech and loss of speech. If any of these occur it is an acute medical emergency – don't dally! You should call an ambulance immediately or get someone to bring you to the Accident & Emergency

Department of a hospital, as the first priority is to see whether you might be eligible for clot-busting treatment (thrombolysis). For this to be effective you need to be assessed and have some blood tests and a brain scan within three hours of the onset of the stroke (the effect is lessened considerably if there is a longer delay). Your local hospital may have an out-of-hours service, possibly by linking to a consultant in another hospital.

For a range of reasons, only about one in six people is eligible for this therapy, and if you are not one of these you will then ideally be admitted to a stroke unit. These are being developed in most Irish hospitals, and you and your family member should ask about being admitted to one if it exists, as being treated in a dedicated stroke unit reduces your chance of death and disability by 25 per cent. It is a ward, or part of a ward, where you will be looked after by a stroke specialist (usually a geriatrician or neurologist), and an associated team of nurses and therapists. A stroke can cause a range of problems in addition to weakness of the limbs and face, and speech and language problems:

- Memory problems
- Disorders of how you perceive space and your body
- Swallowing disorders
- Visual problems
- Continence problems

You will be assessed for all of these, and relevant therapists – physiotherapists, occupational therapists, speech and language therapists (for both language and swallow problems), clinical nutritionists and social workers – will be called in to help, depending on what is found. You should get, or ask for, the Irish Heart Foundation booklet on stroke; this will also be helpful for your family, particularly if you have language or memory problems. In general, most stroke services have a weekly case conference – find out when this is and ask the team what the likely goals for therapy are after the meeting.

Do not get disheartened if it seems to be a severe stroke; it can take up to six weeks to know what the likely shape of recovery will be, and it may take longer than this to be sure what the likely outcome will be. You should be discharged once you are at the point where further recovery can be managed as well as an outpatient, or once your recovery has 'plateaued', i.e. you are unlikely to make *significant* further progress with in-patient rehabilitation. This does not mean that you will not make further improvement, but rather that it will tend to be modest from that point on. In some areas ongoing rehabilitation may be continued in a different rehabilitation hospital. In general, these can allow for a more focused rehabilitation. Although some patients may feel anxious about leaving the general hospital, it is usually a good idea, as long as the other hospital has adequate therapy staff and nurses.

If discharge is being considered and you are left with a significant degree of disability, a *care planning meeting* (sometimes also called a family meeting) should be held with you (and usually your family) to set out a plan for discharge, and a home visit, usually from an occupational therapist, is recommended to see whether any adaptations need to be made to your home. If you (or your family) feel you are not getting enough therapy, or are being discharged too early, discuss this with your therapists and consultant, and if you are still unhappy consider asking for a second opinion.

The care planning meeting will usually try to clarify your care needs and what schedule of input will be needed from either care attendants or family members. It will also examine if this schedule of care is achievable depending on a home care package (if you are eligible for one), whatever private assistance you may be able to arrange, and whatever support your family and friends are willing and able to provide. Usually some form of consensus arises from these meetings; if an appropriate network cannot be arranged, entry to a nursing home may be required.

Wherever you go, a plan for ongoing rehabilitation and support should be clearly outlined, either through a day hospital or community services. If you have ongoing swallowing difficulties, or have a feeding tube, you will need follow-up with speech and language therapy and clinical nutrition, and training in food preparation or managing tube feeds might be necessary. Continuing, if modest, improvement can follow discharge, and it is best to keep an open mind but not to have major expectations.

In terms of preventing future strokes, your doctor will carry out a range of tests and recommend a number of measures. These include lifestyle measures – stopping smoking, improving your diet (especially ensuring you have five portions of fruit and vegetables a day) and exercising. In addition, if you had a stroke caused by a clot your doctors will generally put you on a medication like aspirin to thin the blood and reduce the chances of another clot forming, and often cholesterol medication.

For families this is a difficult time. The key principles are: a) get informed (for example, read the Irish Heart Foundation booklet on stroke), b) advocate for stroke unit care if your older relative has memory or language problems that stop them asking for this themselves, and c) do not rush to early judgement as to what the outcome of the stroke will be – recovery can vary widely from one patient to the next, and nobody with a significant stroke can be said to have plateaued until at least six weeks have passed. Upon discharge there are often contrasting desires and motivations between the patient, their family and the medical team in their assessment that the patient has plateaued or of the services and further treatment required, but with goodwill and trust these can be bridged. With your family member, try to develop a shared position on what you see as the best approach, and do not be surprised if your relative seems willing to be discharged sooner than you might think appropriate. There comes a point where an ongoing stay in hospital might provide benefit from therapy but the older person finds the environment psychologically challenging as they are getting better. With a common position, you can more efficiently help your relatives in determining the support required after leaving hospital in terms of ongoing therapy and support.

Transient Ischaemic Attack

A transient ischaemic attack (TIA), sometimes called a mini-stroke, is where you get the signs of a stroke, but they are resolved within 24 hours. This is also an emergency – you need to get to the Accident & Emergency Department because a) you don't know that it is not a stroke until the doctors check you over, and b) there is a high risk of an acute stroke in the first week after a TIA, which can be reduced if you get early assessment and treatment. Apart from the major risk factors of smoking and high blood pressure, the doctors will focus on whether you have an irregular heart rhythm (atrial fibrillation) or narrowing of the arteries in your neck, and arrange treatment for these if present – blood thinning with warfarin (or one of the newer medications) if it is atrial fibrillation (see page 255), and consideration for surgery if one of the neck arteries is narrowed.

Chronic Stroke Disease

Chronic, or silent, stroke disease is where you may suffer from a range of conditions, including memory problems, dementia and unsteadiness when walking, that are linked to subtle changes in the arteries of your brain, and you may or may not have had an acute stroke at some stage.

In reading this, you may be ahead of your doctors. This section is in this book because some of my patients get alarmed when we tell them that they have 'mini-stroke disease' or 'subtle hardening of the arteries'. You are most likely to get this diagnosis from a specialist and, in general, we do not yet know if we should be as aggressive with medications for stroke prevention for chronic stroke disease as we would be for acute stroke, but the other stroke prevention issues are really important: stopping smoking, exercise, moderating your alcohol intake and ensuring you get five portions of fruit and vegetables daily. The memory problems of chronic stroke disease may be called vascular cognitive impairment (if it doesn't interfere with your everyday function) or vascular dementia (see Chapter 14); the problems with steadiness in walking are caused by vascular gait dyspraxia (see Chapter 11). It is hoped that in the future, as our populations take more care with smoking, exercise, diet and blood pressure, we will see less of these conditions.

From your point of view, this diagnosis at least provides a cause for your gait or memory problems, and the preventive strategies outlined above should retard the progression of the condition.

Heart Failure

Heart failure is one of the major disease conditions of later life. Although the name sounds forbidding, most older people will maintain a good quality of life with it, particularly if treated with due care. Older people can continue to work, travel and have sexual relationships with heart failure, with due consideration for management of the illness. It is not a heart attack, which is when an acute blockage of an artery damages the heart muscle quite suddenly, usually with pain, which is a medical emergency.

Heart failure arises when the muscles of the heart no longer pump as efficiently as they used to, or can no longer relax as well as formerly when the heart is filling with blood from the veins, and the overall effect is to make you breathless on exertion. In addition, you may find your ankles swelling (although other conditions can make your ankles swell), and also that you get breathless lying flat in bed and need more pillows. Many with the condition complain of fatigue, as well as loss of appetite and low blood pressure leading to dizziness.

In general, this condition is related to hardening of the arteries, and is more common in those who have heart disease, high blood pressure, diabetes, have had heart attacks or have smoked, but the condition may occur in those who have not had any of these conditions. In a very small number of cases, it may be due to an over-tight or leaking heart valve.

Diagnosis

The earlier the condition is detected, the better. As well as taking a history from you and carrying out a physical examination, your doctor may do a number of tests, including an electrocardiogram (ECG, a measure of the wiring of your heart), a chest X-ray and an echocardiogram (also called echo, an ultrasound picture of your heart and valves). Your family doctor may mange the heart failure, or may decide to work with a specialist, depending on your response to medications, or the degree to which you are suffering from other illnesses. The specialist may also order an angiogram, a specialised X-ray where dye is injected into the heart and its vessels so that blockages can be seen. A small number of hospitals run heart failure services, sometimes known as heart efficiency services.

Management

Ideally, you will start a number of measures to manage your heart failure, not just medications, although they are important. These will include following a healthy diet (including reducing your salt intake), taking as much exercise as possible, avoiding smoking and reducing or cutting out alcohol, which has a negative effect on heart muscle. Control of other illnesses, such as diabetes and high blood pressure, is also important. Ideally, you should avoid medications which cause you to retain fluid, particularly anti-inflammatory medications, known as NSAIDs.

Your doctor may also recommend reducing your fluid intake and checking your weight to check daily for fluid retention. This should be done at the same time each morning, after emptying your bladder, and a record kept in a diary. If you gain more than 2 kg in two days, you should contact your doctor. It is also particularly important that you get the flu and pneumococcal vaccines every year.

Medications for heart failure include diuretics (water tablets) to remove fluid from the body, ACE inhibitors and ARB inhibitors to open blood vessels and reduce strain on the heart, beta blockers to help the heart pump more slowly and effectively, and sometimes digoxin if you have a particular form of heart rhythm disturbance called atrial fibrillation.

You will in most cases be on low-dose aspirin, or stronger blood-thinning agents (such as warfarin or newer agents, see below) if you have atrial fibrillation.

This can mean quite a lot of medications, especially if you have other illnesses which require medication. Do keep a list, and bring it with you each time you visit a doctor or the hospital.

Side Effects of Medications

The most common side effect of medications for heart failure is postural (also known as orthostatic) hypotension, when your blood pressure drops when changing posture, say from sitting to standing, leaving you unsteady or light-headed (see Chapter 11). Discuss this with your doctor if it occurs, as it is not only uncomfortable but is also a risk factor for falls. They can look at altering your medications so as to get the best balance between controlling your heart failure and minimising the postural hypotension. With ACE inhibitors you may get a cough – again, discuss this with the doctor who can change the medications around.

Change in Symptoms

The symptoms of heart failure can wax and wane, but if they get worse you should contact your doctor. The symptoms you might notice are an increase in breathlessness when lying down with your usual number of pillows, increased breathlessness on exertion (or even at rest), increased swelling of your ankles and chest pain.

New Technologies

A small number of those affected by heart failure may benefit from technologies to assist their heart rhythms, either a *pacemaker* (to aid the heart's rhythm) or an *implantable cardiac defibrillator* (ICD, to prevent dangerous abnormal heart rhythms that can lead to cardiac arrest). For a very small number of people, a tight heart valve may need to be repaired, and this can now be performed by using a device pushed through an artery, without cutting the chest open, although this technology is relatively new.

Communication, Communication, Communication

As with all chronic diseases, the key to success is learning as much as possible about the illness and, together with your doctor(s), taking as much control as possible of your own condition. Write down your list of questions ahead of seeing the doctor, always bring your list of medications with you, and ask what you should do if your symptoms get worse at night or during the weekend.

Atrial Fibrillation

With both stroke and heart failure, your doctor may detect an irregular heart beat, known as atrial fibrillation, which if untreated is a significant risk factor for stroke. You may or may not be aware of its presence – some experience palpitations, but most do not. Once detected, your doctor will almost certainly perform an ECG to confirm that it is there; it may also be detected in the investigations after stroke, when the doctors will routinely monitor your heart rhythm for at least 72 hours. Sometimes your heart will alternate between normal rhythm and atrial fibrillation, a condition known as paroxysmal atrial fibrillation.

After the age of 65, if detected, it is likely that you will have atrial fibrillation or paroxysmal atrial fibrillation for the rest of your life, and, for most people, it is strongly recommended that you should have a form of blood thinning medication which is stronger than aspirin to protect you from stroke. This can be warfarin or one of the newer medications; at the time of writing these include dabagatrin (Pradaxa) and rivaroxaban (Xarelto). The most compelling reasons why you should not be on these medications are a) you have an existing condition likely to make you bleed, such as a stomach ulcer, b) you fall frequently and therefore could suffer from bruises or bleeding, c) you have significant memory problems and no reliable way of ensuring that you do not under- or over-dose, or d) chronic alcohol dependency. If you do not have these exceptions, have atrial fibrillation and are not on warfarin or one of the new medications, you should ask your doctor why not.

Warfarin is a tried and tested medication, originally arising from a rat poison, and when carefully controlled by your GP or a warfarin clinic is a safe medication with a long track record. You need to be careful about taking alcohol and other medications (your doctor/the clinic will advise you) and the drawback for some is that it needs constant monitoring, usually between every two and six weeks, for the rest of your life.

The newer medications do not have the same need for monitoring, so why does everyone not take them? In the first instance, the track record in terms of safety is not as long, and, secondly, the ability to reverse the blood-thinning effect with an antidote should you get severe bleeding or a 'bleed' stroke is not possible for one of them, and limited for the other. The lack of monitoring at a clinic may also mean that your compliance may not be as rigorous as with warfarin. In addition, older people with kidney disease may be more susceptible to bleeding. The new medications are also significantly more expensive than warfarin, and the health service currently requires a special form from your doctor justifying the reason to use them if you want them reimbursed under either the drug refund scheme or the Medical Card scheme.

In the final analysis, the decision of whether to go for warfarin or one of the new agents is a quite personalised choice, and one that you need to discuss with your doctor.

17

Sleep Problems

It is not uncommon for all of us, as we age, to feel that our sleep is not as good as it was in earlier years. In general, however, although we may have a sense that we do not sleep as continuously or as well, we will still get enough sleep to deal with our body's need for rest.

If you are concerned about your sleep, the first thing to do is to look at a number of fairly simple sleep hygiene principles, and if these don't work out then talk to your doctor to see if an illness could be causing you to sleep poorly.

Sleep Hygiene

Sleep hygiene is simply a set of principles that help to ensure you sleep as well as possible. These include:

Routines

- Fix a bedtime – your body is much more likely to develop a sleep pattern if you can adopt a regular bedtime, and whether working or retired this remains the case.

- Exercise as much as possible, ideally in the afternoon, but not just before you go to bed.
- Avoid daytime naps, which eat into rest time; if you must take one, the afternoon is probably the best time, and limit it to 30–45 minutes.
- Avoid drinks (non-alcoholic and alcoholic) near bedtime, and in particular those with caffeine; this includes tea as well.
- Keep your alcohol intake as low as possible.
- Avoid heavy, spicy foods in the evenings.
- Avoid watching television in the bedroom; listening to the radio is less stimulating.

Environment

- Reserve the bed for sleep and intimacy. Using the bedroom as an office, workroom or study can take away from its sense as a haven of rest.
- Keep the temperature comfortable – neither too hot nor too cold.
- Get as comfortable a bed and bedclothes as possible – as in the old Odearest ad put your money in a good mattress.
- Eliminate as much light and noise as possible; consider ear plugs and blackout curtains.

If you are still concerned about your sleep patterns, discuss it with your doctor. A number of medical conditions can interfere with sleep. In particular, watch out for:

- Depression and/or anxiety: difficulty getting to sleep or waking up very early can be a sign of depression or anxiety. Treatment that reduces your depression can also help your sleep patterns.
- Sleep apnoea: this is a condition where your sleep pattern is disturbed, so that you have restless sleep, loud snoring and periods where your breathing stops, followed by a sudden loud snore. In addition, during the daytime you will fall asleep 'at the drop of a hat'. If sleep apnoea is suspected your doctor will send you to a respiratory specialist who will do what are called sleep studies. If this confirms sleep apnoea this can be treated with good effect.
- Restless legs syndrome: this is exactly what it says on the tin. It is an eminently treatable (and often neglected) syndrome, which may be associated with either a shortage of iron or of a chemical in the brain known as dopamine. Assessment and treatment of these deficiencies can make a big difference to both the uncomfortable feeling and your sleep.
- Urinary urgency and frequency may be the result of a treatable condition and getting up frequently can disturb your sleep. Again, this is very much worth discussing with your doctor.
- Night cramps are common, and may keep you awake, or awaken you. They may respond to a medication called quinine.

Dementia can cause disruption of the sleep–wake cycle. This is very challenging for others in the house, but not a danger to the older person. Talk to your PHN/GP/specialist about the best way to deal with this. Adapting to their new sleep–wake cycle is less problematic for the older person with dementia, but may not work if their live-in carer or spouse/partner has a day job. In such circumstances there may be trade-offs between the need to keep the carer caring (and working) and cautious use of night sedation, and this should be openly discussed with all parties.

Sleeping Tablets

Sleeping tablets generally only give you the sense of having had a good sleep but don't actually improve its real quality, and may only store up problems. They have a very limited role in certain situations, for example after a bereavement, but are habit-forming and only licensed for four to six weeks' usage. In general, geriatricians try to avoid them, but once people become dependent it is risky to stop them without a planned withdrawal. Most older Irish people surveyed who have been on sleeping tablets for a long time do not want to stop them. It is important to let doctors in the hospital know if you or a family member is on sleeping tablets if going into hospital, as if they are not maintained there is a risk of a form of 'cold turkey'. The longer-acting sleeping tablets are associated with an increased risk of falls, so think twice before asking for sleeping tablets from your family doctor.

18

Bladder and Bowel Incontinence and Constipation

Bladder Incontinence

Bladder or urinary incontinence, or leaking of urine, is a problem for at least 30 per cent of people over the age of 60. It is more common in women than in men and can range from occasional dribbling to total loss of bladder control. Many people who have incontinence do not tell their doctor or public health nurse because they are embarrassed or feel it is not a major problem.

The most important message from this chapter is to emphasise that incontinence can be better managed for all, considerably improved for most and cured for a smaller number. To get to this point, you need to be able to a) get over any embarrassment or reluctance to discuss this, and b) get the highest level of assessment and treatment needed.

Whether the incontinence is mild or severe, everyone with incontinence should be seen by a healthcare professional. A medical condition might be causing the incontinence, or making it worse – for example, diabetes or a bladder infection – and if so this should be treated. Incontinence is almost always treatable with review of your medical condition, and the treatment may involve any or all of:

- Bladder training
- Pelvic muscle exercises
- Medications
- Surgery

In the first instance, your GP and PHN should be consulted, but if things do not improve you may be referred (or ask to be referred) to a specialist, usually a geriatrician, urologist or gynaecologist (if you are a woman). Your PHN will have training in continence management, and a specialist nurse called a continence adviser may also be available in your area.

There are four patterns of urinary incontinence, although you may have element of more than one of these patterns:

- *Urge incontinence* is the most common form of incontinence; it is a sudden urge to pass water but not having enough time to reach the toilet. People with urge incontinence often have an overactive bladder muscle. Bladder over-activity can also cause frequent urination and awakening at night to urinate (which doctors call nocturia). When urge incontinence occurs the bladder contracts with little or no warning and urine leaks as a result. There may be no clear reason, or it can be caused by stroke, Parkinson's disease, bladder infection or disorders that affect the spinal cord.
- *Stress incontinence*, which is most common in women, happens during or after coughing,

laughing, bending or other activities that apply pressure on the bladder. Common causes are weak muscles around the urethra and bladder opening as a result of childbirth, surgery or lack of oestrogen after menopause. 'Stress' incontinence has nothing to do with emotional stress, and almost invariably any woman troubled by stress incontinence should be seen by a gynaecologist.

- *Overflow incontinence* occurs when urine leaks from a full bladder that cannot empty properly. This condition can be due to damage to the nerves that control the bladder and can occur, for example, in those with diabetes or injuries to the spinal cord, making the bladder weak and unable to empty. It can also result from conditions that block the exit to the bladder and prevent it from emptying, such as an enlarged prostate in men.
- *Functional incontinence* occurs when the bladder and the urethra are functioning normally but the person either cannot physically get to the toilet, or has an impaired mental function that interferes with recognising the need to urinate and getting to the toilet on time. This condition is common in patients with Alzheimer's and other types of dementia.

For carers, you may be involved at several different points. It is helpful at all stages to start by sensitively discussing the problem with the older person. The first step is to help them accept they have a problem by discussing it with tact and sensitivity. Your goal is to support the older person to ensure the incontinence is appropriately assessed and treated. At later stages in the process your role may change from advice to hands-on support, and this will be discussed below. If the person you are caring for does not wish to be assessed this may in itself be a sign of an illness, and tact and patience are important.

What Should I Do?

Any incontinence should be reported to your doctor or healthcare professional. Buying pads from the chemist's may seem to help, but actually might be condemning you to unnecessary expense and also distracting you from the possibility that this incontinence might be curable – it needs to be evaluated by a doctor or other healthcare professional.

Incontinence is not usually a life-threatening problem, but you should seek medical help quickly – within a day – if any of the following symptoms happen suddenly:

- Sudden loss of ability to pass urine
- Great difficulty urinating
- Uncontrolled dribbling
- Pain with urination
- Blood in the urine

These symptoms could be caused by a urinary tract infection or urinary retention. Both conditions can become very serious if untreated.

In general, your doctor's assessment will often include the following questions, so consider them before you go in:

- What are the symptoms?
- When did the problem start?
- Has it ever happened before?
- Do you have other health problems?
- What medications are you taking? (Be sure to include non-prescription medications, and herbal and other remedies.)

The assessment will often include examination of your tummy, back passage (constipation, and an enlarged prostate in men, can worsen incontinence) and for women an inspection of your vagina, particularly to check for a condition called atrophic vaginitis (insufficient oestrogen to the vagina) or to look for an obvious prolapsed womb. A sample of urine should be sent and the doctor may suggest some blood tests.

Management of Early Stages of Incontinence

After the doctor and nurse have checked you out, considered your medications, performed tests, recommended exercises and possibly prescribed medications, you can try the following things to gain some control yourself:

- *Set up a routine* – it can be helpful for people with stress incontinence or urge incontinence to urinate about every two hours to avoid having too full a bladder. They should keep a record of when they go to the toilet for about two days and then make a schedule of trips to the toilet just before they would normally feel the urge to go.

- *Review fluids, caffeine and alcohol* – limit caffeine (coffee and tea) and alcohol, but do not decrease fluid intake. Older people should drink four to six glasses of water or other clear fluids a day. Too little fluid reduces cues to urinate regularly and concentrated urine can cause bladder irritation. If there is an incontinence problem at night restrict drinking for two to three hours before bedtime.
- *Pelvic muscle exercises* – these can be useful in treating stress and urge incontinence. In the past they were mainly recommended for women, but now they are also recommended for men, especially after prostate surgery and if there is a tendency to dribble after passing water (see pages 271–272).
- *Avoid constipation* – constipation can exacerbate any tendency to incontinence and should be vigorously treated. Ask your doctor about how best to do this and, if you have a new onset of constipation, whether or not it should be further investigated.
- *Choose your clothes carefully to facilitate speedy toileting* – there is nothing worse when the urge comes to lose control because you are struggling with zips or tight clothing. Reduce garments to a minimum, and consider loose clothes with a minimum of fastenings, e.g. elastic-waisted skirts or trousers.

Plan Your Environment

If you have both mobility problems and continence problems you have a reduced chance of getting in a timely fashion to that toilet up those stairs. Reconsidering where you go to the toilet can be of major benefit; this is where the eye of an occupational therapist or skilful PHN can see opportunities. The use of a commode, a urinal bottle or the Housing Adaptation Grant for People with a Disability Scheme to build a downstairs toilet can all make your life easier.

In Moderate to Later Stages

After all the above has been implemented incontinence may still be present, and the use of pads, absorbent garments and various types of urinary catheters may be needed. These should only be used after full assessment and trial of all the steps mentioned above. Do not use them in place of a doctor's evaluation.

There is quite a variety of incontinence pads, from small pads to insert into your underwear to larger nappy-like pads. In conjunction with the PHN and/ or continence adviser you might find yourself using a range of appliances; for example, you can manage day-to-day life with a small 'slip' pad, whereas a larger pad may be helpful for extra protection on long trips. In general, we try to advise the use of the smallest pad practicable, as the pad itself can slow you down when using the toilet, due to the time taken to actually take it off. If pads are necessary, they should be changed often to avoid odour, leakage and skin rashes.

Catheters should only be used if absolutely necessary because they can increase the risk of serious urinary tract infections. For men a type of catheter, called a condom catheter, can be attached around the penis to collect urine without the same risk of infection.

Carrying Out And Adjusting Your Plan

Incontinence can be emotionally upsetting to both carers and the older person with the problem. It should be discussed with tact and sensitivity, but it should not be ignored. Incontinence is one of the common reasons for placing people in nursing homes. Therefore, it should be addressed early. The first step is to have an evaluation by a doctor or other healthcare professional, and then develop a plan based on their recommendations. Progress might be slow and might require setting up new routines and exercises.

If Your Plan Does Not Work

If incontinence is becoming more of a problem, or if the person is becoming more and more bothered by it, ask the doctor or nurse for help. Explain what you have done and what the results have been. The doctor may refer you to a nurse or therapist who is specially trained to deal with incontinence problems and in therapies such as pelvic muscle exercises and bladder training. These specialists will also be knowledgeable in using bio-feedback or other aids in helping to strengthen the pelvic muscles and to use them correctly to prevent urinary accidents. The doctor may also recommend seeing a geriatrician, urologist or gynaecologist.

Late Stages

In conjunction with the PHN/continence adviser try to plan a schedule. People who are unable to remember to go to the toilet in time can be helped by reminding them when to go to the toilet, assisting them in getting to the toilet and helping with their clothing and hygiene. If necessary, provide a urinal or portable toilet by the bedside at night.

Pelvic Muscle Exercises

What are pelvic muscle exercises?
They are exercises used to strengthen the pelvic muscles that help to control the outlet from the bladder and urination.

How do you learn to do the exercises?
The best way to learn to control urination is to stop the flow of urine in the middle of urinating. This helps you get an idea of the muscles being used to control urine flow.

It is very important that only the pelvic muscles are used and not the muscles of the stomach. The stomach should stay relaxed during these exercises.

Breathing in and out while doing the exercise will help keep the stomach relaxed.

How are the exercises practiced?
Once you get the feel of using the right muscles, you should do the exercises as follows:

Squeeze the muscles and hold for ten seconds (you may have to gradually build up to this long).

Relax for ten seconds.

Repeat, gradually building up to fifteen squeezes and fifteen relaxations three times a day.

You should do no more than fifty per day, divided into three to four sessions. After one to two weeks of these exercises you should start to be able to use these muscles to prevent accidents (both urge and stress).

When should the exercises be done?
You can practice anytime, while you are sitting, standing or lying down. But to prevent accidents the exercises must also be done at times that normally cause you to leak, such as when coughing, laughing or straining, or when a very strong urge to urinate begins, for example when putting a key in the door, or when you hear running water.

How long do the exercises take to work?
If they are practiced properly, you should begin to notice a difference within four to six weeks.

Can the exercises be harmful?
No. If you get any stomach or back pain with the exercises you are not doing them correctly. You should only contract your pelvic muscles. Do not use your stomach or abdominal muscles to do this. The exercises do not require great effort and should not cause discomfort or fatigue. Hold contractions only as long as comfortable, usually eight to ten seconds.

Remember: Like any other exercise, pelvic muscle exercises must be practiced regularly in order to work.

Bowel Incontinence

Bowel or faecal incontinence is less common, but is clearly a very troubling problem when it occurs.

However, it can also respond to assessment and management, and it is very important to get nursing and medical help for it.

There are two major causes of faecal incontinence in later life, and both tend to occur in the presence of other disabilities. The first is known as *overflow incontinence* and is paradoxically due to constipation. In this type of incontinence the lower part of the bowel becomes blocked by constipation, and a bowel motion above this tends to liquefy and leak around the constipation. It is important that this is picked up and diagnosed by a doctor as it is possible to treat it by treating the constipation. The faecal incontinence tends to be more liquid than solid, and you should discuss this with the public health nurse and/or your doctor. They will check the pattern of your bowel motions and should examine your tummy, and often the back passage as well. The treatment should start with removing any medication that might cause constipation (for example, medications for your bladder, some antidepressants and some sedatives) as well as the use of laxatives, either by mouth or sometimes as a suppository or enema. A review of your diet can also be helpful, with an increase in fruit and vegetables, the use of wholemeal bread, and the addition of bran or linseeds to foods such as porridge.

The second most common form arises for those who have illnesses where *they no longer recognise, or are able to appropriately respond to, the need to pass a bowel movement*. This tends to occur in the later stages of illnesses such as dementia. With proper assessment, advice and support this problem can be improved. In the first instance, it is important that your doctor/nurse ensures that this is not overflow incontinence. Occasionally they may recommend an agent to give the bowel motion more bulk to help the lower bowel sense the bowel motion if your stool tends to be more liquid.

Management is largely about trying to make use of unconscious reflexes and routines that enable a bowel movement to take place. This can be by regular toileting, if tolerated, in particular after meals, as there is a reflex called the gastrocolic reflex which stimulates a bowel motion after eating. So, toileting about 20 minutes after a meal can maximise the chances of having a bowel movement in a controlled way.

It is also important to review whether there are any barriers to using the toilet, such as:

- Distance
- Adequate lighting
- Sufficient aids – such as a raised toilet seat or grab handles if appropriate
- Easily removable clothes

If unsuccessful with these manoeuvres, you and/or your family will need to discuss pads with the public health nurse, and it is likely that some experimentation will be needed to find the right balance between acceptability and practicality. Specialist advice should be considered if the problem is not improved with these measures.

For carers, faecal incontinence is one of the most challenging areas. The strategies outlined above may help, and it is absolutely critical that you seek nursing and medical help with this problem rather than trying to deal with it on your own. Enlist as much help as you can from public and private carers and your family if you are trying to ensure a roster for toileting. It is important to remember that nobody wants to have faecal incontinence, and no matter how troubling it is for you, the older person may be equally distressed but unable to tell you this because of the dementia. Showing irritation or crossness will only aggravate the situation, and patience and tact will be required in large quantities.

Constipation

Constipation is a more common problem in later life than in younger ages. However, the patterns of younger and middle life tend to continue and sometimes are exaggerated in later life. In addition, illness and medications can make a tendency to constipation worse. There are a number of things you can do to reduce the chances of getting constipation, and these are also effective should you develop constipation.

- The first element of this is to *increase natural fibre in your diet*, and in particular fresh fruit, wholegrain bread and cereals, and green leafy vegetables. If you are not used to taking high fibre cereals such as All-Bran you should probably start this in a fairly gradual way. The use of linseed or bran scattered in cereal is another way of getting fibre, and linseed also provides a natural lubricant with linseed oil.

- The second element is to ensure *plenty of fluid intake*, particularly as fibre works by absorbing fluids and therefore can't work in a dry stomach or bowel. The equivalent of eight glasses of water a day is the standard recommendation for fluid intake but even four to six will help to keep the bowels moving. The fluid intake does not have be water and can be pretty much any drink, such as tea and coffee (while being mindful of the advice given above should there be co-existing urinary incontinence) or juice.
- The third element is *adequate exercise*, which helps to keep the bowels regular. As discussed in Chapter 4, exercise routines can be arranged to suit those who are more frail or unable to get out of the house.
- The development of *good bathroom routines* is a further help; in particular try to use the body's natural reflex to have a bowel movement after a meal. Try to ensure that you lessen any habit to 'hold on' or ignore the urge to have a bowel motion or to wait for a more convenient time or place: if you need to go, go!

Laxatives are commonly used over-the-counter medications. Ideally you should discuss it with your doctor if you start using these. There are a number of types, including bowel stimulants (such as senna), medications which draw water into the bowel (such as lactulose/Duphalac), and lubricants such as liquid paraffin. The most immediate concern is that you would continue to use these medications over a long period of time without checking why your constipation is occurring. It may well be that you are unnecessarily taking laxatives when altering medication or changing your diet could achieve the same ends. It is also important to discuss laxative use with your doctor because when overused laxatives can lead to a form of lazy bowel and the need for ever-increasing doses.

If the above measures do not work discuss your constipation with your doctor because many medications, including antacids, blood pressure medication and antidepressants, can cause constipation. In addition, if you get any change in your bowel habit that lasts for longer than a week or two – a new tendency to constipation or diarrhoea – you should discuss this with your doctor to rule out any possibility this could be due to a more serious bowel problem, and in particular so you can be screened for bowel cancer.

19

Medications

Ideally, we would all like to live without taking tablets or medication, but in the end the benefits can be important. However, as previously discussed, as you age you are more likely to have multiple illnesses and therefore multiple medications. In addition, there are increasing numbers of tablets used for prevention, such as those for hypertension (to prevent heart attack and stroke) and osteoporosis (to prevent fracture).

The two biggest challenges in later life are:

- Making sure you have as few medications as possible, giving due consideration to whether you might benefit from preventive medications
- Organising the medications in such a way that you can access them safely and effectively

The danger in later life is that one doctor, or a series of doctors, may put you on a pill for every ill; the next thing you know they are impacting on each other, or else you are getting one medication for the side effect of another medication. Alternatively, your condition might change, for example a tendency to high blood pressure often becomes a tendency to low blood pressure, particularly when you stand up, and continuing your blood pressure tablets may only make things worse.

The best solution is regular, and focused, reviews of your medication. Ideally your GP should review your medication at least every three to six months, particularly if you are on four or more medications. Also, should you see a geriatrician you should have your medication reviewed. If you are not sure this review is happening, do ask your GP, geriatrician or old age psychiatrist.

In addition, try to learn the name of each medication and what it is for; in this the pharmacist (in your local pharmacy or in the hospital) can be very helpful. It is also good to be aware of the main side effects of each of your medications, particularly when you are starting them.

Reducing Medications

Reducing the number of medications assumes more importance should you develop memory problems, and some trade-offs may need to be made. For example, medications to reduce cholesterol may be less important than medications to increase bone strength when you are in your nineties.

Another way of reducing the number of dosages is through reducing the frequency of each medication by using longer-acting versions of the medication, or by avoiding splitting up the doses unnecessarily; for example, the laxative lactulose may be prescribed three times a day, but it is just as effective when prescribed twice a day. Ask your doctor can any of your medications be given in a long-acting form.

Organising Your Medications

As you get more and more medications, there are a number of simple measures which might help you.

The first is a small box with compartments into which you (or a helper) can place the medications. This is called a dossette box and can be purchased cheaply from your pharmacist.

The next level is to ask your pharmacist to arrange the week's medications in a blister pack; not all pharmacies can provide this service, but it can be very helpful when you get it. It is a bit challenging when this needs to be changed, but organising the medications in this way can make a difference should you have a memory problem, or if your carer is giving a hand in ensuring your medications are taken.

Helping to Supervise Medication

If you are helping an older relative with their tablets it might be helpful to have a sheet outlining the tablets in the home, identifying each tablet and the time at which it is to be taken over the course of a week, as well as what it is for. If your older relative has a memory problem, as well as asking the doctor whether any of the medications can be eliminated or their frequency of dosage reduced, you should explore how you can help prompt them to take their medications. A telephone call at the time of key dosages may be helpful. Home helps generally do not administer medications, but informal carers or agency staff may help with medications.

Crushing Tablets

Be careful about breaking and crushing tablets, as you may change their efficacy. Some medications, particularly those that are long acting, need the tablet to be unbroken to work, so crushing it means you get a very high dose initially and then very little over time, rather than a slow, steady and constant dosage. If you have a feeding tube at home your doctor should aim where possible to prescribe the medications in a format that suits the tube best (for example, in liquid form). If you or your carer is administering the medications discuss how this is best done with a hospital/community pharmacist, as the order in which the medications are taken is important (some are neutralised by the feed and some can clog the tube if it is not flushed with water after administration).

Section III

The Final Years

20

When Home Is No Longer Possible

Less than 5 per cent of older Irish people live in nursing homes or other residential care, but this still means that at least one in twenty older Irish people has to prepare for this difficult change. Indeed, hidden within this figure is the fact that up to one-third of women and one-quarter of men will spend some time in a nursing home before they die.

Entering a nursing home is a difficult decision for you and your family, but there may be no other choice. It is likely that you will have exhausted your options for care at home and are not able to manage (or find a place in) the two less intensive options to your own home: sheltered housing and welfare/residential homes. The decision may also need to be taken at relatively short notice. It is *vital* that you have been fully assessed by a geriatrician or old age psychiatrist to ensure there is no aspect of your present condition that can be improved, and to check if there are alternative solutions to going into a nursing home; the advice of a social worker can also be very helpful.

While this is a moment you and your family may have dreaded, there does come a time when your disabilities and care needs may be so great that you and your family will just run into more difficulties by trying to stay at home. At this stage, entry to a nursing home may be the only helpful solution. For many older people this will happen during a significant illness on top of other background illnesses – for example, a stroke or fractured hip against a background of arthritis and memory problems. It is not uncommon that this will occur following a hospital admission. It is absolutely critical that you and your family discuss this fully with the treating doctor, as an *adequate period of rehabilitation* (for example, at least six weeks in general after a stroke) should be offered prior to any decision about entering a nursing home.

As an older person, you need to be aware that one of the most common reasons for entering a nursing home is dementia, and that your family or those close to you will need to have a significant input into this choice. You can either leave this to your family in an informal way or else try to choose someone to make this decision in advance, through an Enduring Power of Attorney. There are potential benefits and challenges to both approaches.

Making the Decision

For families, the pathway of decision making is hugely variable. If entry into a nursing home arises from a significant illness, such as a stroke, it may be relatively clear to all that this is needed, even if painful. More difficult situations arise where the older person with significant memory problems, such as those caused by moderate to severe Alzheimer's disease, becomes less aware of their needs and begins to engage in risky behaviour. In general, when counselling families about the risk, the biggest issue tends to be the fear of a future risk, the what-if factor. However, despite the fact that many people use gas cookers, there have been almost no gas explosions caused by people with Alzheimer's disease. Indeed if leaving on the gas is a problem isolators can be fitted to cut off the gas supply to an unlit cooker. The determination that an older person is no longer able to make decisions on their own is one not to be taken lightly, and in my practice it involves demonstrating formally a major gap between what an older person can do and what they think they can do; in cases of uncertainty the benefit of the doubt rests with the older person.

In general, admission to a nursing home from the community tends to be event driven, either through an exacerbation of an existing illness or a deterioration of a condition such as Alzheimer's disease. Your older relative may find it easier to consider a nursing home if they have become used to a particular nursing home through the provision of respite care or day services.

Relatives often wonder whether the older person can be removed from their homes without their consent, but in fact this is limited to a few very specific instances, such as elder abuse or psychiatric committal, and in practice is almost never used.

Finally, research shows that older people can improve in health and well-being in the stable environment of a nursing home, and it may be that after six months or a year the situation can be reviewed. Advice from a geriatrician or old age psychiatrist can be helpful if a re-insertion into the community is considered.

Making the Choice

Your choice will be dictated by a number of factors:

- The workings of the 2009 Nursing Home Scheme
- Cost
- Geographical location
- Availability
- Quality and style of care

Below we describe the main types of care, then discuss funding, and finally look at issues such as how to access and choose nursing home care.

The background to making choices is coloured by three main themes:

- The system of funding nursing home care, which at the time of writing generally consists of a mixture of 80 per cent of your income, an equity release scheme by the state to claim back (after your death) up to 15 per cent of the value of your house and 7.5 per cent per year of your other assets, up to the value of the nursing home loan, which will generally be between €40,000 and €180,000 a year. This system replaced an entitlement to publicly funded care, less 80 per cent of your State (Non-Contributory) Pension. If you, or a relative, were admitted to a nursing home from hospital before 27 October 2009 because you needed ongoing nursing and medical care or therapy, and you were not informed of this eligibility and could not be discharged home, you should consider asking your manager for services for older people about exercising this eligibility retrospectively.

- The failure of successive Irish governments not only to fund and develop an adequate number of public nursing home places in the major urban areas but also to update the physical fabric of existing homes so that many no longer meet regulatory standards.
- Lack of clarity from the HSE as to the provision and structure of medical officer and therapist support to those in nursing homes.

There are also some other issues, such as a lack of residency rights for those who move to nursing homes. While this does not pose a concern for the vast majority of those taking up their new residence in a nursing home, it is a cause of concern that all nursing homes (public, private and voluntary) can decide to no longer maintain a contract of residency. This usually relates to care needs and is something that needs to be attended to by the government.

In this chapter, we will describe the main forms of nursing homes available, and then discuss the issues involved in choosing a nursing home.

What Is Available?

In most parts of Ireland there are two main forms of nursing home care, private nursing homes and HSE nursing homes/community hospitals, with a

third option available in some parts of the country –
voluntary nursing homes.

Private Nursing Homes

Private nursing homes are, as the name suggests,
privately run. They have to be registered with the
Health Information and Quality Authority (HIQA –
www.hiqa.ie) and this depends on them fulfilling a
certain minimum number of basic criteria: generally
there must be a nurse available at all times (although
the ratio of trained nurses to patients is not specified), the staff must be able to dispense medications
and provide palliative care (though the nature and
extent of this is not specified), the nursing home
must comply with fire and health and safety regulations, and so forth. HIQA has inspection teams which
review private and public nursing homes at varying
intervals and will inspect on foot of complaints about
adequacy of care. HIQA has developed a detailed set
of criteria for the inspection of nursing homes.

Private nursing homes do not have to take every
one who presents to them (even if they come with
significant public funding) and this may be of some
concern to you if you have a significant disability.
Occupancy will generally be in rooms of one to three
occupants. Bathrooms may or may not be shared.

Public Nursing Homes

These are nursing homes run directly by the HSE. The
accommodation varies from renovated workhouses,
through community hospitals to purpose-built

community units. Their position within the health system structure means that in general there has been a reasonable overview of care, with nursing staff at a level of twice that of the private sector noted in a recent survey. Unfortunately, the physical fabric of the older units can be poor, with some dating from the early Victorian era. Accommodation is generally in multiple occupancy rooms or wards of up to twenty beds. Bathrooms are generally shared.

There had not been any formal inspection of public nursing homes up to 2009 but these are now conducted by HIQA.

Voluntary Nursing Homes

These are nursing homes run by religious orders, charities or foundations that are run independently by boards of management. The majority of their funding come from the HSE and is supplemented by contributions and fundraising. Accommodation ranges from open wards to single rooms. These institutions have been inspected by HIQA since 2009.

Which Do I Go To?

This will depend on four main factors:

- What is available in your location
- The balance between geography, cost and personal preference
- Your disabilities
- Timely availability within a specific institution

You or your family may have a preference by location which may trump the type of nursing home. For example, if the only facility in your remote part of Donegal is a community hospital then it is unlikely that you or your family will look elsewhere. On the other hand, if you are in a suburb of Dublin there may be a potential choice between private, public and voluntary options, and the role of the Local Placement Forum (a group organised by the health service in each locality which processes applications for nursing home care) in negotiating this choice is evolving. You may find, however, that availability and cost loom large; for example, there may be no places available in private nursing homes that will take you at your current level of disability.

In the greater Dublin and some other urban areas, public beds are very scarce. Prioritisation may occur on the basis of serious disability (as private nursing homes may not take you). For many, the final steps to nursing home take place during a critical illness which finally exhausts the capacity of you and your carers to manage, and the application will take place from a hospital. You may find yourself waiting in a general hospital bed or respite bed while this is happening.

How Is Extended Care Funded?

Although you and/or your family may choose to fully fund nursing home care (an expense which is allowable at the standard rate of tax), most will now use the equity release loan scheme of the Nursing Home Support Scheme, the so-called 'Fair Deal'. There is a budget for the amount of money which can be used for this in any one year, which we will come to in Appendix A.

The Process from Home

If you, or your family, arrive at a situation whereby you are looking for a nursing home bed from the community your public health nurse can start the process with you and/or your family. As well as a needs assessment (i.e. an assessment of whether you have problems managing activities of daily living, etc.; they may also ask therapists in the community to carry out assessments) and a financial assessment, you should be referred for assessment by a geriatrician and/or old age psychiatrist to ensure that you are not foreclosing early on your independent life at home. The specialist will try to ensure that your health is as good as it can be and that all rehabilitation and support options have been exhausted. A further benefit of this assessment is that it may allow you and your family to discuss the nursing home option(s) in your area with the social worker on the team (if they have one). They will usually have significant experience in this area and can save you some headaches.

The PHN and other staff coordinating the process should check whether or not you have the capacity to understand the financial contract, and if not to guide your family towards the appointment of a care representative (see Appendix A), who will look after this aspect for you and also assist in choosing a nursing home.

Going to a Nursing Home from Hospital

A significant number of people go to a nursing home from hospital, often after a critical event that does not get better, even with rehabilitation. For example, a broken hip, a severe stroke or a worsening of dementia may cause this. After you and your family have ensured that you have had appropriate rehabilitation (in consultation with the treating consultant and the geriatrician/old age psychiatrist), either you or family will be faced with a choice with the hospital team. Your consultant's team will fill out the needs assessment and will support you and your family in filling out the financial needs assessment.

The hospital staff coordinating the process should check whether or not you have capacity to understand the financial contract, and if not to guide your family towards the appointment of a care representative (see Appendix A), who will look after this for you and also assist in choosing a nursing home.

The Choice: The Least Worst Compromise

As most of us wish to be at home for as long as possible, entry to a nursing home represents a significant compromise. Your goal must be to make this the best (or least worst) compromise, by matching the nursing home to you and your family's personal preferences, and the deliberations of the Local Placement Forum.

The challenge here is the appropriate balance between what is available and what is best for you, and the decision must be taken with your consent or with the agreement of your family if you are unable to make that decision. In general, in most situations this is resolved after discussion between you, your family and the medical team, and increasingly involves you (or your family on your behalf) visiting the nursing home and/or a nurse from the nursing home coming to the hospital to see you. While an appropriately planned agreed discharge should take place as soon as possible, it is also important that you or your family are not inappropriately pressurised by the use of phrases such as 'we need the bed urgently'–you, like all older people and their families, know how much pressure the system is under, but you also have the right to an appropriately planned and agreed discharge. This is particularly important in urban areas where there is a shortage of suitable nursing home beds available.

At this stage, you hopefully will have a sense of what is available in your area and what the Local Placement Forum is suggesting. The choice may be restricted in terms of what is available, unless you or your relatives are willing to consider travelling significant distances. In the greater Dublin area there is a major shortage of public nursing homes and also places for those with heavy dependency or dementia-specific care needs. While social worker support may become available through the primary care teams, for those placed from hospitals the social work support is most easily accessed through the hospital team.

Medical Care and Therapies in Nursing Homes

The Leas Cross Report found that the HSE and the Department of Health and Children had failed to clarify the expectations and supports for medical and therapy care in nursing homes. This is clearly a very important issue for a frail and complex group of older people, and somewhat astonishingly the contracting process by the government (through the National Treatment Purchase Fund) for private nursing homes in the so-called 'Fair Deal' in 2010 specifically excludes the provision of therapies.

For medical care, only a very small number of older people will have the luxury of being in a nursing home where their family doctor can continue to provide cover. In most cases, a GP near the nursing home will take over (or be enjoined upon by the HSE), and will receive a fee for providing care 365 days a year. This will probably involve some visits during the week, and out-of-hours cover (nights and weekends) is often by some form of doctors' cooperative or deputising service. This GP is your primary doctor, and you should make it your business to meet him or her at a very early stage in your stay. The GP may refer you to other specialists – old age psychiatrists or geriatricians – *but the specialists do not take over your medical care*; their advice on your care is communicated to your nursing home GP, and he or she is the person charged with implementing your healthcare and is the key contact point for discussing your progress and medications.

As mentioned above, access to therapists is a potentially vexing area; it is hoped that the HSE will provide clarity on its responsibility in this area. Many of the public and voluntary units have developed therapy services; provision of therapies is specifically excluded from the contracting process for private nursing homes.

Your starting point should be to clarify your or your relative's needs in terms of these therapies. If you have been discharged from hospital you should ask for written recommendations from each of the therapists to be sent to the director of nursing in the nursing home and keep in touch with him or her as to how these will be implemented. In general, the table below outlines who you should seek a review from.

Difficulties	Need review by
Swallowing or speech difficulties	Speech and language therapist
Balance or walking difficulties	Physiotherapist
Requirement for specialist seating or splints	Occupational therapist
Difficulties with feeding or weight loss	Clinical nutritionist
Concerns over family stress	Social worker

In some public and voluntary nursing homes some of these therapists may be available in-house. In private nursing homes there are in general two options – some invoke the community/primary care team therapists if they cover nursing homes in the locality, and some make options available for you to pay for these services. There is a reasonable case to be made that as a nursing home is a new 'home' such services should be provided by the community/primary care team therapists, but the reality is that these teams may be under-provided, or individual disciplines may be completely missing, in your area. Recent studies on the provision of services for those with stroke in Irish nursing homes show a grave under-provision of necessary therapy services. In particular, swallow problems require the input of speech and language therapists with specialist training in swallow, as well as liaison with clinical nutritionists (also known as dieticians).

So what to do? In the first instance, establish the need or not for therapy input as suggested above, and/or discuss this with the GP/medical director and/or director of nursing. If the relevant therapists are not available from the nursing home or community/primary care team therapists then the choices are to either pay for these if available, or to make the case to the local health manager that your or your relative's needs are not being met.

The director of nursing may also call on specialist nursing services from the community services, such as specialist nurses in continence management or tissue viability (dealing with leg wounds and pressure sores).

If the GP/medical officer calls in a consultation with an old age psychiatrist there may also be visits from a community psychiatric nurse, who may advise the nursing staff on the best way to manage any behavioural and psychological problems that you or your relative may be suffering from.

What Should I Consider in a Nursing Home?

The nursing home is going to be your new home, so it is important that you have an opportunity to visit it and see it for yourself. Should you have very significant dementia then it is reasonable that your family should help with this decision, perhaps even doing the visit, but otherwise it is important that you should see it.

While we may all differ hugely in our expectations of nursing home care, it is my experience that the ethos, atmosphere and care are more important than the physical fabric of the nursing home for most people. However, the physical fabric is also important.

On the visit, be in listening and observing mode and ask questions. Below is a checklist of things you should look for.

Home-Like Atmosphere

Does it feel like a comfortable place to live? Is the lounge cosy and are the bedrooms adequate? Is there a garden for summer?

Caring Staff

The quality of the staff is the key determinant of your care. Did you get a sense of helpful and welcoming staff who had no difficulty in dealing with your questions? Do they seem to get on well with the residents?

A Clean and Tidy Environment

Cleanliness is a very important marker of overall maintenance, particularly as nursing homes have to deal with potential infection issues. Is the nursing home clean overall? Is it in a state of good repair? Is there an odour of urine? (There should not be.)

The Other Residents and Day-to-Day Life

You must remember that stroke and dementia are the most common causes of entry to a nursing home, and therefore you are likely to encounter significantly disabled people among the other residents. This is often uncomfortable for you, and in particular for your family, as it brings them face to face with the reality of your disability. In your visit it is perhaps more important to see whether the daily schedule and any activities that are available are suited to both to you and to the residents who are there. Is independence encouraged? Are there any activities provided? Does your family feel encouraged to visit, to bring you out or to carry out activities? Is there a residents' committee?

Medical Care and Therapy Cover

Can your own GP provide cover for you (if willing)? Is there a GP who visits, and how often? Are unnecessary restraints used? Is there access to physiotherapy or any other therapies? Can you or your family buy in physiotherapy or other therapies?

Type of Room

How many residents are there to a room? Is the bathroom en suite? If not, where are the bathrooms and toilets situated? What condition are they in?

Food

Is the food to your liking, given the likely constraints of any institutional catering? Can they cater for your special needs diet? Will they facilitate family or friends who wish to bring in food?

Your Own Possessions and Their Security

Can you bring in your own mementoes, photos, etc. and display them in reasonable safety? If you have your own room, can you bring small pieces of furniture? Will you have somewhere reasonably safe to keep and charge a mobile phone?

Privacy and Belonging

Is there somewhere you can have a private discussion with your family and friends? If you are sleeping in a shared room, are there regulations to protect you from the noise of communal television and radio? Is there a residents' committee? This is still relatively uncommon in Ireland.

Special Care for Dementia

A relatively small number of nursing homes will have (or claim to have) special care units for dementia. Does it seem to be well-staffed with adequately trained staff? Is there a good mix of calm and stimulation?

Preparing for the Move

Once you have decided on your place, a number of matters must be settled before you move in. A full medical report will be important if your GP is not going to look after your care. If you are being trans-ferred from hospital a full nursing report as well is the very least that is required, and ideally thera-pist and social worker reports as well. These and your prescriptions will be required by the nursing home before you go there. Any financial arrange-ments should be clarified. Agreement over transfer of mementoes, small items of furniture and so on should be arranged.

Settling In

This is a very major move, so be sure not to make any hasty decisions about pulling out. After a few days, the rhythm of the nursing home will become clearer. If you have significant memory problems you and your family should be aware that these might become more pronounced for a few days after the move, and it is important not to overreact at this time.

Over time, it is important that you and your family and friends establish a routine that allows you to maximise your own sense of being at home while at the same time adapting to some extent to the rhythm of the nursing home. For the staff in the nursing home care has to be given and meals need to be provided, so the schedule therefore involves some compromises.

Visiting, Outings and Stimulation

Visiting is usually a very important support and link with the outside world. A balance must be struck; whatever illness or disability has been the cause of your admission into the nursing home may reduce your stamina and tolerability. Outings may therefore need to be planned with a little bit more time and possibly with a relatively small number of objectives than you might have been accustomed to previously. If you are able, and you have the appropriate support from friends or family for transport and personal support, the limits of what you can do are largely determined by what you are able to manage.

For families and friends, this can be a difficult time; visiting represents a new rhythm and pattern of seeing your older relative. However, please do try to visit as regularly as possible. Your older relative may at this stage be disabled or suffer from memory problems and there will be many changes in their life. Just sitting and providing company is the most important part of visiting. Do not be unnerved by silence, and avoid the temptation to cut the visit short. Try to imagine how it might be at home and consider bringing a book or newspaper, some knitting or whatever might help both you and your older relative to adapt to the new circumstances.

With dementia, other helpful tips are:

- Play music – a small CD player and a selection of the music that your older relative likes can provide a supportive environment for both of you.

- Consider modest activities that allow you both to do something together – Carmel Sheridan's book *Failure-Free Activities for the Alzheimer's Patient* might give you some tips in this regard.

If you have the resources, consider paying someone who might sit with your older relative as a personal companion and who might also carry out these activities. This will need to be discussed and cleared with the director of nursing in the nursing home.

Some people may also feel guilty that their older relative is in a nursing home. The best way to alleviate this is to be certain in your own mind that everything had been done to avoid this; this is one of the benefits of a geriatric medical assessment, as this is not only designed to maximise your relative's chances of managing at home but also may provide you with the opportunity to discuss the process with a professional (the geriatrician/occupational therapist/social worker) who has knowledge of what you are going through.

Quality of Care

Part of the new change for you and your family is a dependence on others for things that you would have formerly done yourself. This is a big compromise and there will always be things done in a way that doesn't quite suit you. Meal times may not be when you want them; you may not have your needs attended to at the time or in the manner to which you are accustomed.

However, there is usually goodwill and professionalism on the part of the nursing home staff and the key issue is to remember that you should approach this as a new relationship. You and your family will get to know the staff and get some sense of their style of working. The best approach is to develop a sense of collaboration and work out the conflicting needs and demands.

In the event of a more major concern over quality of care, you (or your family) may need to consider other avenues for discussion. In general, the director of nursing is the first point of contact, and will usually take your concerns seriously. If the director does not seem to take your complaint seriously enough you can express your concerns to the nursing home inspection team in HIQA.

If the care seems to involve any abusive elements you should talk to the director of nursing, who will usually take your concerns seriously and initiate an investigation. If the director does not seem to take your complaint seriously enough you can express your concerns to the elder abuse officer of the HSE or to HIQA (www.hiqa.ie).

It is well recognised that relatives often fear negative consequences for their older relative if they raise issues of abuse or inadequate care. However, it is invariably the case that not raising the issue will lead to a continuation or worsening of the poor care or abuse, and all parties are better served in general by raising the issue. Unless the older person is so severely incapacitated that they do not understand the complaint, you should let them know that you are considering bringing forward the complaint, and sound them out on how to progress. That said, as mentioned above, it must be recognised that, as yet, older people do not have residency rights in nursing homes, and no guarantees can be given that the nursing home will not seek to terminate the contract of care; however, this would be very unusual.

The Future

Interesting developments are occurring in other countries which may take place in Ireland in the near future. These centre around a realisation that much nursing home design and procedures are relatively institutional in nature, and may deliver more on the 'nursing' than on the 'home' element of care. Initiatives such as the Eden Alternative and the Green House Project try to bring a domestic element to both the design and living rhythm of the nursing home. These include domestic scale and design (albeit adapted for complex care), and more choices for residents in how they live their lives – for example, having breakfast when one wants, rather than everyone getting breakfast at, say, 8.15 in the morning. This model has been developed already to a certain extent for newer housing for younger adults with disabilities, and a working group in the HSE is looking at developing this model for new public, private and voluntary nursing homes.

21

Advance Care Planning and Preferences

There is increasing discussion about 'living wills' and 'advanced directives' in Irish society, particularly after the publication of the Law Reform Commission report which suggested that legally binding advanced directives should become part of Irish law. These aim to be the health equivalent of ordinary wills, laying out treatment preferences in a legally binding way should you no longer be able to communicate your wishes.

Much of the underlying tone of the debate betrays a degree of prejudice against disability and ageing, and indeed the recommendations of the Law Reform Commission that advance directives should only be for refusal of treatment are indicative of the negative way that young and middle-aged people may view later life, age-related disability and disease, and death.

This short chapter aims to reassure you that, awaiting formal legislation in Ireland, appropriately timed and discussed advance care planning between you and your doctor will carry a strong moral weight and is likely to be given significant priority if you arrive at a stage where you can no longer manage to make your own decisions about healthcare independently. In addition, a form is included to help you tease out some of these issues in Appendix C.

In general, the greatest risk to you in later life should you have a disabling illness is not that you would be kept alive against your wishes in some deeply disabled state, but rather that you will not have adequate access to assessment, rehabilitation and support services. In particular, there are major concerns all over the world that healthcare staff of all grades do not have sufficient training in dealing with people with memory problems such as delirium and dementia in healthcare settings. If we as a society were truly concerned about making our wishes known when we have dementia or delirium, we would be much more likely to be understood, and have our wishes acted upon, by a group of healthcare professionals who have had training in communication with and care of people with dementia.

However, awaiting such developments, it is encouraging that a humane and collaborative approach tends to be used in Ireland when it appears that it is no longer appropriate to provide aggressive treatment if you are very seriously ill with a poor prognosis. Research done in Ireland suggests that senior clinicians are likely to discuss the appropriateness of resuscitation with you, or your relatives, if such life-sustaining treatment does not seem to be reasonable given the gravity of your condition.

The problem with advance care planning, other than for very specific decisions such as resuscitation, is that your care pathway could well be unpredictable, technologies and supports you are not aware of may become available, and also as you get closer to the actual reality of your illness you may change and indeed grow with your illness. Other Irish research shows that older people actually wish to defer their advance care planning to a point quite late in life when they are affected by the disability that is relevant to decision making.

So where to next? I would recommend in the first instance that you raise discussions about intensity of care directly with the doctor who is treating you. The three areas most relevant to everyday practice are most likely to be around resuscitation, decisions on whether and not to transfer you from a nursing home to a hospital in the event of illness, and the intensity of certain treatments for cancer such as surgery, chemotherapy and radiotherapy.

Resuscitation

The discussion on resuscitation really relates to how well or ill you are. In the United States there is a legal obligation to ask all patients admitted to hospital, even for a trivial illness like an ingrown toenail, their preferences for resuscitation or if they would prefer not to be resuscitated. This is clearly so far removed from the reality and the likelihood of resuscitation being required that it doesn't make much sense, whereas if you are admitted with severe heart failure and lung cancer it is much more likely that you would view an attempt to restart your heart, should it stop, as less likely to benefit you. Over the last twenty to thirty years the rate of success of resuscitation has been much the same, with about one in six patients who are resuscitated in hospital leaving it. But it is also important to remember that resuscitation can include several components, including cardiopulmonary resuscitation, the application of shocks to your chest wall, medications, the insertion of a tube into your windpipe and ventilation. It is up to the doctor to explain to you what each of these options might mean for you should your heart or breathing stop, and in general these discussions are started either by the doctor, by you, or your family at a time when you are more likely to be ill. In the past doctors were hesitant to discuss this with the patient, as were family members, but in a society where these things are talked about more openly, it is more common for the patient, i.e. you, to be involved. There are no hard and fast rules, and in general the decision is not one that is taken as an immediate once-off decision, but may be one that is explored in stages over a period of days.

Transfer to a Hospital

In the nursing home setting you and your doctor may take a decision to consider whether or not you should be transferred to hospital should you become unwell. This needs to be approached in an individualised and cautious manner. While on one hand it is likely that there are many conditions that can be treated in a nursing home as well as in hospital, on the other there is some concern that there may be somewhat of an artificial divide suggesting that care in hospital is bad and care in the nursing home is good. Hospitals are not only about acute emergencies but often about complexity of care; for example if you are in a nursing home because you have had a stroke and are getting recurrent chest infections it may well be that you need not only the specialist medical and nursing care attention of the general hospital but also the speech and language therapy and clinical nutritional assessment on how best to cope with your swallow disorder.

In a well-organised nursing home with consistent medical cover and a good relationship with the local hospital it is reasonable to consider advance care planning schedules which cover in general whether or not you should be considered for a transfer to the general hospital if you become unwell at night or over a weekend. It is best that these are general in intention, as there can be exceptions to the rule. For example, if you are to get severe bleeds from a stomach ulcer this might be something that the nursing home would find difficult to manage. Similarly, if you have fallen and fractured a hip this might be best managed in the general hospital. So it is best if you make such advance care plans as a general principle but that some discretion must be left to the assessing doctor and nurses on duty.

Cancer Treatment

Finally, with cancer therapy it is your overall fitness which will determine your likelihood of tolerating the side effects, and in general I find that older people seem to be very wise in making their own decisions about whether or not to take such aggressive therapy.

In general, if you are in a condition where you can no longer make your wishes known it is unlikely that you or your family would be offered the option of these significant therapies.

Discussing Your Relative's Care Options

For families, you are most likely to be asked your opinions and your perception of your parent or relative's opinions about either resuscitation decisions or advance care planning if they are in a nursing home. In general there is a subtle distinction here in that you should be canvassed for your opinion and perceptions, but *it is the senior treating doctor who makes the decision on behalf of a patient who cannot make their own decision*, informed by the insights that family members can give of the patient's values and previously expressed wishes. This is not a licence for untrammeled medical paternalism, and the treating doctor should aim to reach consensus with the family. If consensus cannot be reached the treating doctor should offer to get a second opinion, which is a very helpful option and can help families not to feel trapped within the confines of the decisions of a single doctor. Again, it is important to stress that most ethical decisions are not a matter of crashing urgency, but rather a decision taken over a series of meetings where the patient and family discuss the issues with the doctor and discover their perspective, and equally the doctor comes to learn the perspectives of the patient and family.

One other area where family views may be canvassed is when patients with moderate to severe dementia begin to reduce their food intake and are no longer taking enough calories. In general, it has been established through research that tube feeding for this group of patients does not usually increase their life span or prevent them from getting pressure sores. However, this is not a blanket ban on the technique and some families may have a very strong sense that their mother or father would wish to be fed in these circumstances, so some flexibility is required in this setting.

22

End of Life

While most of us will live more healthily and happily into old age, it clearly is obvious that we are not immortal and despite all our best efforts and care death faces us all at the end. It is helpful that there is less of a taboo about talking about death in modern Ireland, but it still is uncomfortable and painful to think about. In the background however, despite reports of deficits in care, most people and their families report that they consider death occurs with dignity, and increasingly people feel that they have more say in how treatments are used or refused, and in what settings they happen.

It is also reassuring that palliative care services in Ireland, particularly for cancer, are relatively well developed, and it is hoped that in the future there would be more attention paid to the other common causes of death.

Because it is the tougher of us who survive into old age, death is increasingly unpredictable, and one of the greatest challenges in modern medicine is determining the point at which really sick becomes dying. There is an urban myth that older people prioritise quality of life over quantity of life, but studies and clinical experience show that when faced with death people see life as very precious and often will make a sustained fight that may surprise their relatives and indeed care staff.

If you, in discussion with your doctor, become aware that you have a terminal illness it is important to remember the words of Sherwin B. Nuland, author of *How We Die:*[3] 'Death belongs to the dying and to those who love them.' By this he doesn't mean that you should not be in hospital under the care of a doctor; he means you and your family should have some control over your death – not over its cause or timing – but over the sort of life you can live until that point, of what medical treatments will be used, and where you spend those last months and days, with whom, and with what comfort and support.

On receiving the news of a terminal illness many people may go through the phases described by Elisabeth Kübler-Ross, which include in the first instance denial, anger, bargaining, depression and acceptance (or perhaps better described as accommodation or resignation).[4] These are not some sacred writ but rather represent some of the common features than people experience on receiving bad news. Awareness of this pattern may be helpful to you and your family. There is no set course, and some people may stay in any one phase for a considerable length of time.

---

[3] Sherwin B. Nuland, *How We Die: Reflections on Life's Final Chapter* (Vintage Books, 1995).
[4] Elisabeth Kübler-Ross, *On Death and Dying* (Routledge, 2008).

Common concerns at the time of death are a fear that pain will not be controlled, that you will be a burden to others and that your affairs may not be in order. In general, doctors and nurses are more attuned to ensuring as much pain relief as possible, and indeed those who have experience in palliative care are also expert at adjusting painkillers and other medications to help alleviate anxiety and difficulty with secretions as well. There is a fine balance between appropriate pain relief and the deliberate choice of an older person that they actually don't want certain levels of pain relief because of side effects, real or perceived. In general, we would encourage people to adopt the mindset that there is no danger of dependency on opiate medications and you should have as much pain relief as you need. It is important not to be overly stoic at this point.

Avoiding stoicism also means trying to avoid considering yourself a burden to others. It is my clinical experience, and widely recognised in the literature, that most families and loved ones are keen to go the extra mile when death is near. It is often harder to receive than to give, and at this stage it is helpful if at all possible to avoid putting up barriers to those who wish to help you. Just keep in mind what you would have wished to have done when your own parents or valued friends died.

The palliative care services are usually accessed by your family doctor or a hospital specialist. They may make first contact while you are in hospital, where they may visit you. In many parts of the country a hospice home care team is available, and their remit is to deal with symptoms that cause discomfort.

Occasionally people say to me 'But Doctor, I have no symptoms that cause discomfort.' I would still recommend that you make first contact with the hospice home care team to familiarise yourself with the personnel and gain more understanding about the services available. The service does not replace your home help or private home care, but you will often find that the community services make an extra effort to visit when it is clear that death is near. Hospice services may also provide other supports such as day centre care, respite care and spiritual support. Being on the books of the hospice home care team facilitates your access to these other services if needed in due course.

There is much discussion about people's wish to die at home, but actually, if you examine the research in detail, people are more concerned about being where they will have the right services and where their family will not be overly burdened. All other things being equal, people in general prefer to be at home if they can be certain of services and support, but this tends to be a very individual decision between you and your family.

For families this is a difficult time, and very often even approaching the subject in conversation can be too painful to consider. However, when all is said and done, families have their own sometime circuitous or even cryptic ways of letting each other know how they care for each other. Don't be too distressed if there is not an overt discussion between the older person and you and your family, as people communicate in many other ways. On the other hand, if your older relative or parent raises the issue, do engage in open discussion as much as you can. It is common for the proximity of death to cause people to review their lives in terms of what its meaning was, what its value was and what will be remembered afterwards. While it is important that people should be able to express regrets, it is also important to try to encourage them to review all the good things that have happened in life – achievements, milestones, family and friends. This is the basis of a newly developing approach to the end of life called dignity therapy.

If your parent or relative is dying in hospital or a nursing home it is reasonable to ask about a single room if this is what your parent and yourselves would like, which is the case for most people. You may indeed find that the hospital staff have already made some effort to do this for you. If the time comes when your relative becomes less able to communicate or make their wishes known, it will be up to you and your family to check with the nurses as to whether or not your parent is comfortable. Experienced nurses are usually good at picking up the signs of distress; one common condition that often worries families is a small amount of secretion in the upper chest which makes the person sound very chesty, but they may actually be quite comfortable with this. When visiting, if your parent or relative is in a coma it may be that they can actually hear and it is good for you and them to sit, hold their hand and speak gently about the things you would normally speak about.

In general, when it becomes more clear that death is inevitable, a discussion will often take place with the older person, or with the family if the older person is unable to take part in the discussion, about the appropriate intensity of medical care and in particular whether or not to engage in resuscitation. This should be with a senior member of staff and in general there is consensus reached. If you and the medical team differ, then you should seek a second opinion, which is good medical practice.

Usually, death occurs as a slow process and a gradual departure, and the sick person will gradually stop eating and drinking. This is almost certainly more distressing for you, the relative, than for the older person. Studies have shown that patients with cancer who are not eating and drinking show no more hunger and thirst than those who continue eating and drinking. Your parent or relative may become delirious and confused, and communication may be limited.

The final moment is usually quiet and uneventful, but some reflex actions may occur. For example, a person may make a last energetic effort to breathe or sit up, which can be upsetting for the relatives. In fact, this is almost certainly a reflex and is unlikely to be distressing to the dying person. The bowel and bladder may also release. While it is clearly shocking and distressing, you can play your part by your presence, by speaking gently and by human touch. If death has been expected do not feel that you have to rush and call for a nurse, but rather sit and take your time with your deceased parent or relative.

If your relative has died in a hospital or nursing home the staff are usually well versed in how to direct you in terms of death certification, linking up with the undertaker and making the appropriate arrangements. One important thing worth noting, which can take people by surprise, is that the coroner needs to be notified if your relative was a nursing home resident (even if they have been transferred to hospital), or if they have died following a fall and, say, a fractured hip. No funeral arrangements can be made until the coroner has cleared the case. In the majority of cases they will not ask for a post-mortem. However, if they do ask for a post-mortem this is because of legal requirements and cannot be countermanded. Some people get quite concerned at the thought of this, but in fact the process is carefully designed to avoid any disfigurement so that the funeral can subsequently take place without any problems.

If you are the adult child of an older person who has died, and there is a surviving spouse or partner, it is important to offer as much support as possible in the immediate aftermath. They should be advised not to make any major decisions such as moving or selling a house immediately after their spouse's death; it is better to let the grieving process take some of its course before undertaking any major change.

23

Elder Abuse

Elder abuse is a painful subject for many of us to even think about, let alone talk about. However, we know that it affects somewhere between 3 and 5 per cent of all older Irish people, so it is important that you the older person, and your family, have some sense of what it is and how to deal with it if you think it is occurring. The most common forms of elder abuse are psychological abuse, financial abuse and neglect. Less common but important forms of abuse are physical abuse and sexual abuse.

The definition of elder abuse is an act or acts which cause harm to or affect the civil rights of an older person by someone else in a relationship where there is an expectation of trust. In general, the definition excludes abusive behaviour by strangers, for example fraudsters who may leverage money out of vulnerable older people to do things like house repair or re-tarmacing their drive, although this is a problem as well.

Although elder abuse is difficult for people to address, is important to try to plan your life so as to reduce the possibility of it happening and to seek help if it does occur, as there is evidence that it can make a difference to the quality of your life. The good news in Ireland is that the government has set up a network of senior caseworkers, one in each local health authority, who are responsible for responding to cases of elder abuse. In addition, the Gardaí have signed up to the workings of this system and have been very helpful in advising on and sometimes intervening in cases of elder abuse.

The aim of the services for elder abuse is to support you, provide you with help and intervene as sensitively as possible so as not to upset relationships between you and your family unnecessarily.

Psychological abuse includes emotional abuse, threats of harm or abandonment, deprivation of contact, humiliation, blaming, controlling, intimidation, coercion, harassment, verbal abuse, isolation, and withdrawal from services or support networks.

Financial abuse includes theft, fraud, exploitation, pressure in connection with wills, property or inheritance transactions, and the misuse or misappropriation of property, possessions or benefits.

Neglect includes ignoring medical and physical care needs, failure to provide access to appropriate health, social care or educational services, and withholding the necessities of life, such as medication, adequate nutrition and heating.

Physical abuse includes hitting, slapping, punching, kicking, misuse of medication, restraining and inappropriate actions.

Sexual abuse includes rape, sexual assault and sexual acts to which the older person has not consented, could not consent or was pressured into consenting.

If you think you are suffering from abuse in one of these categories you might start by discussing it with your public health nurse or family doctor, who can refer you on to the senior caseworker in your area. The HSE also has a confidential helpline for those who need advice on possible elder abuse: *1850 24 1850.*

In terms of preventing financial abuse, good advanced planning and reasonably open discussion can be very helpful – the disinfectant of sunlight. Sadly, as this book is being written, Irish banks and credit unions remain woefully unprepared to support older people in preventing and detecting financial abuse. Making your will early, and resisting the temptation to change it when you have memory problems, is one helpful strategy. The second is to strongly consider formal arrangements for the management of your money should you begin to have memory problems, in particular Enduring Power of Attorney, where at least two members of your family have to be informed of decisions being taken. In addition, I would strongly recommend you specify that the bank accounts for the Enduring Power of Attorney are scrutinised by an independent person, such as your solicitor, on an annual basis. You should avoid handing over your house or property during your life, and avoid letting others use your bank account or have access to your PIN codes. In particular, you should avoid any financial gifts or loans to home care workers.

With increasing emphasis on community care you should expect the same standards of courtesy, probity and professionalism from home care workers that would be expected in a nursing home or hospital. As it is likely you have some vulnerability if you have engaged a home care worker, or are receiving a grant or care package, any deviation from high standards is best discussed with a trusted family member, or with the homecare package coordinator or public health nurse.

For family members, particularly if your older relative has memory problems, acting on suspected elder abuse is an important task. If a serious crime is suspected, such as rape or bodily harm, urgent referral to the senior caseworker who will involve the Gardaí at an early opportunity is probably the best course. If it is other than a serious crime, and if the older person has a capacity for decision making, discussion with the older person along the lines of this chapter should be your first step. There is often a co-dependency between the older person and the alleged perpetrator, and the older person may be wary of any intervention that threatens their relationship with the alleged perpetrator. However, there is a benefit from these discussions as they may help to move the older person forward in thinking about possible elder abuse. If the older person has significant memory problems and has less capacity to deal with as complex an issue as elder abuse then it is likely that you should have a lower threshold in discussing this with the public health nurse or family doctor, or consider a direct call to the HSE helpline.

Within the nursing home sector, you may come across not only individual elder abuse (which you should report immediately to the director of nursing, and onwards to the

Health Information and Quality Authority (HIQA) if you feel the response is not appropriate), but also institutional elder abuse. Institutional abuse is characterised by poor care standards, lack of a positive response to complex needs, rigid routines, inadequate staffing and an insufficient knowledge base within the service. If you feel that the care your older relative is getting displays features of institutional abuse you should contact HIQA.

Although the subject may seem depressing, as a geriatrician I am cautiously optimistic that the increased publicity given to elder abuse, and increased data suggesting that older people benefit from intervention to support and protect them, will help promote a proactive approach which will give a happier old age to an important minority of older people.

Appendix A

The Nursing Homes Support Scheme

The Nursing Homes Support Scheme, also known as the 'Fair Deal' Scheme, replaced a former eligibility for publicly funded nursing home care less 80 per cent of the State (Contributory) Pensions in 2009. With this scheme, you make a contribution towards the cost of your care based on your income and assets (the state is offering a state-run equity release scheme to fund a loan from your assets and income and the state pays the balance. The scheme covers all forms of nursing homes (i.e. private, voluntary and public nursing homes) – although a small number of nursing homes have remained outside of the scheme (usually those who work on a purely private payment basis) – and is only for long-term nursing home care (i.e. not for respite care or convalescence).

What you get for these 'long-term residential care services' is maintenance and some health and personal care services. The Department of Health has further clarified that this includes bed and board, nursing and personal care appropriate to the care needs of the person, laundry service, and basic aids and appliances necessary to assist a person with the activities of daily living. It *does not* include therapist cover in private nursing homes, and is not clear about the provision of incontinence pads and specialist equipment to facilitate independence, a sad reflection on not only the Irish state, but also what Irish politicians believe the Irish electorate will tolerate. The HSE states that other goods and services may be available under schemes such as the Medical Card or drugs payment scheme, but expecting people with such significant disabilities to get services from a variety of sources seems unhelpful.

There is a set level of funding for the scheme each year, so there may be situations where a person's name must go onto a waiting list until funding becomes available. If this is the case the HSE will let you know when it writes to advise you whether you are eligible for state support. It is uncertain at the time of writing what will happen if you are in hospital; it is not clear whether or not you will be charged for being in hospital.

Applying for the Nursing Homes Support Scheme

You must apply to the HSE on the two standard application forms (known as the Common Summary Assessment Report (CSAR) and the NHSS Application Form), which your public health nurse or hospital team can source for you. You can also download the forms and guidance booklets from www.hse.ie/eng/services/Find_a_Service/Older_People_Services/nhss/. You can contact the HSE Infoline on 1850 24 1850, Monday to Saturday, 8 a.m. to 8 p.m. There is also an FAQ document on the Citizens Information website: www.citizensinformation.ie/en/health/health_services_for_older_people/nursing_homes_support_scheme_1.html.

There are three steps in the application process, which are discussed in further detail below:

- Step 1 is an application for a *care needs assessment* using the CSAR form. The care needs assessment identifies whether or not you need long-term nursing home care; that is, whether you can be supported to continue living at home or whether long-term nursing home care is more appropriate.
- Step 2 is a financial assessment and an application for state support, using the NHSS Application Form. The information that you give will be used to complete the *financial*

assessment which decides how much you contribute to your care and how much state support you get. The financial assessment assesses your income and assets in order to work out what contribution the HSE will pay towards the cost of your nursing home care: this is the state support. Unless you have no assets, do not own your own home and have only the state pension, you will be left with generally a considerable sum to pay per week (equivalent to 80 per cent of your income, 5 per cent of the value of your house each year for a maximum of three years, and 7.5 per cent of your other assets each year (with no maximum). Many, if not most, will bridge this gap between the HSE state support and the cost of the nursing home by applying for the 'optional' nursing loan, which is equivalent to this sum.

- Step 3 is this 'optional' application for the *nursing home loan*; that is, the HSE pays the rest of the costs up front, and you enter into an equity release mortgage on your home and assets. In practice, given the price of nursing home care, many if not most will opt for this. Why would you (or your family) not opt for the loan? It may be that you/they do not wish your house and assets to be sold in this way after your death with the HSE as a priority claimant on its portion of the assets, and may choose instead to pay the difference privately, even if this represents a significant sum each year.

The form for the loan is the second part of the NHSS application form and should be completed and signed by the person who is applying for nursing home care. However, 50–75 per cent of those applying for nursing homes have memory and dementia problems, and many of these will not be able to manage a complex contract such as the equity release mortgage inherent in the loan scheme. In such cases, another person (usually a family member, called a 'specified person' in the regulations, but a care representative generally) may apply on their behalf (see below).

Care Needs Assessment

The care needs assessment will be carried out by the appropriate healthcare professionals appointed by the HSE, for example a nurse. It can be completed at any time in a hospital or a community setting such as your own home, and may involve a physical examination and input from therapists and specialists.

The assessment will take into account:

- Your ability to carry out the activities of daily living, for example bathing, shopping, dressing and moving around
- The medical, health and personal social services being provided to you or available to you both at the time of the assessment and generally
- The family and community support available to you
- Your wishes and preferences

Getting a geriatrician's or old age psychiatrist's assessment is recommended as a national standard to ensure that you are not suffering from undetected and untreated illness(es), which if treated may allow you to continue to live at home.

When the care needs assessment has been completed a report will be prepared. The report is sent to the Local Placement Forum within the HSE, and it must decide whether or not long-term nursing home care is the most appropriate option. Once a decision is made you and/or your family will be notified in writing within ten working days. You and/or your family will be given a copy of the report and the reasons for the decision.

You must be assessed as needing nursing home care in order to be eligible for either state support or the nursing home loan.

The HSE may use the care needs assessment to identify other health or personal social service needs. However, there is no legal requirement for them to provide the services identified.

Financial Assessment

The financial assessment calculates your income and assets in order to work out what the HSE will then pay towards the cost of your care. For example, if the cost of your care is €1,000 and the HSE calculate that they will pay €500, then you will need to pay €500 a week. This payment by the HSE is called state support.

The financial assessment looks at all your income and assets. In the case of a member of a couple, the assessment will be based on half of the couple's combined income and assets. For example, if a couple's income is €600 per week, the assessment of the person needing care would be based on 50 per cent of €600, or €300. In other words, the person needing care would be considered to have a total income of €300 per week.

Income and Assets

Income includes any earnings, pension income, social welfare benefits or allowances, rental income, income from holding an office or directorship, income from fees, commissions, dividends or interest, and any income which you have divested yourself of in the five years leading up to your application.

An asset is any material property or wealth, including property or wealth outside the state. Assets are divided into two distinct categories, namely cash assets and relevant assets.

Cash assets include savings, stocks, shares and securities. Relevant assets include all forms of property other than cash assets, for example your principal residence or land. In both cases, the assessment will also look at assets which you have divested yourself of in the five years leading up to your application. Be very wary about divesting yourself of assets prematurely, as in many geriatricians' experience you will lose flexibility in managing your care later in life, and promises to look after you may not come good – remember *King Lear*. The assessment will not take into account the income of other relatives such as your children.

Your Contribution to Care

Having looked at your income and assets, the financial assessment will work out the HSE state support on the basis that you will contribute:

- 80 per cent of your income (less deductions below) and
- 5 per cent of the value of your house (for a maximum of three years) and 7.5 per cent of the value of your other assets per year (no maximum)

However, the first €36,000 of your assets, or €72,000 for a couple, will not be counted at all in the financial assessment.

Where your assets include land and property, the 5 per cent contribution based on such assets may be deferred and paid to Revenue after your death. This is known as the nursing home loan.

Your principal residence will only be included in the financial assessment for the first five years of your time in care. This is known as the 15 per cent cap or 'three-year cap'. It means that you will pay a 5 per cent contribution based on your principal residence for a maximum of three years regardless of the length of time you spend in nursing home care, although a recent government report suggested raising this amount.

In the case of a couple, the contribution based on the principal residence will be capped at 7.5 per cent where one partner remains in the home while the other enters long-term nursing home care, and, again, the three-year cap applies. If you opt for the nursing home loan in respect of your principal residence your spouse or partner can also apply to have the repayment of the loan deferred for their lifetime.

If you have already been in a nursing home for three years, then you do not pay the 5 per cent on your principal residence.

After three years, even if you are still in long-term nursing home care, you will not pay any further contribution based on your principal residence. This three-year cap applies regardless of whether you choose to opt for the nursing home loan or not. All other assets will be taken into account for as long as you are in care, but the three-year cap also extends to farms and businesses in certain circumstances.

There are safeguards built in to the financial assessment which ensure that:

- Nobody will pay more than the actual cost of care
- You will keep a personal allowance of 20 per cent of your income or 20 per cent of the maximum rate of the State (Non-Contributory) Pension, whichever is greater
- If you have a spouse or partner remaining at home they will be left with 50 per cent of the couple's income or the maximum rate of the State (Non-Contributory) Pension, whichever is greater

A couple is defined as a married couple who are living together. It also includes heterosexual or same-sex couples who are cohabiting as life partners for at least three years.

Summary Table for 7.5% Yearly Contribution re: Assets

Asset	7.5% per Year	Three-Year Cap	Option to Take Up Nursing Home Loan	Option to Further Defer
Chargeable asset	Yes	No	Yes, if the asset is a land-based asset in the Irish state; otherwise no	No
Principal private residence	Yes	Yes	Yes	Yes
Farm/relevant business	Yes	Yes (but certain qualifying criteria)	Yes, if farm/business is a land-based asset in the Irish state	No

Deductions

In relation to income, the following deductions are allowed:

- Income tax, social insurance contributions and levies actually paid
- Where a person owns their principal residence, interest on loans for the purchase, repair or improvement of the principal residence
- Where a person rents their principal residence (i.e. is living in rented accommodation), rental payments in respect of the residence where the person's partner or a child of the couple aged under 21 lives in the residence
- Health expenses allowable for tax purposes, excluding contributions payable under the Nursing Homes Support Scheme
- Maintenance payments in respect of a child, spouse or former spouse made under a separation agreement, or divorce or court order

In the case of assets the net value of the asset is assessed; that is, its value minus any borrowings incurred specifically for the purchase or improvement of the asset.

Payment of Your Contribution

If you select a public or voluntary nursing home, you will pay your contribution to the HSE or voluntary nursing home as appropriate each week and the state will pay the balance on your behalf.

If you select an approved private nursing home, you will pay your contribution to the nursing home provider each week and the state will pay the balance on your behalf.

Financial support will only be paid where a nursing home is identified as being appropriate to your needs.

Applying on Behalf of Someone Else

If the applicant is not able to apply himself or herself, a specified person can act on his or her behalf for Step 1; for Step 2 (financial assessment), most banks and financial institutions are relatively obliging, but in the future will probably seek more formal procedures for families in these circumstances, as this discretion with the financial dealing of older people in other settings may permit financial abuse of older people. This may be by way of a court-appointed representative, as is currently required if applying for the nursing home loan for an older person who no longer has the capacity to do so.

Only a court-appointed care representative can act on the applicant's behalf for the nursing home loan (Step 3); in this case, one member of the family engages to become a care representative. If they wish to do this themselves, there is a four-part form which they can download from the Courts website: www.courts.ie. Parts 1 and 2 of the Form are the application to the Court for the appointment of a care representative; Part 3 is an affidavit outlining the attributes of the older person and the care representative (including permission from closer relatives who may be unable or unwilling to be the care representative). For Part 4 the care representative needs to arrange for two doctors (i.e. the family doctor and a specialist) to certify that their older relative is no longer capable of managing their financial affairs, using Form 4. They then need to present the completed form to the Circuit Court, along with a fee of €68 and €11 for the affidavit. Alternatively, you can ask a solicitor to arrange this for you, although this will clearly increase the costs of the process.

Existing Nursing Home Residents

You will not be affected if you are already in a fully funded public nursing home or a HSE contract bed in a private nursing home, as was the eligibility up to October 2009, or in a subvented bed. You will contribute to your care on the same basis as you do at present, usually 80 per cent of the State (Non-Contributory) Pension.

If you are already in a private nursing home which is approved for this scheme but do not have a subvention, or you are not happy with the amount of the subvention, you can apply for the Nursing Homes Support Scheme. If your private nursing home is not approved for this scheme you can retain your current subvention arrangements or you can opt to apply for the scheme and change to a nursing home which is on the list.

If you have been resident in the nursing home for three years or more, the financial assessment will only be based on income and assets other than your principal residence (and your farm/business in certain circumstances); that is, the three-year cap will apply.

If you are happy with the amount of subvention you get you can continue with that arrangement. You can claim tax relief on nursing home expenses that you pay for yourself or another person or relative at your highest rate of tax.

You can choose to take up the new scheme or continue with your present subvention, whichever is the best option for you financially.

After You Send in the Application Form

When the care needs and financial assessments have been completed, the HSE will write to you and inform you of your contribution to care, and your eligibility for state support and the nursing home loan (if applicable).

At this stage you will also be provided with the list of nursing homes that are participating in the scheme. This list will include public nursing homes, voluntary nursing homes and approved private nursing homes.

You may choose any nursing home from the list subject to the following conditions:

- The home must have a place for you.
- The home must be able to cater for your particular needs. The nursing home will have to carry out an assessment to determine whether it can meet your particular needs.

Your choice of nursing home is not connected in any way to the level of your contribution to care.

Appeals and Reviews

The HSE will inform you of the appeals process and provide details of your local appeals office when it writes to you to inform you of the outcome of your care needs and financial assessments. If your care needs assessment found that you did not need long-term nursing home care you can appeal the decision to your local appeals office.

Any care needs assessment can be reviewed six months after a previous assessment or earlier if either:

- The HSE is satisfied that there has been a material change in your health or circumstances.
- A registered medical practitioner states that in his/her opinion there has been a material change in your health or circumstances since your most recent care needs assessment.

Reviews are carried out by your local nursing home support office and you should contact it if you want to have your care needs or financial assessment reviewed.

Once the HSE has made a decision regarding the review, you will be notified of the decision and the reasons for the decision, in writing, within ten working days.

If Asked to Pay for Hospital Care while Awaiting a Nursing Home Place

It is common that older people will enter nursing home due to an illness which is the straw which breaks the camel's back, and it is quite appropriate that you should seek a full assessment in the general hospital to make sure that the decline in function caused by the most recent episode is not reversible. If you are waiting to move to long-term care in this situation, then you should apply for the Nursing Homes Support Scheme as soon as possible. One issue that may raise its head is that of being charged for your stay in hospital while awaiting a nursing home place. You will *not* be charged if you are on a waiting list for the Nursing Homes Support Scheme, or if you have particular needs and there is no suitable accommodation available or if there is no suitable accommodation nearby, of which more below.

Delays in going to a nursing home generally arise from the shortage of nursing home places in urban areas (often half that required), and in particular a shortage of high-dependency/dementia-specific places, or in nursing homes that are reasonably near your relatives. In addition, if you do not have decision-making capacity, there may be uncertainty in your family about who will start the process of appointing a care representative.

In this setting, you should resist any effort to ask you to pay for hospital care because you no longer need 'acute care'. The term 'acute care' is misleading as it suggests that there is a clear cut-off between when frail older people need the broad range of services of a general hospital and when they don't. In fact, because the illness that sparks a need for nursing home care is usually at a point where the older person has complex care needs, this means you are medically vulnerable. For example, one in four older people awaiting nursing home placement die in the hospital. Also, the medical literature increasingly suggests that older people attend general hospitals not so much for acuity (i.e. how urgent the illness is) but because of the complexity of their care needs and the instability of their condition.

So if you, or your family, are faced with these charges for being in hospital you should discuss this with the hospital consultant (who has to sign a form stating they think that you no longer need 'acute care' for these payments to be imposed, and who should have discussed this with you or your next of kin around the time of signing) and social worker. You should determine whether this classification is appropriate. If you think not and cannot come to an agreement with the consultant on this, you or your representative should consider asking for a second opinion to establish some consensus.

There is still a lack of clarity as to what constitutes a 'reasonable rejection' of a nursing home place offered to you, and in particular with regard to the issue of distance. The HSE currently considers this distance to be within 60 km of your home, which might be reasonable in a country area but not in a suburb, and reasonable access to ongoing visits by family and friends is important to the health and well-being of you, the older person.

In the end, if there is actually no nursing home near your home, or one that is willing to take you in your current circumstances, you and your relatives will have to cut your cloth accordingly.

Appendix B

Aids and Appliances

Aids and appliances to support you in later life have become part of our everyday landscape, so much so that they feature in the Argos catalogue, and frequently in the weekly special purchase sections of Aldi and Lidl. On the one hand, this is a good sign of the 'mainstreaming' of supports to keep you independent in later life; on the other hand, without proper tailoring to your needs the danger is that the piece of equipment may not be maximally effective or sometimes (particularly with mobility aids) may actually be harmful. In addition, you may be spending your hard-earned or long-saved resources on equipment that the HSE might provide without cost to you.

Most aids should be matched to your physical and cognitive abilities, ideally be reasonably simple and intuitive to use, and their design as domestic and smart as possible so that their use does not demean or stigmatize. If not available from the health service, cost is also an issue.

The key advice is not to buy any significant piece of equipment without discussion with an occupational therapist or physiotherapist. Ask your GP or public health nurse to refer you to a physiotherapist or occupational therapist in the first instance; if you are not able to get the aid or appliance from the HSE the therapist will advise you as to where they can be purchased.

This appendix will provide an overview some of the areas where aids and appliances can make a big difference, but cannot be exhaustive, so again you should consult with your therapist(s) first.

Mobility Aids

A wide range of mobility aids are available. Each of us may have different reasons for needing a mobility aid, depending on the illness that made us less mobile; the main purpose may be distribute weight differently in the case of pain, or to increase speed and/or balance. Remember that for you it may be the first time you encounter this need, but for your therapist you may be their thousandth client with mobility problems, so use that experience. In addition, you might need a variety of mobility aids, for example a stick indoors, a frame in the garden, and perhaps a wheelchair for longer outings as a back-up, and matching these varying needs can also benefit from skilled assessment.

The humble *walking stick* is the most common mobility aid. Its very simplicity conceals the fact that it needs to be the right height and strength for your needs, and ideally you should check this with your physiotherapist. In addition, should you have arthritis of the hand you may require a particular handle shape. If a therapist recommends a walking stick, do not let a misplaced sense of pride prevent from you using it; no therapist will recommend one unnecessarily, and it will give you added stability.

The walking stick should have a tip (also called a ferrule) made of rubber or similar material, and this should be reviewed regularly to ensure that it is not worn or cracked; if it is, the tip should be replaced. If you get a pain in your arm or hand from using the walking stick discuss this with the therapist.

A formerly common variation on the walking stick is the *tripod or quadripod stick*, which has three or four feet, respectively, at the bottom of the stick. While they are more stable than an ordinary stick, they should be used with caution as the broader spread of the feet means that it is easier to trip on them. They are less often prescribed in current times.

There are a variety of *walking frames*, including Zimmer frames, wheeled Rollator frames (with two or four wheels) and triangular wheeled frames. The choice largely relates to size, stability and your ability to manage wheeled or non-wheeled frames. A wheeled frame can clearly move more easily, but you need to be able to control this or else it might run ahead faster than you can manage and you might fall. Those with no wheels are more stable, but may take more effort to move. Options include a combination of wheels and legs, or lever brakes in the grips, usually found in the triangular frame. The triangular frame usually folds to allow it to be packed away easily, for example in a car, but can also be quite heavy.

A helpful variant is the use of a special *trolley* within the kitchen and house, which allows you to carry food, crockery and so on from cooker to table to sink. As with the frames and stick, an occupational therapist can advise on height and suitability, as well as sturdiness.

The choice of a *wheelchair* is also quite specialised, and ideally should involve both you and the person who is most likely to be using it with you, as well as an occupational therapist. It is not a one-size–fits-all solution, and purpose, weight, comfort, rigidity and ease of folding are among the issues that need to be considered. In addition, the provision of the appropriate cushion is also an important factor in terms of comfort and preventing pressure sores.

Motorized wheelchairs definitely need an occupational therapist's assessment, as they are quite heavy, and require specific skills to be able to use them in terms of vision, perception, reaction times and manual dexterity, as well as also factoring in what to do should you need to use a car as well. The same advice applies for *electric scooters*.

Within the house the use of *rails* can be a valuable assistance, particularly on stairs, in toilets and bathrooms, and on longer stretches of corridor. They need to take account of your individual characteristics, and should only be fitted in consultation with an occupational therapist.

Should you have difficulty using stairs, one possible option is the installation of a *stair lift*. This is usually quite expensive, and you should absolutely engage with an occupational therapist before purchasing one. If you are hoping to avail of a grant from your local county council to pay for installation, you will need the report of an occupational therapist. You need to have preserved skill in balance, memory and some dexterity if you want to use the stair lift on your own.

For those with difficulty in bed mobility, a range of devices are available but requires matching to you and your circumstances. These include a *bed pole*, *bed rope ladder* and *bed rail*, but this is a category of aid where you need a therapist to advise you on what is suitable.

Assistance with Transferring to/from Your Bed or Chair

Should your mobility be compromised to the point that you require help in getting in and out of bed or on and off a chair, a range of aids and appliances can help, but these absolutely require therapist advice, as it is critically important that the person or persons helping you with these transfers gets training in lifting and handling – so as not to harm either you or themselves – as well as in the use of the aids. The aids include *transfer boards*, *transfer discs*, *easy-riser cushions* and *hoists*, to name but a few. A *hospital-type bed* may be appropriate to enable you to raise or lower the height, as well as an appropriate mattress to protect you from pressure sores.

In the Bathroom

As one of the most frequently used rooms in the house, a range of aids and supports are available for use in the bathroom. These include *raised toilet seats*, a *toilet frame* and *grab rails*. For the bath, *transfer devices, bath seats, bath boards* and *grab rails* can be helpful. If you cannot travel with ease to the bathroom, a *commode* may be helpful, and a range of *male and female urinals* are available. An occupational therapist should advise on obtaining and using these devices.

Aids for Everyday Activities

A very wide range of aids are available for assisting in dressing. These include *long shoe-horns, button hooks, dressing sticks, elastic shoe laces, devices for assisting with putting on a bra*, and *aids for putting on tights and socks*. An occupational therapist will not only advise, but also provide training in how to use these aids.

Cooking and Eating

A wide variety of aids and appliances can help with the preparation of food and snacks. A *kettle stand with a spring* can help with pouring a kettle or a teapot, *built-up handles* can make kitchen utensils easier to use for those with arthritis, and a wide range of *grippers* and devices can help with opening jars and bottles, as well as turning taps on and off. A *board with spikes* can make cutting easier, and *electric can openers* can also be helpful. If you have difficulty with eyesight and knowing when a glass or cup is full, a small *electronic aid* can tell you when the liquid reaches the appropriate level, and prevent spillage.

For eating and drinking, the use of cutlery with *built-up handles* can help those with arthritis, as can a *rocker knife and fork* for those who can only use one hand (for example, after a stroke), or *weighted cutlery* to reduce the shake in those with a marked tremor. An *over-sized bowl* can also help reduce spillage in those with tremor, and a *thermos plate* can keep food warm if you eat slowly. On the table, *non-slip mats* can assist as well.

For other activities, as well as dressing and cooking, *grab devices* can extend your reach, or help you to pick up things from the floor.

For Carers

As you can see, there is a huge and ever-evolving range of aids and appliances that can help the person you care for to maximise their independence, or make the task of caring easier.

As you may have also gathered, you should really avoid making any significant purchase ahead of discussion and agreement with your relative's physiotherapist and/or occupational therapist, as nearly all aids and appliances need to be matched to the older person's capabilities and needs, as well as those of the people aiding them. I have often seen families pre-emptively making a major investment in stair lifts or an electric scooter, for example, only to find that they lie idle.

In addition, discussion with the public health nurse and therapists will clarify what is available from the health service – virtually all aids are available for those with Medical Cards, but the situation is not clear for others. If an aid is needed at the point of leaving hospital for discharge to take place, this sometimes provides more influence than for those who are in the community all along.

Appendix C

Advance Care Plan

The key challenge of planning into the future in later life is the enormous variability of potential outcomes that you might be faced with. Add to this the experience of those who bought houses at inflated prices at the height of the Celtic Tiger period, and who are now caught with huge mortgages and nega- tive equity – future-forecasting left them locked into a dismal outcome, but you might say that at least it was only a house, and not their life.

Despite this clear challenge in trying to plan such momen- tous decisions for the future, there is a movement towards 'living wills' and 'advance directives' which seems oblivious to the fact of this diversity of options, and which seems to try to crystallize a part of the future that will not necessarily fit this pre-conception. They are nearly always phrased in terms of what you should not have rather than what you should have, and the lawyers seem alarmingly keen on them.

These 'living wills' and 'advance directives' seem to tap into a vision of ageing which is negative and prejudiced about disability, and probably over-fearful of over-aggressive treat- ment; most evidence suggests that most older people die with a reasonably appropriate level of intensity of care.

In addition, most advance directives seem to consider decision-making as we age into the future as some sort of on– off situation of either full decision-making capacity or none; in fact, most people with dementia can make some input into decisions, even if only to pull out a nasogastric tube in their nose, or refusing thickened fluids if they have a swallow disorder.

Older people are sensible about decision-making into the future, and generally wish to make any such preferences near the time of a likely threat to their independence (and when they know a bit more about it) and also are happy to place trust in, and devolve some decision-making to, knowledgeable and caring health staff. Also, we all commonly make decisions with trusted others, whether choosing a jacket or picking a holiday, or considering medical treatment when in command of all of our powers; our autonomy is exercised in the embrace of others.

So, this is a 'living will' with a difference, one that recognises that should we lose significant capacity to make important care decisions:

- I want to be cared for by professionals who have specific training in care of older people, and particularly in dementia care.
- I want my voice, no matter how diminished, to be listened to.
- I would like to nominate a chief co-decision maker – not someone who runs the whole show, but one who helps in interpreting not only previously expressed values and attitudes, but also those I embody when unwell.
- I want positive interventions as well as potentially not wanting some others.
- I want some flexibility in interpretation of this Advance Care Plan, recognising that in our earlier life our fears expressed about the future may no longer truly represent our current state, that treatment options change with time and that the future can never be forecast with 100 per cent accuracy. I want it to have *a strong moral force* rather than to be legally binding in a narrow and rigid way.
- I am best positioned to make this plan at a time when we best understand future threats, and ideally develop it with

a professional who knows something about the conditions and options which will commonly affect me.

- I should regularly review my Advance Care Plan, given that research shows that those who make such advance plans commonly change them quite significantly if reviewed six months later.

My Advance Care Plan

I, _____, of _____, _____, am making an Advance Care Plan, with advice from Dr _____, who has expertise in the care of older people and dementia, and also with _____, _____ and _____ (suggested others who might collaborate with you include trained senior nursing staff (such as the director of nursing in a nursing home), members of your family and friends.

My current age is _____, and I would like this document reviewed again in ___ months time, unless I am incapable of doing so. If I am unable to review, I would like my chief co-decision-maker and my care staff to review it.

In general, I wish the eleven points of this Advance Care Plan to have **a strong moral force**, as I understand that it is hard to forecast not only the future, but also how I may change as I age and through the experience of my illness(es), so I do not wish it to be followed rigidly if my chief co-decision-maker or family or care staff think that doing so would cause me suffering or diminish the quality of my life.

1. As dementia and related illnesses are the most common causes of older people losing capacity to make decisions for themselves, **my first advance care preference** is that those looking after me – care attendants, nursing staff and doctors

– have due training and competence in both the care of older people and of those with dementia, and renew their knowledge and skills at appropriate intervals.

2. My second advance care preference is that maximal efforts will be made through the use of dementia care skills, allied with appropriate support (such as speech and language therapy and occupational therapy), to communicate with me to help those who are looking after me in the interpretation of my wishes.

3. My third care preference is that I would like to nominate _____ of _____ to be considered as my chief co-decision maker by those providing my care, so as to help interpret and support decision-making. I wish this co-decision-maker to liaise with _____, _____, _____, _____ and _____ (and others as per appended sheet) on the progress of my care.

4. My fourth advance care preference is that those caring for me, whether at home or in a nursing home, have adequate skills in the detection and management of pain, including appropriate pain-rating scales for use with those with memory and communication problems.

5. My fifth care preference is that my personal tastes in activities, leisure and recreation are attended to. I attach a copy of the pleasant events schedule which I would like to be respected, as well as an indication of the types of music, radio and television I like, and those that I definitely do not like.

6. My sixth care preference relates to food and drink: the following are those which I like: _____, _____, _____, _____, _____ and _____, and the following are those which I do not like and do not wish to have offered to me: _____, _____,

_____, _____, _____ and
_____.

Should I find myself in a nursing home:

7. My seventh care preference is that should I find myself in a nursing home, my family and friends should treat it as my home, with the ability to visit me in a manner that they would do if I were in my own home, with due privacy for visits, and due celebration of events in life that are important.

8. In addition, **my eighth care preference** is that I would wish to have place for my personal effects in my room with due security for them.

End of life care:

9. My ninth care preference is that I wish to have my end-of-life care decisions shaped by the knowledge, skills and attitudes of palliative care, both through the skills of my care staff, and additional input from specialist palliative care services as required.

10. My tenth care preference is that if a) I should not have capacity to make the decision myself in terms of the intensity of resuscitation (cardio-pulmonary resuscitation (CPR)) if my heart or breathing should stop, and b) should I be sufficiently unwell or frail that it appears highly unlikely that I would gain overall from an attempt at resuscitation, I would wish that this should be discussed between my chief co-decision-maker, my treating doctor, and the senior nursing staff in the nursing home, and the decision noted below.

____ **Attempt Resuscitation/CPR** (Selecting CPR **requires** selecting Full Treatment for next section)

___ **Do Not Attempt Resuscitation/DNR** (**A**llow **N**atural **D**eath)

Other wishes _____

_____

Such decisions do not lend themselves easily to 'tick-box' answers, as there may be a variety of levels of resuscitation, such as the use of defibrillators to provide a shock in the event of my heart rate becoming fast. The decision should depend on my state, and the resources and training in the setting where I am cared for, and discussed with my chief co-decision-maker.

11. My eleventh care preference in end-of-life care relates to whether or not I should be transferred to hospital for certain acute illnesses. This is a complex decision, and requires a degree of flexibility in its execution, and the three options below should be discussed, but *in general* I would wish that I/ my doctor/chief co-decision-maker would aim for *one* of the three following levels of intensity, annotating any other specific requests below:

__ **Comfort Measures Only**: Relieve pain and suffering through the use of medication by any route, positioning, wound care and other measures. Use oxygen, suction and manual treatment of airway obstruction as needed for comfort. *Transfer to hospital* **only** *if comfort needs cannot be met in current location.*

__ **Limited Additional Interventions**: In addition to care described in Comfort Measures Only, use medical treatment, antibiotics and IV fluids as indicated. Do not intubate. May use non-invasive positive airway pressure. Generally avoid intensive care. *Transfer to hospital* **only** *if comfort needs cannot be met in current location.*

__ **Full Treatment**: In addition to care described in Comfort Measures Only and Limited Additional Interventions, use intubation, advanced airway interventions, mechanical ventilation, and defibrillation/cardioversion as indicated. *Transfer to hospital if indicated, including to intensive care.*

Additional Requests:

_____
_____

_____
_____

Suggested Further Reading

The biological basis of ageing
Tom Kirkwood, *The Time of Our Lives* (Phoenix Press, 2000, ISBN 9780753809204).
A very clear guide to what ageing is, and how it can be influenced.

The longevity dividend
Thomas Dormandy, *Old Masters: Great Artists in Old Age* (Hambledon Continuum, 2000, ISBN 9781852852900).
Wonderful survey of how the art of great artists matures and enriches with age.

General guide on care in later life
Virginia Morris, *How to Care for Aging Parents* (Workman Publishing Company, 2004, ISBN 9780761134268).
Useful guide, although based on the perspective of adult children, and geared to the health and social care system in the United States.

Life with ageing and dementia
Nancy Mace and Peter Rabins, *The 36-Hour Day* (Grand Central, 2012, ISBN 9781455521159).
The first, and still the most comprehensive, resource in dementia care; may cause anxiety in those in the early stages of dementia, as everything described may not come to pass.

Mark Agronin, *How We Age: A Doctor's Journey Into the Heart of Growing Old* (Da Capo Life Long, 2012, ISBN 9780738215587).

A very interesting insight into how we retain our personhood, even with late stage dementia.

Anne Basting, *Forget Memory: Creating Better Lives for People with Dementia* (Johns Hopkins Press, 2009, ISBN 9780801892509).
A thoughtful perspective on how we are much more than our memory, and how to support those with dementia in a positive and engaging way.

Carmel Sheridan, *Failure-Free Activities for the Alzheimer's Patient: A Guidebook for Caregivers* (Palgrave Macmillan, 2002, ISBN 9780333554555).
Very helpful guide to activities for those with Alzheimer's disease.

Life with ageing and Parkinson's disease
William J. Weiner, Lisa M. Shulman and Anthony E. Lang, *Parkinson's Disease: A Complete Guide for Patients and Families* (Johns Hopkins University Press, 2006, ISBN 9780801885464).
Useful guide to living with, and caring for, Parkinson's disease, although geared to the health and social care system in the United States.

Booklets on stroke, dementia/Alzheimer's disease and Parkinson's disease
A range of helpful booklets are available from the Irish Heart Foundation (www.irishheart.ie) on stroke, such as *Step-by-Step through Stroke*, the Alzheimer Society of Ireland (www.alzheimer.ie) on dementia/Alzheimer's disease, and the Parkinson's Society of Ireland (www.parkinsons.ie) on Parkinson's disease.

Reflections on death and dying
Sherwin B. Nuland, *How We Die: Reflections on Life's Final Chapter* (Vintage Books, 1998, ISBN 9780679781400).

Elisabeth Kübler-Ross, *On Death and Dying* (Routledge, 2008, ISBN 9780415463997).

Tastes differ ...
There are a range of books in the United States which promote exercise, nutrition, mental stimulation and social connectedness, but often in language which stigmatises ageing as a bad thing, to be avoided, instead of talking in more positive terms about being fitter or less frail. An example is:

Henry S. Lodge and Chris Crowley, *Younger Next Year* (Sphere Books, 2005, ISBN 9780316731508).

Useful Resources

Government and Statutory Organisations

Citizens Information Board

The Citizens Information Board is a statutory body that provides information and advocacy on a broad range of public and social services. It is particularly helpful in providing information on eligibility and entitlements, as these schemes can change quite rapidly.

The Citizens Information Board hosts the Citizens Information website, supports the voluntary network of Citizens Information Centres and the Citizens Information Phone Service (0761 074 000). It also funds and supports the Money Advice and Budgeting Service (MABS) (0761 072 000).

Tel: 0761 079 000; Email: info@ciboard.ie, helpline@mabs.ie; Web: www.citizensinformation.ie, www.mabs.ie

Health Service Executive (HSE)

The HSE provides public health services in Ireland. For most Irish people, the main point of access is their local health centre. The corporate headquarters is at Dr Steevens' Hospital, Dublin 8.

Infoline: 1850 241 850; Tel: 01 635 2000; Email: infoline1@hse.ie; Web: www.hse.ie

Pensions Board

The Pensions Board is a statutory body set up under the Pensions Act 1990. It regulates occupational pension schemes,

Trust Retirement Annuity Contracts (Trust RACs) and Personal Retirement Savings Accounts (PRSAs) in Ireland.
LoCall: 1890 656 565; Email: info@pensionsboard.ie; Web: www. pensionsboard.ie

Pensions Ombudsman

The Pensions Ombudsman investigates and decides complaints and disputes from individuals about their occupational pension schemes, PRSAs and Trust RACs in cases of maladministration and financial loss. The ombudsman is completely independent and impartial.
Tel: 01 647 1650; Email: info@pensionsombudsman.ie; Web: www. pensionsombudsman.ie

Active Ageing and Advocacy

Active Retirement Ireland

Active Retirement Ireland (ARI) is a national network of over 500 local active retirement associations. ARI believes that older people have the right to be full and participative members of our society.
Tel: 01 873 3836; Email: info@activeirl.ie; Web: www.activeirl.ie

Age Action

Age Action is a charity which promotes positive ageing and better policies and services for older people. Working with, and on behalf of, older people, Age Action aims to make Ireland the best place in the world in which to grow older. Age Action helps about 30,000 older people a year, providing services such as an information phone line, computer training and Garda-vetted volunteers to assist you in light DIY. It also participates in advocacy and lobbies government on behalf of older people.
Tel: 01 475 6989; Email: info@ageaction.ie; Web: www.ageaction.ie

Age-Friendly University Initiative – Dublin City University
Dublin City University has blazed a trail in making the university a place in which older people feel they belong, from introductory courses and intergenerational learning to special sports programmes.
Tel: 01 700 8995; Email: registery@dcu.ie; Web: www4.dcu.ie/agefriendly/index.shtml

Age & Opportunity
Age & Opportunity is a national not-for-profit organisation that promotes opportunities for greater participation by older people in society through partnerships and collaborative programmes. Age & Opportunity works in a developmental way with public and private organisations to deliver practical programmes like the Bealtaine festival, the Go for Life sports and activity programme, Ageing with Confidence courses and the anti-ageism AgeWise workshop.
Tel: 01 805 7709; Email: info@ageandopportunity.ie; Web: www.ageandopportunity.ie

Irish Association of Older People
The Irish Association of Older People is a membership-based organisation set up with the support and encouragement of the National Council for the Elderly. It advocates on behalf of older people based on the principles of respect, dignity and choice with the overall aim of informing, enabling and empowering.
Tel: 01 214 0737; Email: iaop@oceanfree.net; Web: www.olderpeople.ie

Irish Senior Citizens' Parliament
The Irish Senior Citizens' Parliament is a representative organisation of older people in Ireland. It is a non-partisan political organisation working to promote the views of older people in policy development and decision-making.
Tel: 01 856 1243; Email: seniors@iol.ie; Web: http://iscp.wordpress.com

University of the Third Age (U3A)

U3A is network of groups around the country with the purpose of providing an educational forum for their members. Members learn from one another by sharing knowledge and experiences and engaging in shared activities. University in this context refers to the university of life – no qualifications are given, nor are any required. Anyone can join; all you need is interest and enthusiasm. U3A is a part of a wider international initiative and groups are developing around Ireland, with Age Action providing a common point of reference.
Tel: 01 475 6989; Email: u3a@ageaction.ie; Web: www.ageaction.ie/lifelong-learning-u3a

Support and Services

ALONE

ALONE works with vulnerable older people, providing long-term housing, a befriending service and support in the community. Trained volunteers befriend and support older people in the community, and provide them with crucial companionship.
Tel: 01 679 1032; Email: enquiries@alone.ie; Web: www.alone.ie

Alzheimer Society of Ireland

The Alzheimer Society of Ireland is the leading dementia-specific service provider in Ireland. It is a national voluntary organisation with an extensive national network of branches, regional offices and services that aims to provide people with all forms of dementia, their families and carers with the necessary support to maximise their quality of life.
Helpline: 1800 341 341; Tel: 01 207 3800; Email: info@alzheimer.ie, helpline@alzheimer.ie; Web: www.alzheimer.ie

Bethany

The Bethany Bereavement Support Group is a voluntary parish-based ministry which aims to help the bereaved and grieving. Bethany members are trained to listen with under-standing, accept those suffering loss as they are, and support them through the grieving process.

Tel: 087 990 5299; Email: bethanysupport@eircom.net; Web: www. bethany.ie

Carers Association

The Carers Association is Ireland's national voluntary organ-isation for and of family carers in the home. Family carers provide high levels of care to a range of people including frail older people, people with severe disabilities, the terminally ill and children with special needs.

Careline: 1800 240 724; Tel: 057 932 2920; Email: info@carers ireland.com; Web: www.carersireland.com

Diabetes Federation of Ireland

The Diabetes Federation of Ireland is an advocacy and support group for people in Ireland with diabetes. Through its network of support branches throughout the country, information on diabetes and related matters is sourced and shared.

Helpline: 1850 909 909; Tel: 01 836 3022; Email: info@diabetes.ie; Web: www.diabetes.ie

Friends of the Elderly

Friends of the Elderly is an Irish charity, part of an interna-tional network that works to alleviate loneliness and isolation amongst older people who live alone or feel alone. It believes in supporting people to remain independent and to live at home for as long as possible.

Tel: 01 873 1855; Email: info@friendsoftheelderly.ie; Web: www. friendsoftheelderly.ie

Irish Wheelchair Association

The Irish Wheelchair Association (IWA) is committed to improv-ing the lives of people with physical disabilities in Ireland. It is

an important provider of quality services to people with limited mobility throughout the country.
Tel: 01 818 6400; Email: info@iwa.ie; Web: www.iwa.ie

Meals on Wheels
The Meals on Wheels service is available to people in the community who are unable due to age, illness or disability to cook their own meals. It is operated on a voluntary basis. Referral and access to Meals on Wheels services is by word of mouth, through social workers, GPs, hospitals and self-referral. Please check with your local public health nurse to see if your area is covered.

National Federation of Pensioners Associations
The National Federation of Pensioners Associations was founded in 1976 and currently has twenty pensioners associations affiliated to it, representing in the region of 29,000 pensioners. The federation represents pensioners from the public service, semi-state bodies and private industry.
Tel: 01 831 2851, 086 813 7672; Email: nfpasec@eircom.net; Web: www.nfpa.ie

Parkinson's Association of Ireland
The Parkinson's Association of Ireland is a charity is based in Dublin, with branches throughout the country, assisting people with Parkinson's disease, their families and carers, health professionals and interested others, by offering support, a listening ear, and information on any aspect of living with Parkinson's.
Helpline: 1800 359 359; Tel: 01 872 2234; Email: info@parkinsons.ie; Web: www.parkinsons.ie

Senior Help Line
Senior Help Line is a national confidential telephone listening service for older people provided by trained older volunteers.

The LoCall number (1850 440 444) is available for the price of a local call anywhere in Ireland. Senior Help Line is open every day from 10 a.m. to 10 p.m. Trained volunteers listen empathically, providing information and practical and emotional support to callers. Senior Help Line is a Third Age programme. *LoCall: 1850 440 444; Web: www.thirdageireland.ie/what-we-do/14/ senior-helpline*

Retirement Planning Council
The Retirement Planning Council promotes the concept of planning ahead for retirement. It provides support, information and guidance to people planning for retirement. It is a not-for-profit organisation with charitable status and is supported by almost 250 private and semi-state bodies.
Tel: 01 478 9471; Email: information@rpc.ie; Web: www.rpc.ie

St Vincent de Paul
The Society of St Vincent de Paul is the largest voluntary charitable organisation in Ireland. Its 9,500 volunteers throughout the country are supported by professional staff, working for social justice and the creation of a more just, caring nation. This unique network of social concern also gives practical support to those experiencing poverty and social exclusion, by providing a wide range of services to people in need.
Tel: 01 838 6990; Email: info@svp.ie; Web: www.svp.ie

Sonas apc
Sonas apc is dedicated to enhancing the lives of older people with impaired communication, especially those with dementia. It is a charitable organisation which provides workshops and services.
Tel: 01 260 8138; Email: info@sonasapc.ie; Web: www.sonasapc.ie

Third Age
Third Age is a voluntary organisation promoting the value and contribution of older people. Based in Summerhill, Co. Meath,

Third Age has over 1,000 volunteers working throughout Ireland as listeners, befrienders, tutors, advocates and more. Third Age also promotes the third age, before and after retirement, as a positive life stage. Third Age has a vibrant local programme offering activities, programmes, services and outreach to local members.
Tel: 046 955 7766; Email: info@thirdageireland.ie; Web: www.thirdageireland.ie

Volunteer Stroke Scheme
The Volunteer Stroke Scheme is a registered charity that provides help for people with stroke in Ireland.
Tel: 01 455 9036; Email: vss@iolfree.ie; Web: www.strokescheme.ie

Private Sector Representative Organisations

Nursing Homes Ireland
Nursing Homes Ireland is the representative organisation for the private and voluntary nursing homes sector.
Tel: 01 429 2570; Email: info@nhi.ie; Web: www.nhi.ie

Home and Community Care Ireland
Home and Community Care Ireland (HCCI) is the trade association representing private home care providers in Ireland.
Tel: 01 484 7499; Email: enquiries@hcci.ie; Web: www.hcci.ie

Index